and re'
the g
lear
tio
o

Not Minds Alone

Not Minds Alone

Some Frontiers of
Christian Education

BY

KENNETH IRVING BROWN

*Former President of Hiram College
and Denison University*

HARPER & BROTHERS PUBLISHERS

NEW YORK

Library of Congress catalog card number: 53-11839

TO M. H. B.

*with the deep affection
born in our days of
high-school friendship
so long ago
and growing continuously
through our years
of joyous companionship
together*

Contents

Preface   ix

CHAPTER ONE   *Questions Both Pertinent and Impertinent*   1

INTERCHAPTER   *Seeds of Hope*   21

CHAPTER TWO   *Can Education Be Meaningfully Christian?*   38

CHAPTER THREE   *"And Gladly Wolde He Lerne"—We Hope*   61

CHAPTER FOUR   *"The Terrible Responsibility of the Teacher"*   85

CHAPTER FIVE   *Some Problems of Creative Leadership*   111

INTERCHAPTER   *The Measure of a Christian College*   140

CHAPTER SIX   *The Way Ahead*   161

Acknowledgments   193

Footnotes to Chapters   195

Index   203

Preface

This book is born of a series of convictions. But the major faith on which it is based is a belief that unless American education, in all of its major manifestations in American life from kindergarten to graduate school, can be brought to a deeper appreciation of the place of ethical and religious values in the classroom and the goal of spiritual maturity for both the learner and the teacher, American education will continue to fail its own high objective.

I believe in education's dynamic power. But it is in an education that is concerned for all phases of a man's growth that significance and power make for prosperity and happiness and peace. When education becomes partial, provincial, and dwarfed, the consequences are blindness and confusion.

America is emerging from a moral depression, which has been the more devastating for the reason that we did not recognize the seriousness of our ethical and spiritual poverty. In fact, we did not even know that we were poor in these realms of the spirit. Our jolly, easygoing paganism was so pleasantly sophisticated and so obviously adequate for most of the needs of our inconsequential living that it was only in crisis or in hours of high aspiration that we recognized its unworthiness.

The signs of hope for a better day lie in our reaching for new bases of moral security, knowing that these must be laid not alone for our own safety as a nation, but for the peace of the world. "Our wealth and our material resources are only a Maginot Line." There are other signs of hope, too, in our growing awareness that graft and corruption must be rooted out of our national and community life, and in the fresh quickening of faith in the truth of freedom, provided freedom becomes a responsibility as well as a right.

Our patterns of education, with their emphases upon tangible evidences of prosperity and their secularistic ignoring of ethical values and that which gives validity to values, have had their part in leading

us into our years of depression, and into the characteristics of lostness and wistfulness which Dr. Nels Ferré lists as qualities of our age.[1]*
Education, with revived and enlightened ethical and religious patterns, may provide us the leadership that shall point the way to wiser and better days. These are straws in the wind, but we shall be blind indeed if we fail to see that the wind also carries its amber burden of chaff which ancient poetry made the symbol of uselessness and godlessness.

These are generalizations which have feeble life until they can be translated into the routines and the duties, the specific objectives and the personal opportunities, of the student, the instructor, the administrator. So to translate is the endeavor of this book.

This is definitely not a book with all the answers. It is not a book written by a man who knows all the answers. Rather, it is a book of many questions—questions which grow out of years of struggle with education. To some of those questions answers are proposed. If the book has significance, however, it is because there is suggested a frame of reference for the educational process within which the questions must be received and the answers sought.

For want of a more exact label, that frame of reference is called "Christian." I wish there were a word that opened the door to the great traditions of both the Jewish and Christian faiths. I know of no such word. "Judean-Christian" and "Hebraic-Christian" are a scholar's terms and not easily adapted to conversation.

* * *

GENTLE PROTEST

I am plagued by the memory of a conversation of some years ago, in which an extremely intelligent and cultured young Jewish matron said to me:

"Why do you always talk about Christian education? We Jews are a part of the American community. We Jews send our children to the public-school system. Indeed we Jews send our sons and daughters to the colleges you talk about, and whenever you speak of them as Christian colleges, I feel as if you were trying to push us out in the cold. I feel as if it were a slap in the face, although I know you have no such intention."

"But what is there to use in place of 'Christian'?" I asked.

"There is, of course, the adjective 'religious,' but its use is so

* Footnotes are grouped for easy reference, beginning on page 195.

diluted. It includes too much, it includes everything, it includes nothing."

Reluctantly she agreed.

"It is in no strictly doctrinal sense that we speak of Christian colleges and Christian education. I am sure that few who make use of the phrase give thought to the dogma which may divide your people and mine." She nodded.

"Is there no chance that with the full recognition that Christian values are built upon Hebraic values, and Christian truths grow out of Hebraic soils, that the Jew of liberal faith might come to feel himself included in the phrase 'Christian,' even though he remained loyal to a synagogue?"

She was slow in answering. Finally she spoke: "Perhaps it could be; perhaps it should be. It would be hard, but some of us might try."

* * *

"Christian" is a label sometimes used for purposes of exclusiveness. It has too often been made a means of keeping the other fellow outside the circle. In using it I hope most earnestly that in the spirit of the Master it may suggest inclusiveness; I want the other fellow to feel that he can share in the anticipations and the efforts of Christian education.

Most assuredly I use it in no sectarian sense. Too often, in the religious life of America, sectarianism has drowned out the voice of Christianity. In education, sectarianism is in large part responsible for the divorce of religious teaching from the classroom. A century or less ago, if the churches of America had been able to agree on the deserved place of religion, and particularly the kind of religion, in the public schools, we would not today be faced with the censored education which is our portion. The contemporary patterns of religionless education are the work of a disagreeing Christianity more than a proselyting secularism. If religion can be brought back into education, particularly on the level of college and university where the outlook is hopeful, it must be an inclusive, cooperative Christianity—ecumenical in the unity of spirit of all Christians.

I hope, too, that I do not use the label in any narrow Protestant sense. I would welcome the agreement of Catholics and Protestants on the endeavors that must be made.

I choose the adjective "Christian" rather than "religious" for the reason that "Christian" is in accord with our strongest American cultural and religious traditions. It has historical significance for our country. It is not easily defined, unfortunately, and explanations will range from the easy tolerance of humanism, with a Christian coloration, to the strictest fundamentalist interpretations, with a doctrinal creed attached for every man's signature. Nevertheless, for the purposes of education, Christianity has a body of concepts which are recognized; it has a code of ethics which is generally known although not adhered to, and a Person to attract the supreme commitment of a man's life.

The word "religious," on the other hand, has become a catchall. When used exclusively to denote the faiths of the great religions of the world, it has meaning; but so often the thoughtless and the uncritical have made of it a wastebasket into which they toss all loyalties, both those which are high and those which acknowledge no deity; all attachments, both those which are worthy to stand in first place, and those which are given to political systems and to recreational devotion, such as communism and bridge. There is not much substance, and still less authority, left in a word which can be stretched to contain the exalted faith of a St. Francis and the Sunday-morning worship of an ardent golfer.

* * *

HELLO . . . HELLO!

There is the story of a mother who called the headmaster of one of the great Episcopal private schools and asked for an appointment. She wanted her son registered at a religious school—and this was "a religious school?" Might she see the headmaster?

The reply was given that the day was a holyday; since it was Ascension Day the headmaster would not come to his office.

The mother made this reply: "Oh, a church holiday! I think I'll come anyhow. I would like to see your campus when you have a holy holiday; and tell me, what time will the ascension be?"

* * *

The word "Christian" is used, moreover, at times as synonymous with the Good with its concern for human welfare and the development of that kind of community living which shall offer the opportunity of meaningful days to the greatest possible number of men and women. There is always danger, of course, that what pertains to the Good shall be appropriated as inherently and basically Christian, whereas that particular item of goodness may belong to a far larger constituency of all religious faiths and indeed to all men who seek the Good whether with or without a group label. Honesty can be both a pagan and a Christian virtue. Integrity was esteemed in days of old by the lovers of Zeus as well as in later days by the followers of Jesus of Nazareth. Righteousness is not a Christian monopoly. But for the American reader, if righteousness, whether corporate or individual, is to have a religious validity, that validity has historically been Christian.

With this explanation, let the subtitle "Some Frontiers of Christian Education" stand.

The chapters are written against a background of thirty years of educational effort, as student, as teacher, as college administrator. Because my own thinking is of necessity molded by the events of these three decades, I have felt free to draw upon them, even to the extent of local impressions and personal experiences. Because those experiences came on the campuses of undergraduate colleges, much of this book deals with the problems of higher education. I dare to hope, however, that some of the conclusions reached may have their application for the other areas of education as well.

This book comes directly out of one man's stumbling effort to think through the perplexing problems and demanding needs of the American classroom. It comes out of his sincere but often mistaken endeavors to put the conclusions of that thinking into the forms of actuality. To say that the thinking is partial, and the attempts inconclusive, is only to say that man is fallible.

* * *

Our Two Ultimate Dangers

Charles Malik, the distinguished delegate from Lebanon to the United Nations, has written in The Commonweal:

"There are two ultimate dangers besetting present-day preoccupation with the problem of human rights. The first is . . . the danger of materialism. . . . There is a deadly danger that in our enthusiasm for economic and social justice we forget that man cannot live by bread alone. . . .

"The second danger is . . . the danger of humanism. We

*have been endlessly speaking of human rights, as though
there was nothing except man in the universe, as though he
was the center of existence. . . .*

*"If we have our rights, God always has His rights over us;
and in vain shall we seek our rights, until, confessing our sins,
we recognize in all brokenness and humility, the dominion
of God over the course of history and of human life."*[2]

* * *

The conclusions drawn in these chapters that follow have been
coming upon me through the years. I have struggled to find light,
and to share it in the speaking and the writing which I have done.
Parts of the chapter on "Can Education Be Meaningfully Christian?"
and the second Interchapter on "The Measure of a Christian College"
are sufficiently close in outline to the form in which they originally
were printed in *School and Society* and *The Intercollegian* (*motive*
later reprinted from *The Intercollegian*) that I should be ungracious
if I did not express my thanks to these publications for their permission to make use of this earlier material. Sections of Chapters 3, 4,
and 5 have appeared in *motive, The Christian Scholar,* and *The
Journal of Higher Education.* Several of the "Interludes" are taken
from the small monthly leaflets *from Hiram* and *at Denison.* I am
grateful to the editors of these periodicals for their permission to use
this material.

Without the encouragement the Trustees of the Danforth Foundation have given me and the leisure they have made possible, I should
never have been able to bring this work to its present stage of com-
pletion. Let me tender my sincere thanks to them, and, also, to Dr.
Elizabeth Stanton and my wife for their helpful criticism, and to my
secretary, Miss Lillie Mae Rose, for her untiring efforts in the preparation of the manuscript.

I would express, too, my appreciation to two great Christian educators whose recent books have summed up in superlative fashion
the best of British and American thought on our present efforts to
educate man: Sir Walter Moberly, author of *The Crisis in the University,* and my friend, Howard Lowry, author of *The Mind's Adventure.* If the reader should ask why still another book on education is
necessary when so much has already been written, let him know that
there have been hours when the author in all sincerity raised the same
question. The decision to continue was made, not with any egotistic

hunger for the printed word, but in response to a contemporary need that every man stand up and be counted.

The educational world is sorely divided and every vote is needed, although not every vote need be a volume. There is the mighty struggle whether education shall deal alone with minds or the men who possess the minds; there is the struggle whether education shall effect a religious neutrality which in truth becomes propaganda for non-religion, or shall, within legal framework and with the support of the great majority of Americans, present religious faith and thought as appropriate parts of American culture, necessary to the needs of every maturing person.

This book is one man's vote on these fundamental issues.

Not Minds Alone

Chapter One. Questions Both Pertinent and Impertinent

Fear not waves nor winds that bring
The unbridled hurricanes;
Fear not cold nor the sleet's sting,
Flaming heat nor levelling rain;
Fear not even fear itself,
Fear not pain.

Only fear the eye grown dull,
Only fear the heart grown bland
That applauds the beautiful
With condescending hand,
Only fear the green fields covered
By the sand.[1]

ELIZABETH COATSWORTH

IN A RECENT year, 425,000 young men and women enrolled as college freshmen. Presumably, in saying good-by, their parents bestowed upon them the blessing of good advice. Presumably, also, many a father and mother used the early letters of that year to pass on to their absent son or daughter some of the hopes, aspirations, and quavering anxieties that were in their hearts.

One father, a businessman serving as chairman of his local board of education, wrote to his son as follows: "The college will do its part; of that I have no doubt, although I sometimes wish that colleges were less wedded to tradition. The faculty will teach competently. I believe that, although again I wish that more of our American teachers would bring an adventuresome enthusiasm to their classrooms. I am aware, and I guess you are, that the burden of effort lies largely on you. If you are determined to fail, you can; and all that the college or the faculty or your fraternity brothers or your mother and I can do will not alter that consequence. But knowing you, I have no fear of that failure. If I have any fear at all it is that your college experience may be less significant than it might be because of the temptation to easy satisfaction and uncritical success. That is why I am sharing with you some of the ambitions and prayers that I have in my heart for you.

"One of my great desires is that the college will give you a reasonably complete intellectual introduction to the world in which you are destined to live. I hope you will come through the four years knowing a considerable amount about its past and also its present. I hope you will know much about the peoples of the world and their institutions. All this can't be done in four years, but four years of honest effort added to your high-school education can give you a good foundation for becoming an intelligent and a well-informed man.

"I am hoping most earnestly that the college years will help you to choose wisely the purposes that will control your life. Here your fraternity brothers, your college activities, your social contacts, will play a large part, together with the teachers and the teaching in the classroom. I doubt seriously whether there is in you any ability or capacity that earmarks you as a genius, but I do believe that you have a chance to become a first-rate man. Remember, there is no substitute for a first-rate man. It certainly would be worth your effort to make the hardest try you have in you to make.

"Your mother and I are hoping, also, that the college experience will reconfirm within you the religious impulse to seek and to obey God as best you can conceive Him. We have tried to help you in this regard, and we have been proud of the response that you have made. Neither your mother nor I ask that you search for God by the same ways that we have sought Him, but we do ask that you seek and continue to seek Him. And we pray that you may find Him. It is of utmost importance that you constantly reinterpret your experience in religion, whether it be large or small, in your daily life: what you do with your time, how you use your money, where you bestow your friendship. What you choose to do with that self which is in your keeping is the answer that you will make to the invitation of religion. Deep within our hearts we want you to be a good man.

"Because of our family background and because also of our American culture, it is probable that your religious life will be within the framework of the Christian faith. As you come to study the great religions of the world, I think you will find that they give new meaning and enlarged dimensions to the Christian religion with its claim on the best of a man's mind and heart and life. Looking toward the years that lie ahead for you, your mother and I are hoping that you may be a growing, working Christian, even as you have been through your years of adolescence. I think that means that you must find a position both in Christian faith and Christian activity that gives promise of offering maximum truth and maximum hope for your own personal maturity, and a promise too of maximum usefulness for you in an ailing society. If you decide to continue your membership in the church where your mother and I have had our spiritual life, we shall be happy. But what is vastly more important is that you take your place somewhere actively, creatively in the Christian community of the Church, both for your own needs and for the needs of your day.

"You know that I have faith in American education, for I have spoken of it often to you. You know, too, that I have large faith in you, my son. Neither education nor you is perfect. There is too much humanity hanging around for that. But of this I am confident: that if you at your best take your educational opportunities at their largest, in the next four years something significant can happen to you, as a man with both a mind and a heart.

"I sign myself, with proud love, your father."

IT'S DIFFERENT FROM A PARTNERSHIP

Baccalaureate sermons speak easily of the great partnership of religion and education. The subject is appropriate, the audience responsive; the speaker usually contents himself with generalizations which picture a farm scene of idyllic beauty in the Millet mood: two great oxen in a companion yoke slowly, somewhat sullenly, and certainly not too ambitiously dragging a plow which turns the furrows of earth.

The analogy, though common, is inadequate. It suggests that either ox alone could do the job, though less speedily. This assumption is basically false. Education cannot be complete without attention to the inner urges of man, and his outreach beyond himself—this is the stuff of religion. In turn, religion cannot be complete without the activities of the mind, which gather and evaluate facts, assumptions, and opinions and put them together into some creative pattern for judgment and action—here is the stuff of education.

Education and religion are not in partnership. They are basic units of a single process which requires a wise and complimentary integration of both. Neither is complete in itself; neither is at its best when attempting to stand alone.

* * *

THIS INTERNATIONAL FAMILY

In the summer of 1950, 120 young people from 26 nations came to the Friutjof Nansen International Student Haus, Gottingen, Germany, to see if men and women from many walks of life might together create a genuine community. Their wish was to discard the traditional prejudices which tend to divide human beings of different national, religious, racial, economic, and social backgrounds.

For periods of three weeks they studied and discussed, worked and played together under a common roof. They elected a self-governing council and appointed social, cultural, and house committees. Each student took his turn at every-thing from leading a debate to peeling the potatoes.

They probed deeply into the basic issues which they will have to face some tomorrow. More important, though, than the things said were the things done.

Through the mutual living experience, hurdles of nationalism and ignorance were met by understanding and consideration. Indonesians and Dutch, Germans and French, Indians and English, lost many a preconceived notion about one another while drying dishes side by side. This international family set the foundation for something positive: a democratic ideal given life through the pattern of "Love thy Neighbor."[2]

* * *

Realistic thinking demands, however, that it be said that neither education nor religion has always found it easy to endure each other's company, much less to yield graciously to the union. In recent years, at least, education has frequently been contemptuous of religion and religion frequently anxious with fear toward education.

Education is aware that the historical record holds abundant evidence of days when the Church sought to close the door on truth, being more concerned for the protection of her own inaccuracies than for the discovery of new understanding of God and His ways with man. In the list of the Church's heretics have stood many a distinguished scholar to whom time has brought justification, but too late to extinguish the contemporary flames of public hate and of the execution pyre. Too often the educationalist—the generalization is at least 51 per cent true—makes no effort to distinguish between religion and the Church. In his thinking the two are one, and religion must bear the blame for the sins of her daughter. The questions are asked, asked with pertinence: What reason is there to believe that the Church's door is open wide today to truth, new truth disclosed and supported with all the scholarly procedures of education?

Religion has answered with no single voice; her children are divided. Some churches have minds sealed against new truth or fresh understanding of old truth. Some churches have swung the door wide open, almost with appetite for novelty and the untried, believing in the unity of truth and certain that God's truth cannot suffer, at least ultimately, at the hands of honest inquiry.

RELIGION RAISES HER QUERY

Religion, too, asks her question with its measure of pertinence and impertinence: Recognizing that religion, like education, has its strong and its weak, its low and its high, its wisdom and its foolishness, why will not education eagerly recognize the component of religion insofar as religion is willing to stake its future on the unity of God's truth and the complete freedom of inquiry?

* * *

ONE MAN's JUDGMENT

In a public lecture at Washington University, Gerald Heard listed the three virtues which in his opinion were most necessary for our day:

1. *Anonymity and the willingness to work without public recognition for one's effort.*
2. *Frugality and the continuing endeavor to escape the entanglement of the materialistic world.*
3. *Continued training which refuses to give up the search for enlarged vision in any area of understanding.*

* * *

Men of religion have brought their criticism that large areas of American education appear to be founded upon an inadequate concept of man. They suggest that education is tempted to emphasize only the lower animal hungers—food, shelter, rest, play, sex. Man, they plead, is more than animal heritage; and within him are the higher hungers for meaningfulness and creative craftsmanship and love. It is the responsibility of education to point the way to the satisfaction of these hungers. Such satisfactions, they argue, are not to be found without recourse to the truth and the inspiration of religion.

The answer of education has too often been given in the strident voice of the dogmatic scientist: Animal-man we can measure, but what do we know of the spirit-man that you claim we are neglecting? How can we use our test tubes and our laboratory flasks, our experimental procedures, on him? If we have been concerned with animal-man, it is because we are scientists and hold the methods of science to be the wide avenue leading to truth.

But of late years the psychologist has been less certain than the natural scientist that the problem of values and the realm of the spirit can be wholly isolated from the classroom and the laboratory. He, too, like the psalmist of old, has asked the eternal question, What is man? and at least a few of the profession have returned with reverence and an answer that appears to be the combination answer from men of both science and religion.

Nevertheless, religion and education have seen more clearly their points of disagreement than the unity which is rightfully theirs. They differ on means to the discovery of truth as well as truth itself. They do not see eye to eye on the life goals which each is sponsoring.

* * *

The Education of Little Jack Horner

The legend does not reveal how far Jack went with his formal education. He may have quit his school after eight grades, since presumably he was not affected by our modern educational laws. He may have gone on through high school, scorning college as offering nothing that was worth knowing. He may indeed have had the advantages of four years of college training, and still have been the nasty little moral isolationist that he was.

Concern for the common welfare is highly desirable in all educational effort; it is absolutely indispensable in Christian education. Too many students, reinforced by home training of silence and parental example, see college and their world through the eyes of little Jackie. They see it as a place to learn how to make one's corner larger and more exclusive, how to ensure one's Christmas pie being bigger and better tasting, how to secure one's own personal satisfaction through the most trivial accomplishment, as if pulling a plum out of a pie were a proper cause for excitement and self-congratulation.

*Jackie Horner must have been an unendurable prig, insuf-
ferably smug and self-satisfied, completely engrossed in his
own small existence, and isolated from the world of human
need.*

*G. Roy Elliott has commented ". . . if he had handed his
plum or even half of it to his younger brother he might have
exclaimed with still more satisfaction (in private, of course)
'What a good boy am I!' "*

*The thought never came to Jack's restricted mind; maybe
his home was to blame, maybe his church, maybe his school.
Jack's education was left ragged and incomplete. If Jack alone
suffered it would have been serious enough, but Jack's community suffered too. It lost Mr. John Horner as a responsible
Christian citizen.*

* * *

Education through its agent, the school, has largely fostered the
"success pattern" with its emphasis on tangible achievement—grades,
honors, membership in honorary societies, and then a job where
significance is measured by salary. Religion through its agent, the
Church, while by no means free from the influence of this success
pattern, has looked on, troubled and fearful, still convinced in better
moments of the essential truth that the man with the full barn and
the contented stomach somehow finds his soul "required of him"
by his treasury of accumulated things. When education sets personal
or professional success as the sole goal for a man's life, religion cries
in protest of spirit "No." When education in the mood of compromise says, "We'll shift the goal to make it a man's loyalty to his
group; let that be his *summum bonum* in life," religion still will
not yield, saying that the measure of a man must be his obedience to
a divine will. Then education snorts in disgust and uses such words
as "obscurantism," "mysticism," "silly nonsense."

THE CRUELEST WORD OF CRITICISM

When religion and education have attempted to face each other
on a basis of equality, there has been a still more fundamental misunderstanding between them—greater either than the misunderstanding that religion was dangerously anti-intellectual or that education belied itself by promoting a popular brand of materialism
wherein man's life was made to consist primarily of TV sets and
electric refrigerators. Religion and education sitting together on a

love seat were unanimous in their acclaim of the importance of education, at least so far as education did not intrude upon sectarian
doctrine or belittle that which the Church magnified. But religion
and education, side by side, were not unanimous on the importance·
of religion. The major and most destructive criticism which the
friends of education have propounded is simply the irrelevance of
religion, both to education and to the contemporary culture which
education represents. Too often the educationalist, like the poli-
tician, fearing the interference of social-visioned religion, has cried,
"Religion is personal. It is man's choice in his solitude and, like
man's shaving, should be kept for his moments of privacy. It is
something apart from and something extraneous to the whole province of learning; it is like romance, primarily an emotional choice,
riding the wind and as unpredictable and impermanent."

When the educationalist pronounces this interdiction of irrelevance, he is thinking of the Church rather than of religion, and of the
Church at its dramatic worst—divided, loving superstition, ineffec-
tive, other-worldly. It is a judgment of prejudice made in ignorance
of the high importance of religion in its fullness or the Church at its
royal best.

* * *

Two Horns of a Dilemma

*It seems to me that one of the really great problems now
affecting education is: How can state-supported schools provide spiritual growth and yet maintain the American concept
of separation of church and state? One serves as an indispensable tenet for the preservation of a good life and the
other as a preservation of a democratic way of life. These
basic tenets are compatible and must be so found on every
college campus.*[3]

* * *

The Harvard Report, *General Education in a Free Society,* is an
example of American education in its secular strength, rejecting
theology as no longer capable of serving as an architectural cornerstone and not bothering to note in passing that religion is more than
theological controversy and might conceivably have valuable contributions to make to the education of the whole man.

The concern of the writers of the Harvard Report for the education of the whole man was, however, indirectly a triumph of a religious point of view. Indeed, the religious implications of the Report are strong; the assumptions of the committee are not without their religious foundations. The committee takes its stand, for example, on "belief in the dignity and mutual obligation of man," and affirms faith that man can reach "agreement on the good of man at the level of performance without the necessity of agreement on ultimates." Gordon K. Chalmers, in a brilliant analysis of the affirmations of faith within the Report (quoting these as two such affirmations), has commented, "This . . . involves Christian and other religious belief. . . . It is the faith of humanism. . . . Indeed many theologians, Catholic, Jewish, and Protestant, regard humanism as essential to religious faith. They are right, for without humanism religion can find no adequate account of man's nature."[4]

Nevertheless, without greed, one wishes for more. Man grows restless in the halfway house of the spirit which humanism provides. When education concerns itself with the moral norm, if not "on the level of agreement on ultimates at least on the level of performance," is there not need to embody in the pattern of education some attention to the forces of religion which since the days of Judaism have been the heart beat of the moral norm? Is there not reason to expect at least some recognition of the relevance of religion? But the reader seeking in the Report for some recognition of the place of theistic religion in contemporary American education might conclude that the committee counted it an unimportant sideshow on the periphery of the fairgrounds, or a decorative piece of bric-a-brac for the family mantle, valuable as an antique, interesting as a curio.

In response to the Harvard committee's words, "we must perforce speak in purely humanistic terms, confining ourselves to the obligations of man to himself and to society," Harold C. Phillips says, "To use [this] as a reason for omitting religious instruction . . . is to reveal either an astonishing blind spot or surprising ignorance of the true nature of the Christian religion. Actually it would be hard to find two better reasons for its study than precisely those for which this committee has deemed it wise to omit it."[5]

The irrelevance of religion is one of the predominating attitudes to be found during the first half of the twentieth century, when the structure of modern secular education, splendid in its strength, magnificent in its extensiveness, but nevertheless faulty and incomplete, was being refashioned.

Even the church-related colleges came to be apologetic for their church connections and more than one sloughed off a relationship which had become an embarrassing tradition. The fetish of objectivity restrained many a conscientious instructor from making witness to his religious faith. With glorious exceptions, the campus attitudes of many colleges, both independent and tax-supported, made any active practice of Christianity a halfhearted art. The churches had their student work, foundations they called them, and occasionally the leadership was creative and the support generous, but in too many situations these were appendages to the college life, located on the circumference of the campus and touching only a handful of the minority who still held to their Christian faith in spite of the prevalent paganism, or those desiring companionship in their Sunday-evening loneliness.

It was assumed that our American paganism was adequate as a national philosophy—adequate at least to those American pagans who appeared to find it adequate.

There is much to be admired and much to be praised in the standards and achievement of American education during this period; but that appreciation and praise need not blind one to the thoroughly secular character of the dominant educational pattern.

THE DUEL OF OPPOSING THEORIES

In that pattern there were two theories of education struggling for mastery. There was on the one hand the conception of education exclusively as the training of the mind. Those who held to this theory would take the mind of a child and sharpen it as an instrument. They would take clay and, on the potter's wheel, fashion a vessel they might fill with the heritage of the world's wisdom and the world's finest experience, even as one might pour water into a jar. They were not blind to the fact that it is men who possess minds. But their first concern was not with the man, but with the mind of the man. They saw themselves dealing not with children, with all the individualities and the uniqueness of a child, but rather with a single aspect of individuality, the process of mentality, and as they developed this process of mentality they did so with disregard for the spiritual needs of man, for in their eyes religion was irrelevant.

It would be unfair to suggest that the concern of these educators actually stopped with the mind. They had high hopes of what the child and eventually the man would do with the sharpened instrument at his disposal. They looked with pride upon the heritage of human knowledge which their educational forefathers had passed on as a gift to be wisely used; they in turn were transmitting it to the next generation, enriched and enlarged like the Biblical talents that were productively invested.

But these hopes and desires and high expectations were for the most part disassociated from the educational process through which they worked. They were hopes and expectations taken for granted if—and the "if" needs to be written in italics—the training of the mind was accomplished. Basically and traditionally our American education from the elementary grades to the college years has been grounded on the assumption that the one thing to be sought first and foremost is the trained mind—and any second emphasis came far in arrears.

Then during the decade of the First World War there was developed a new emphasis, although in fact it was as old as Greek education, an emphasis on the wholeness of the man of whom the mind was part. It was essentially a religious emphasis, but unfortunately the development came through educational leaders who were still deeply convinced of the irrelevance of religion in education.

John Dewey and his disciples are responsible for pointing out to us the necessity of activity combined with learning. They have insisted rightly that education shall provide means whereby the child may interpret the idea which the mind entertains. With the endeavor to develop group activity there has come to the child a concept of "belonging," together with some understanding of the importance of community. These new enlightenments were essentially religious and it is unfortunate that their full implications were not made clear at the time.

These developments are based on the assumption of the rightful importance of the child; "child-centered" our educationalists wisely though pedagogically call it. They recognize that there is a heart to be trained as well as a mind. They know that behind both heart and mind the person stands, including both and more. They are intent to do all they can to make education an avenue to full and desirable living, as well as to wise learning.

THEORIES IN ACTION

These movements spread from the grade school to the college campus. Whereas forty or fifty years ago the students were responsible themselves for their own activities in such cultural areas as dramatics and music and debate, engaging their own coach and arranging their own contests, now the college has brought these interests into the circle of the curriculum. Professional direction is given; academic credit is established. A phenomenal change in college life is the advent of appreciation for the best in classical music, sung and played by well-directed college choirs and orchestras. The elderly alumnus who may recall with nostalgia, the days when students were "their own masters," and given a large measure of responsibility for their use of leisure time, may be expressing a preference for barbershop harmonies rather than Palestrina, Mozart, and Bach. One need not be the oldster to prefer with hearty enthusiasm the productions of Shaw, Ibsen, and Maxwell Anderson, designed with skillful care and played with finesse and strength, to Charlie's Aunt and the painful efforts of collegiate Thespians of not so long ago.

As they care for their daily assignments of the classroom and the laboratory, our faculties today (for the most part) believe that it is not minds alone, but men, with whom they are working. Through the participation of college students in the experience of great music or well-interpreted plays or the struggle through debate with major issues of our day, our administrators recognize that here are experiences that aid in the making of men and women capable of leading interesting and serviceable lives.

The changes that have come in the physical living of our college students are an expression of the new concern for the total man. The effort of colleges to build dormitories is not alone a means of caring for the fundamental problem of housing; it is that, to be sure, but it is more. It is a philosophy of housing, based on the theory that group living, if wisely directed, can be an experience that makes for rich maturity. The new concern for counseling and the plan which many colleges have of assigning every student a faculty counselor for at least the first year—this, too, is recognition of the college's obligation to provide every possible opportunity for the full growth of the full personality.

MORAL LEUKEMIA

Then, in the decade of the forties, America fell into a depression. It came with the war and as a consequence of the war. To be sure, it had been foretold according to the patterns of other wars, but as Americans we did not really expect it, and when it came, as Americans, we did not recognize it.

* * *

REFLECTION OF AN AG SENIOR

It was at the end of a summer-camp session where students from colleges had gathered for a program of study and sport, inspiration and recreation. A senior from an A. and M. school was talking with the man who had taught the course in ethics.

"Why can't we have this kind of thing in college? Here I am an Ag senior, and never along the way have I had any teacher help me in any way to see what makes right right and wrong wrong. I guess I never stopped to ask the question myself. I know all about cows and chickens and pigs. I can raise stock and breed them. But it seems to me that every man in college, no matter what he is going to do, ought to have a good, strong course in right and wrong. It wouldn't keep us from doing wrong, but it might make us think twice."

* * *

It was not an economic depression like our despair of 1931 when production wheels ground to a slow stop and men sold apples on the street corner. It was a moral and ethical depression when college students debated whether there was significance to existence itself, believing less than halfheartedly that through their words and air-tight arguments a simple answer might be found to so tremendous and profound a question. Cheating in our high schools and on our college campuses was strongly on the increase. Students justified their dishonesty on the score of over-emphasis upon grades, the demands of the employer for good records, and the easy "everyone does it." Men in high places sold themselves for high prices, and men in low places tried to get something better than a low price. Integrity became more a dictionary word and less a moral center of American life. One commentator noted that the roots of our virtues had withered for lack of sustenance. "They push deep but there is no water. They spread far but the land is parched. They shrivel, they weaken, they no longer sustain the growth above."

The awareness of inadequacy may be an introduction to adequacy; a sensitiveness to weakness can become an approach to strength. The individuals and the groups of individuals who, even when public morale was falling, held fast to an ideal of a national integrity never failed to speak with courage that without a foundation of religious convictions and spiritual strength, our national absorption in military might would be the cause of our national destruction. And men and women, believing with Robert M. Hutchins that "civilization is the deliberate pursuit of a common ideal [and] education is the deliberate attempt to form human character in terms of an ideal,"[6] looked to our schools and colleges as sources of renewed hope and moral security.

The years since the war carried their tumultuous problems for these institutions, problems of peak enrollments followed by valleys of budgetary difficulties—and if the former demanded additional work, the latter brought additional worry—and always the big question on those infrequent occasions when the flood crested high: What is the measure of education's fidelity to its main purpose of caring not alone for minds but for men—the total man with a soul as well as a parcel of gray matter?

A mounting awareness that the moral supports of our national life were being eaten into by corruption and greed brought many thoughtful Americans to a new consideration of the need for a revitalized and cleansing spirit in education. To save our democracy and us, it was agreed that it must be an education of more than facts and skills and patterns of dollar success. When a visitor from Australia told us that our absorption in the Lincoln legend was caused less by the spiritual greatness of the man than by our inordinate pride in his climb from log cabin to White House, some Americans began to wonder if the prevalent success patterns of American life, so largely extolled by schoolteachers, business executives, and government officials, were, after all, responsible for the popular standard of dollar-success-at-any-price. Shocking, indeed, was the knowledge that hundreds of thousands of young people in schools and colleges were totally lacking any commanding sense of purpose or clear arrow of direction, which the home and the Church together with the school are expected to offer; and that these young people in consequence were drifting with a dangerous inclination to say "Yes" when the right answer was "No," and to say "No" in reply to those invitations for creative and constructive effort when "Yes" might have brought new meaning to an empty life. Somehow we must make the spiritual values of honesty and honor, integrity and brotherhood, inescapably important. There must be built foundations sufficient to support significant living.

THE AGENTS OF MORAL RECONSTRUCTION

The churches in their divided ways have been deeply concerned with the situation and have followed their concern with new plans for action. The home, being without organization and understanding less than the Church and the school wherein it has failed, did little except to pass the responsibility on to the Church, if interest was there, or else to the more accessible school.

And the school with its older sister, the college, responded to the new situation according to the measure of the enlightenment of its leadership. The situation was obviously one too large for the school to remedy alone. The Church, the home, the school, with all the community agencies for public welfare, must cooperate; and the school heeded the alert. The problem was clearly one to which new buildings, larger facilities, better recreation, more equipment, could give only partial answer. It was essentially a spiritual problem, and the American people with their practical-mindedness shy away from the uncertainty of the spiritual. They cannot get their hands on it. It is not something to be added in an account book or measured by a yardstick; in consequence, they avoid and evade it.

More and more people were seeing a need with renewed clarity. The magnitude of the problem was inescapable. The problem was more than an educational problem, and yet the local educational groups and the community leaders were inclined to say, "Here at least we can make our first approach to some solution." And they turned their gaze of criticism and hope inward upon their own schools.

They soon discovered that the schools and colleges, which are intended to bring to the young American a worthy, commanding purpose in life, too often themselves have been purposeless. Our schools and colleges, which are intended to aid the student in his choice of direction, his choice of ultimate goals, have too often themselves been directionless, too deeply concerned with the tangible question of immediate vocations while ignoring the more difficult problem of ultimate goals. Our schools and colleges—theoretically, at least, responsible for the teaching of those spiritual values which give meaning to life—have so often, because of problems involved in that teaching, quietly shelved the difficulty and allowed the courses to become valueless. It is true that the schools and colleges were never intended to serve as substitutes for the Church. Teaching the doctrines of the Church and pointing the way evangelistically to an accessible God to whom man is responsible is not the primary task of the school; some would say not the task, either primary or tertiary. Nevertheless, neither has it been intended that the schools should, by their complete silence in the matter, present to the student a cosmic picture from which God is conspicuously absent, and man without accountability to anyone save his banker and then only when his account fails to balance. As our leaders looked with care upon our educational scene, they found to their dismay that in our rightful loyalty to the doctrine of separation of Church and State, we have gone to perilous extremes and separated education from religion in ways in which our forefathers and their children never intended.

HANDS OF DESPAIR AND ALSO OF HOPE

The piously sentimental among our leaders have raised their hands in horror at the stories of dope-peddling among the high-school students and the fixing of basketball games on the college level; and, content with pious ejaculations, they have done nothing. Some among the secularists have in genuine anxiety longed for the days when religion was for them a source of intellectual and moral security, but having cut the umbilical cord they were without power to restore it. The materialist consistent with his loyalty has often seen the answer only in terms of more buildings and higher salaries, rather than in the new uses to which buildings could be put or in the character of the men and women who struggle on undignified salaries to maintain a professional competence.

* * *

What American Democracy Really Is

In 1946-47 few, if any German students had come to America for study. A young captain in the Nazi Army, whom

I had met at a Hitler Labor Camp in 1938, wrote regretting his participation in the Hitler regime and asking if he might enroll at our college for study. I did not know whether he would meet our academic qualifications; neither did I know whether the students were ready to receive a German, for many of the young Americans on the campus had had military service.

Through the Social Action Committee the situation was brought to the students at one of their assemblies, and they were asked to vote in the fraternity and sorority meetings that evening on their willingness or unwillingness to have an ex-Nazi captain on the campus. We were still close enough to the war to be deeply moved by the prejudices and the vivid memories of suffering which those years had brought.

It was at the supper hour that my telephone rang and a voice which I recognized as the voice of a splendid young Jewish student from New York asked if he might see me at once. An appointment was made, and as I waited for him to come I thought that perhaps it was a mistake to consider bringing a German student so soon after the war. The Jewish students on the campus were in a small minority, but was it fair to them, considering what their people had suffered at Hitler's hands? I was certain I knew what the young man wanted. He was going to protest in the name of justice—and maybe there was justice, if not mercy, in his claim.

Max arrived at the appointed time, and we sat together in my study. "I have come to ask a great favor. I hope you will grant it if you can."

I waited for him to go on.

"In our assembly this morning it was announced that a German student might come to the campus."

I nodded, feeling certain that I knew what he would say next. Then to my surprise I heard him say: "If that German student should come, would you do me the very great favor"— he seemed to be groping for his words—"of letting me be his roommate? If I could live with him for a year, I think I could show him what American democracy really is."

When the vote was taken that night, it was 99 per cent in favor of the admission of the German student, if he was qualified; 19 per cent stated that they would not be too happy about receiving him, but that they would not be unfriendly; only 1 per cent insisted they would be hostile to him.[7]

* * *

There has come, nevertheless, a growing demand on the part of many persons, who may find themselves in less than complete philosophic agreement, that the time is ripe in American education for a reorganization of our program that shall take larger concern for values, purposes, and ideals, and even larger concern for the presentation of a world view which shall include a recognition of God and His expectation of man.

In no sense is this a demand that ecclesiastical institutions assume control for public education. Let them do a better job in the institutions for which they are responsible, the private preparatory school and the church-related college; for although these may have been intended as lighthouses in the decades of moral storm, in many cases the light of Christian purpose has been shining dimly and in some cases has faded into blackness.

The American churches of all faiths, however, may well raise their voices in support of the efforts to bring spiritual emphases into our public schools, and their voices will be heard, like the voices of other institutions; but the authority for reorganization will not rest in the hands of religious bodies. Any effort on the part of any church to reach for authority in the area of public education—outside, of course, of that educational domain which churches control by right of its disassociation and separateness from public education—must be steadfastly resisted whether the movement come from Protestant or Jew or Catholic or some group without known label.

Any solution that may be offered must be one of spiritual remedy for spiritual needs. And the *spiritual* can never be completely divorced from the *religious*. Any solution must come inherently and fundamentally from our American way of life, not from any single group. It must needs be a solution-in-emergency to which many will give partial consent even though withholding complete agreement.

THE CHRISTIAN ANSWER AND EDUCATION

The question both pertinent and impertinent which this chapter raises is: In the emergency in which American educational life finds itself, is not the most far-reaching and best remedial answer that of a pattern of Christian education? Let it be a pattern that shall maintain all of the best in educational standards and ideals which we now hold. But let it be a pattern which shall infuse those standards and ideals with a new and a far greater concern for the religious hungers of man.

The answer cannot be identical for the private and the public institute, but in direction and pattern is it not essentially the same? A pattern of education in which religion takes its rightful place with other academic disciplines, and religious-minded teachers, supported by religious-sensitive administrators, are daily serving the religious needs of American young people, seeking to support our American living with a faith that can stand the strains and tensions of our contemporary world. When I give this the name of Christian education, I do so with sympathetic recognition of the Judaic contribution to Christian faith. I do it with every hope of warm tolerance for other faiths which have their part to play in our world. But I do it with conviction that the fullest answers to our major needs are to be found in the teachings and the compelling example of Jesus of Nazareth who called men to follow Him in sacrificial self-forgetful service and dedication to Almighty God.

And yet, men talk so glibly about Christian education! One might think it a peculiar kind of brew, compounded of special herbs, that one makes in the teakettle, and that all that is needed is to go into the herb garden, select with care, and put the kettle on the stove. So often we have been guilty of using the words "Christian education" easily, far too easily, and, too frequently.

Let the reader face with all honesty and a sense of basic reality whether Christian education is a human possibility in the world of American schools and colleges and universities as we know it today. Occasionally from that picture there shines forth isolated examples which give reason for hope—the well-trained teacher who makes his faith a contagion, and students, seeing it, recognize instinctively that great living can grow out of great faith; the course in history or English literature or science that provides a sense of world perspective; the course in religion, where such course is possible, that gives an intellectual grasp on intangibles and the reason for the faith that can be in man; the contact of students and teacher in the classroom or on the school grounds whereby the virtues of honesty and integrity, or purity and honor, become living realities, accessible and attractive.

Educated minds, wedded to uneducated hearts, like concealed and exploded mines, are dangerous to the neighborhood. It was never intended that education should exist in a vacuum apart from and unrelated to the emergencies and the daily demands of life. Education was intended for the service and the welfare of mankind.

I do not know for certain whether or not it is possible for education on any of the levels of human need today to be basically and vigorously and completely Christian. But I hasten to add this: I can imagine no more significant, more urgently needed task in all our living than the effort to make education in the elementary school, the secondary school, the college, and the university intelligently, intrinsically, fundamentally more Christian than we now find it.

Interchapter.* Seeds of Hope

There is no formal religious revival among the young. God, for most young Americans, is still a vaguely comforting thought, theology a waste of time, and denominations beside the point. To large numbers of them, religion is still merely an ethical code. But God (whoever or whatever they understand by that word) has once more become a factor in the younger generation's thoughts. The old argument of religion v. science is subsiding; a system which does not make room for both makes little sense to today's younger generation. It is no longer shockingly unfashionable to discuss God.

Church attendance among the young has increased partly because churches have made strong efforts to win new followers through social and sport activities. But there is an unquestioned spiritual need at work, too. Says Dean Robert Strozier of the University of Chicago: "They all have a conscience." Says Historian Viereck: "They believe they believe; they do not necessarily believe. Not many of today's young people say they have seen God, but they think everybody needs to see God."[1]

TIME

THE decade of the forties was a decade of paradoxes and contradictions. In retrospect to many Americans, they were the Frightening Forties. The war and its aftermath, the lowering of generally accepted moral standards and the blurring of ethical codes, the tendency to call evil good and good evil—all of these are items in the history of the decade. Nevertheless, the American who sees only this discouraging collection of grays and blacks will gain a much-distorted understanding of the decade. In particular, he will be overlooking the testimony of an impressive number of endeavors and organizations which were struggling valiantly and conscientiously throughout the decade to strengthen those national forces of mor-

* This Interchapter is not a look ahead, it is a glance behind. It is an endeavor to see in brief retrospect the leaven working on our campuses in the last twenty-five years. Perhaps the most amazing thing in the picture is the amount of leaven which has been available, the numerous sprouting seeds of hope in the educational garden—and also the way efforts have multiplied during the decade 1940-50, at the very time that national standards of morality were falling. It is called an Interchapter for the reason that it is in essence a detour from the major thesis. It is an effort to get a cursory glance at some of the organizational instruments which are available. Those readers who have firsthand acquaintance with these groups, and are aware of the number of significant books and studies written on the subject, may choose to turn at once to the next chapter.

21

ality and religion which might stem a tide of ethical uncertainty
and restore a nation to sanity and morality. Throughout the period,
first in importance has been the sustaining work of the Church and
the Synagogue. Secularism, materialism, and our own special American brand of paganism might attack the men and women who con-
stituted the membership of the Church and the Synagogue, but the
institutions themselves never wavered in their foursquare stand for
personal and national righteousness, and for the daily demand of life,
lived under the continuing judgment of Almighty God.

The forces of institutional Protestantism, Catholicism, and Judaism have, nevertheless, been hesitant once again in the flow of history
to recognize the national necessity of close *rapprochement* between
religion and education, in some broad, cooperative pattern. Each of
the great faiths holds a strong allegiance to education with religion
playing an integral part; but each of the great faiths has been tempted
to see this need in less than community-wide and nation-wide terms.
Their answer too often has been the private, parochial school where
the Church was free to determine the measure and the kind of religion which should be mixed with education; whereas by this partial
solution—if solution at all—the major need of those outside these
schools was never met.

The last twenty-five years, and especially the last decade, have
seen a number of efforts in the area roughly designated as "religion
in higher education" which, although they were sympathetic with
the Church, were nevertheless without ecclesiastical connection. De-
scribe them, if you wish, as the cousin-agents of the church. And
as one examines these endeavors, one wonders if the province of
Christian education is slowly slipping away from the Church; and,
like the areas of community health and philanthropy, finding its
leaders among church-bred people who believe they can work more
effectively outside the institutional limitations.

Where does the Christian teacher or administrator look for aid in
his endeavor to make religion an integral part of higher education?
In terms of movements and significant endeavors, where have the
seeds of hope flourished most promisingly?

Among many—and it will obviously not be possible to mention
all—two movements which have given full support to the troubled
teacher and the seeking administrator are the National Council on
Religion in Higher Education and The Edward W. Hazen Foundation. Both work quietly without trumpets but with great effectiveness;

the spiritual content of American education today is significantly richer because of their efforts.

THE NATIONAL COUNCIL ON RELIGION IN HIGHER EDUCATION

Although 1922 is the official date of organization, it was in 1923 that Charles Foster Kent and his board of directors elected the first group of Kent Fellows. For the first thirty years of its history approximately four hundred carefully selected men and women were given appointment and membership in the Society of Fellows. The large majority of them were chosen during their graduate years and aided with financial stipends. A few were appointed after the promise of success was well established.

The careful selection of the Kent Fellows, together with the organization of the Society of Fellows and the annual Week of Work, have been the major accomplishments of the National Council although by no means all. The purposes of the Council have been to work "for the inclusion of religious experience as a proper subject in the curricula of our colleges and universities,"[2] as well as to aid young men and women "showing promise of outstanding leadership in relating the concerns of religion to higher education" to complete their graduate training which will "best equip them for the specific academic area in which they plan to work."[3]

Early in the Council's history Dr. Kent and his cohorts worked valiantly to select and train men and women for the chairs of religion in American colleges. They held the conviction that too often these appointments were given to those whose good intentions were inadequate substitutes for graduate study and tested strength as teachers. Within the quarter century much has been accomplished to effect within the colleges a recognition of religion as a discipline acceptable on a par with other academic disciplines. Instructors of religion have gradually won their place as full-fledged faculty colleagues, and the steadily increasing academic competence in this field has been owing in large measure to the wisdom and persistent efforts of the leaders of the National Council. In more recent years larger attention has been given to the selection of Kent Fellows from all the academic fields of subject matter, although the record still finds the group largest in philosophy and religion.

Through the quarter century the Kent Fellows have joined in corporate activities, such as the two excellent collections of essays, *The Vitality of the Christian Tradition*,[4] edited by George F. Thomas, and *Liberal Learning and Religion*,[5] edited by Amos N. Wilder. It is, however, in the field of graduate fellowships and the encouragement given to college teachers, both in their graduate preparation and in the early years of their establishment, that the Council has made its largest contribution to American education.

THE EDWARD W. HAZEN FOUNDATION

The Hazen Foundation, established in 1925, bears the name of the donor, Edward W. Hazen. The purpose of this foundation is to aid the cause of religion in higher education. In 1950 the trustees issued a twenty-five-year report which gave ample warrant for a sturdy belief that Mr. Hazen's objectives had been magnificently fulfilled in the first quarter of a century of the Foundation's endeavors.[6] With limited funds the leaders have achieved results worthy of the highest commendation.

The inquiring teacher will recognize the pattern of Hazen Associates. This is a program by which hundreds of men and women in colleges throughout the country have been encouraged in their teaching and enabled through a small grant to increase the student entertaining which they delighted to do. In recent years the Foundation has been experimenting with a larger grant made directly to the colleges on condition of a dollar-for-dollar matching. The total sum is then administered by a faculty committee for the purpose of enriched faculty-student relationships.

Through the annual Hazen Conferences, teachers of all disciplines from all corners of the country have been encouraged to probe into the multitude of problems in this area. The group thinking resulting from these conferences has spread like ripples on a pond to influence many faculty men and women and through them the spiritual living on scores of campuses.

* * *

FIVE TESTS OF THE VALIDITY OF A PROGRAM OF LIBERAL ARTS

1. *The right and the ability to think.*
2. *The capacity to appreciate values, both moral and social and religious.*
3. *A sense of the historic past and the prophetic future.*
4. *The step from contemplation to action.*
5. *The experience of commitment to a cause greater than self.*

* * *

The work of the Hazen Foundation, however, for which the Christian teacher will give most earnest praise is the series of pamphlets, issued intermittently but always dealing with pertinent subjects, by scholars who write with authority. A few of these titles, together with mention of their authorship, will indicate their importance:

The Place of Religion in Higher Education—Robert L. Calhoun.

Teaching Economics with a Sense of the Infinite and the Urgent—Patrick M. Malin.

Spiritual Problems of the Teacher—Ordway Tead.

The Contribution of Religion to Cultural Unity—Reinhold Niebuhr.

A Christian Context for Counseling—Albert C. Outler.

Written to "arouse, inform and stimulate thought, discussion and action," they have fulfilled their mission well.

Not content with treatment of isolated problems in the field of college teaching, the Foundation turned in 1947 to develop a plan which "enlisted the aid of scholars who were not only deeply interested in the relations between religion and higher education, but who had made substantial contributions to their respective fields of learning."[7] These men were invited to discuss religion as it affected their own field of scholarship, particularly in relation "to the conception of the teacher's intellectual and spiritual responsibilities to his students, to the institution which he serves, and to society in general."[8]

The result was a series of essays in pamphlet form entitled "Religious Perspectives of College Teaching," with nationally known scholars speaking for their own disciplines. In 1952 the committee in charge of the project, under the chairmanship of Professor Hoxie N. Fairchild, brought the pamphlets together in book form, with a slight change in title, *Religious Perspectives in College Teaching*. This book, with its introductory chapter "Religious Perspectives in College Teaching: Problems and Principles" by George F. Thomas and the concluding chapter "The Preparation of Teachers" by Robert Ulich, is the most significant book that has been published in the field of Christian education in the last quarter of a century. The chapters on the twelve disciplines include: English literature, history, philosophy, classics, music, physical sciences, biology, experimental psychology, sociology and social psychology, anthropology, economics, and political science.

The volume is the first concerted, well-conceived effort on the plane of high scholarship to bring religion into the curriculum, not as a special, separate department (although the study expresses no antagonism to departments of religion), but as a motivating force, a high spirit of men's endeavoring in all fields of learning that deal with men and man's outreach and understanding, and his appreciation of the world, both the world of nature and of human nature.

The leaders of the Foundation will be the first to recognize that much needs to be done to follow up these initial studies; nevertheless, to those leaders goes the major credit of offering the fundamental blueprints for studies which it may take many years to complete.

THE DANFORTH FOUNDATION

The Danforth Foundation has sought to make its contribution to Christian education in the major areas of need, supplementing and strengthening at times some of the endeavors of the National Council on Religion in Higher Education and the Hazen Foundation. Mr. and Mrs. William H. Danforth established the Danforth Foundation in 1927 as a family trust fund broadly chartered and operating on the objective of "aiding the spiritual development of young people, particularly through the schools and the colleges."

The Danforth Associate, like the Hazen Associate, has sought to enrich the faculty-student relationships on his campus. Mr. Danforth's interest in small meditation chapels in which the harassed college student may find privacy for prayer and silence has been the stimulus for the building of these centers on close to a dozen campuses. Through the program of the Danny Grads, more than one hundred and fifty carefully selected young women have been chosen at the end of their undergraduate study for a year of internship in Christian service on a college campus in a section of the country far from their own home and college. For these girls the year has been one of growth and maturity achieved through the experience of working with the student religious groups and with individuals on the assigned campus.

Since the turn of the mid-century, the Foundation has sponsored two new endeavors. A series of Teacher Summer Scholarships has enabled both college and secondary-school teachers to have training in contemporary religious thought at academic centers where special courses devised for teachers have been established. The institutions offering the courses have been given the responsibility for assigning the scholarships. In one recent summer, 175 tuition-fees-board-lodging scholarships were made available to qualified teachers.

The program of Danforth Graduate Fellowships in many ways parallels the Kent Fellowships. It is an attempt to aid and encourage the student of major promise who is preparing himself for a career of college teaching and who sees in this vocation his particular form of Christian service. Approximately fifty appointments are given annually to college seniors throughout the country. The appointment, however, is not primarily a financial stipend, although financial aid is offered according to the individual's need; rather it is the establishment of a relationship. It is hoped, through the means of an annual conference on Christian teaching and the fellowship of the group, that this relationship will encourage the prospective teacher to realize the full promise of his intellectual capacity and religious commitment, which the Council members believe they saw at the time of their invitation to him to become a Danforth Fellow.

Behind those two more recent endeavors lies the purpose of encouraging those men and women now teaching, and recruiting and training a supply of spiritually able young men and women preparing for the teaching profession.

"WHAT IS A CHRISTIAN COLLEGE?"

An additional aid and stimulus to the Christian teacher and administrator has been the research-study project, "What Is a Christian College?"

The pattern for the study was laid in the late forties in the Commission on Christian Higher Education of the Association of American Colleges. The research committee of that commission, working under the able leadership of Raymond F. McLain, has been responsible for the series of annual workshops which have brought together the representatives of the participating colleges. Over the four years some 350 colleges have taken part in these workshops which have served to bring an intercollegiate point of view to the studies already in progress on the individual campuses.

Dr. McLain in his introduction to *The Consolidated Report of the Six Faculty Workshops of 1952* has suggested what he believes to be the major values of this study. First of all there comes to the faculties of the colleges engaging in the study the opportunity to clarify their own philosophy of Christian higher education and "the improvement of its processes in light of that philosophy." It is to be hoped, moreover, that out of the total project there will come generalized judgments that will be of value to all institutions which are endeavoring to find a place for religion in their curricular and extracurricular life. "Such judgments may well make explicit the hitherto implied nature and role of the Christian college in today's world." An additional value is the sense of kinship in a common task that has arisen among the hundreds of faculty members who have engaged together in study.

It is planned to complete the present phase of the study with a volume, *The Nature and Role of the Christian College*, which will be both a review and a summation of the endeavor.[9]

THE FACULTY CHRISTIAN FELLOWSHIP

The Faculty Christian Fellowship was organized in October, 1952, at Berea, Kentucky; it held its first annual conference at Park College in June, 1953. The Fellowship is an independent, self-governing movement which intends, as the name implies, to provide channels of communication and relationships of fellowship to the thousands of college teachers throughout America who are attempting to understand the implications of their Christian commitment for their responsibility as effective, competent college teachers. Its genius lies in its particular characteristics of being national, nondenominational, and professional.

The United Student Christian Council in November, 1951, called the initial consultation, composed of representatives of agencies and denominations, to consider the possibility of some loosely organized association of faculty men and women. This was followed by a second conference in March, 1952, which led to the meeting of organization in Berea. It was early agreed "that the work [of the Fellowship] should be oriented upon the basis of genuinely Christian and ecumenical perspectives and that it should find its primary rooting in the Protestant Churches."[10] At the present time the Fellowship looks to the Commission on Christian Higher Education of the National Council of Churches for "administrative services." The Faculty Christian Fellowship, however, is no longer a matter of representation from the denominations, as might have been suggested by the original consultation, but rather an autonomous gathering of college teachers.

The organization is still too youthful to be open to evaluation. There is the possibility that it will mean much and there is the possibility that it will mean little; but of all the services that it is given to perform, perhaps none is greater than the experience of "belonging." The lonely teacher sometimes comes to feel an isolation that can dry up the roots of inspiration—or bring forth a cry of exultant faith.

The Christian Scholar, successor to Christian Education, gives promise of being an important means of bringing unity to the Fellowship. This periodical, born of a recognized need which no other journal was filling, has, from its first issue of March, 1953, served as a channel of communication for Christian teachers.

FACULTY CONSULTATIONS ON RELIGION

There is nothing particularly original in the decision of a college faculty to come together for the discussion of the place of religion in higher education; to be sure, such occasions are becoming increasingly frequent. There was, however, a flare of originality in the program of faculty consultations on religion in higher education which was developed in 1945 under the joint sponsorship of the American Council on Education, the Edward W. Hazen Foundation, and the National Council on Religion in Higher Education. John W. Nason, former president of Swarthmore College, has written of the original design for these consultations.[11] Albert C. Outler has offered an appraisal of the program in his Hazen pamphlet, Colleges, Faculties and Religion. The project extended for a period of three years and brought visitors to fifty-three institutions in twenty-nine states. Sixteen different consultants were used.

Dr. Outler has written that the typical consultation consisted of a three-day visit, during which the consultant usually spoke to the general faculty on some aspect of the theme of religion in higher education and then joined a series of smaller groups of faculty and administrators for further searching of the implications of this thesis. In addition, "an interview with a representative student group was included and infrequently an address in a college chapel."[12] From his appraisal of these consultations, Dr. Outler concludes that the five following points can be made with substantial conviction:

1. A case can be made for religion as a crucial factor in liberal education which will be generally acknowledged as an intelligible and intellectually respectable theory of education.

2. No curriculum which ignores or suppresses a competent and critical examination of the history and literature of the Judaeo-

Christian religious tradition can fairly be called either "liberal" or "general."

3. The secularists have no monopoly on intelligent concern for truth and human values and their loudly proclaimed preference for "the democratic creed itself" is, in fact, a rival creed and metaphysics which deserves, in any liberal education, to be examined on its merits alongside the chief alternatives and not covertly imposed as an arbitrary dogmatism under the ambiguous constitutional concept of "separation of Church and State."

4. Modern college students respond eagerly to the chance for a firsthand investigation of the truth claims of high religion presented by competent scholars who themselves have firm religious convictions, and yet who eschew the impulse to impose these convictions dogmatically.

5. It will be a major tragedy of contemporary education and of the society which it seeks to serve if the cause of religion in higher education goes by default or fails because of the capture of the higher education by implacable and doctrinaire secularists. This need not happen. The evidence accumulates that the influence of liberal religious attitudes and ideas is waxing in American academic life.[13]

A telling consequence of this program was the recognition on the part of faculties generally that here was a technique that could be used to strengthen education. Other faculties set up their own consultations and invited their own guest speakers. The Commission on Christian Higher Education of the Association of American Colleges, the Committee on Religion in Higher Education of the National Student Council of the YMCA and YWCA, and the University Christian Mission[14] each in turn offered its services for organizing faculty consultations, going beyond the individual campus to arrange for such gatherings on a regional or state basis. In Wisconsin the interest has been sufficient to support a continuing committee for an annual consultation.

At least one of the major denominations has chosen to sponsor conferences of this nature for the college teachers within the membership of its church. The Church Society for College Work of the Protestant Episcopal Church has for a number of years held annual conferences for teachers, with a program that has been intended to increase their religious understanding and to strengthen their effectiveness as academic representatives.

RELIGION IN THE TEACHERS COLLEGES

Within higher education lies the special province of teacher education. Some institutions are concerned almost exclusively with this task of training teachers; others through their departments of education have a partial concern; all must admit the importance of this field.

The work of teacher education is a broad bridge between higher education and the institutions on the various levels—kindergarten, elementary, junior high school, high school—which may from point of time be grouped as "pre-college," whether their work be terminal or introductory to the more advanced unit.

It is not the function of this Interchapter nor indeed of this book to survey or appraise the new emphasis on moral and spiritual values which has found its way into the planning of many of our public-school educators. This constitutes a new and exciting ferment in American public education. Insofar, however, as these experimental endeavors have connection with the teachers colleges and the centers of teacher education—and eventually all of them do—they cannot be completely ignored.

Of the many practical demonstrations which are under way, probably none is more significant than that which has been fostered in Kentucky. It was J. Mansir Tydings, executive director of the Lincoln Foundation, who in 1946 approached John Fred Williams, then superintendent of public instruction, and urged the naming of a committee "to study and take appropriate action concerning the need for more effective teaching of moral and spiritual values in Kentucky's schools." A state committee was appointed and in 1948 an advisory committee of professional educators was set up with William Clayton Bower, professor emeritus of the University of Chicago, as chairman, to advise and to assist the state committee. The story is told in Ellis F. Hartford's booklet, *Emphasizing Moral and Spiritual Values in a Kentucky High School.*[15]

In the national scene, on the level of the elementary and secondary school, the most important recent volume is the report of the Educational Policies Commission of the National Education Association, entitled *Moral and Spiritual Values in the Public Schools*, and commonly referred to as the M Report. The writers are outspoken that "intelligent and fervent loyalty to moral and spiritual values is essential to the survival of this nation,"[16] and, moreover, that these values must be given fuller recognition in the program of the schools.

The Report does important service by enumerating definite values which the school is equipped to handle. Named specifically are the following: the basic value of human personality, moral responsibility, institutions as the servants of men, common consent, devotion to truth, respect for excellence, moral equality, brotherhood, the pursuit of happiness, and spiritual enrichment.

Even more significant is the forthright position taken by the Commission on the controversial question of the place of religion in public education. "The public school can teach objectively about religion," the writers of the Report affirm, "without advocating or teaching any religious creed. To omit from the classroom all references to religion and the institutions of religion is to neglect an important part of American life. Knowledge about religion is essential for a full understanding of our culture, literature, art, history, and current affairs."[17]

The M Report puts the mighty National Education Association on record as affirming, first, that religion is relevant to education; and second, that there is a place for the factual study of religion in public-supported education. Both of these are major declarations, and the loyal American will agree wholeheartedly with the condition imposed by the Commission that "the teaching of moral and spiritual values in the public schools of the United States must be done without endangering religious freedom and without circumventing the policy of separation of church and state."[18]

The next step is that of demonstration, whereby we shall begin practicing our preachment. Until we have had that in carefully surveyed experiments and on a national scale that will allow for the varying climate of opinion, geographically, on these important issues, we shall not be certain precisely how far and deep the public school can go in the teaching of values and a factual study of religion within the limitations of law and public opinion.

STUDIES BY THE AMERICAN COUNCIL ON EDUCATION

A most significant endeavor to investigate the legal and legitimate place for the teaching of religion, as well as the teaching about religion, in the public school has been fostered through the Committee on Religion and Education set up by the American Council on Education in 1944 under the leadership of F. Ernest Johnson, distinguished educator and now professor emeritus of education of Teachers College, Columbia University.

This committee presented the educational world in 1947 with an important document entitled *The Relation of Religion to Public Education: The Basic Principles*. Here together with the M Report is a charter for the numerous studies that have been made of the place of religion in the public school. Dr. Johnson's committee takes the unequivocal stand that teaching moral and spiritual values cannot be regarded as an adequate substitute for an appropriate consideration of religion in the school program. Furthermore, the committee affirms that introducing factual study of religion will not commit the public school to any particular religious belief.[19]

It was this same committee that fostered and supervised a major exploratory project, financed by the Rockefeller Foundation through a grant to the American Council on Education and carried on under the personal direction of Clarence Linton, who for the period of three semesters during 1951-53 was released from his teaching at Columbia University to direct this study. The official purpose of the project is stated: "An inquiry into the function of the public schools, in their own right and on their own initiative, in assisting youth to have an intelligent understanding of the historical and contemporary role of religion in human affairs."

The work of this committee has been carefully compiled in *The Function of the Public Schools in Dealing with Religion*.[20] Most significant are the chapters on "Conclusions" and "Recommendations." Dr. Linton and the committee unequivocally cast their vote for a "factual study of religion when and where intrinsic to general education" as the most promising approach to the problem of place of religion in the public schools.[21]

But until pilot experiments can be established in representative public-school systems and teachers colleges, and experiments made under wise scrutiny and with careful evaluation, we shall not have the data to validate the committee's findings. A series of such demonstrations is urgently called for as the next important step.[22]

Summer seminar-workshops on moral and spiritual values are gaining in popularity. In 1952 Union Theological Seminary held the first of a series of annual workshops for high-school teachers and administrators, directed by F. Ernest Johnson. The members of the group were invited to attend courses under the leadership of Union's distinguished summer faculty, and in addition found the core of their study in Dr. Johnson's seminar on "Christian Foundations for School Teaching."

Other groupings of teachers have been brought together for similar studies, notably a selection of teachers from the Missouri State Teachers Association which met in 1953 for a week's study of "Moral and Spiritual Values," with the approval of the parent organization. A summer seminar for high-school teachers from a limited number of school systems was held that same summer at Kent State University. This program had the desirable feature of "follow-up" whereby a member of the College of Education took as a portion of his teaching load the continuing contacts with the members of the seminar and their schools during the ensuing academic year, that he might counsel with them on their endeavors to bring this emphasis on values into their classrooms and their schools.

Any list of the endeavors to recognize the place of religion in teacher education must include mention of the significant national study conference held at the Yale University Divinity School, December 15-17, 1951. The theme of the conference was "Religion in State Teachers Colleges."[23]

Jointly sponsored by the Department of Religion in Higher Education of Yale University Divinity School and the New Haven State Teachers College, the National Study Conference was the first of its kind ever held. In all probability others will follow either on a nation-wide or regional basis. For, in the judgment of the educational representatives at the conference, here was a frank struggle with problems which have too often been held in the category of "unmentionables." Here was a candid facing of the legal tangle involved in the question of religion in the public schools and colleges, and here also a confronting of the problem of what can be done within the present legal pattern, assuming that there is a desire to find a place for religion in the total life of the state teacher institution.

RECENT LITERATURE

If one were in doubt of the public concern for religion in higher education, a cursory survey of the books and reports which have been written since 1940—to take an arbitrary date—would be persuasive. That there is a problem, the educational leaders who have written are distressingly aware. Moreover, there is a growing agreement that the solution is to be found in a new point of view.

Two major works in the field, of thorough academic competence and deep Christian insight, are Sir Walter Moberly's *The Crisis in the University*[24] and Howard Lowry's *The Mind's Adventure*.[25] Both will be referred to many times in these pages. Antedating these studies and containing pioneering thought are Arnold S. Nash's *The University and the Modern World*[26] and the smaller volume by A. J. Coleman, *The Task of the Christian in the University*.[27]

The proposal for "religious perspectives" is meeting increasingly with favor. But, as will be indicated in the final chapter of this book, there is tremendous work still to be done on what we mean by "religious perspectives," how they apply to the differing disciplines, and how they can be assimilated into the classroom with full academic integrity and, for the state schools, with complete compliance with the law and the public opinion behind that law. It is not known when and where the phrase "religious perspectives" was first coined. It was brought into popular educational thinking by the series of pamphlets issued by the Hazen Foundation and later offered in book form, *Religious Perspectives in College Teaching*.

Reference has already been made to the two reports, *The Relation of Religion to Public Education: The Basic Principles* (now out of print) issued by the Committee on Religion and Education of the American Council on Education, and *Moral and Spiritual Values in the Public Schools*, by the Educational Policies Commission of the National Education Association. This latter volume is based in part on *Spiritual Values in the Elementary Schools*, the Twenty-Sixth Yearbook of the Department of Elementary School Principals of the NEA. In turn, these have given encouragement to local and regional studies, such as *Spiritual Values*, a booklet based on the work of the San Diego public schools, and the study of the experiment in values in the Kentucky schools, reported by William Clayton Bower, *Moral and Spiritual Values in Education*.

Some of the faculty consultations have issued study reports that deserve attention, particularly, *Religion in the State University*, edited by Henry E. Allen, accounting for the first of the symposia for state university administrators and faculty together with national religious leaders, held at the University of Minnesota, 1949; and the annual official digests of the College Presidents' Conference, held at the American Baptist Assembly, Green Lake, Wisconsin, in June of each year. This conference is sponsored jointly by the Baptists and cooperating denominations.

There is no need for a complete bibliography of books in this field as a part of this Interchapter. The following titles, taken from a much longer list of books published since 1939, are deserving of careful reading. They are themselves straws in the strong wind which is blowing:*

OF GENERAL CONCERN

God in Education, M. L. Jacks, London, Rich and Cowan, Ltd., 1939.

On Education, Sir Richard Livingstone, New York, The Macmillan Company, 1945.

Education—Christian or Pagan, M. V. C. Jeffreys, London, University of London Press, 1946.

Education and Crisis, Basil A. Fletcher (in "Educational Issues of Today" series) London, University of London Press, 1946.

Glaucon, An Inquiry into the Aims of Education, M. V. C. Jeffreys, London, Sir Isaac Pitman and Sons, Ltd., 1950.

God in Education, Henry P. VanDusen, New York, Charles Scribner's Sons, 1951.

Crisis and Hope in American Education, Robert Ulich, Boston, Beacon Press, 1951.

The Republic and the Person, Gordon Keith Chalmers, Chicago, Henry Regnery Company, 1952.

OF CONCERN FOR RELIGION IN THE PUBLIC SCHOOLS

The Public Schools and Spiritual Values, ed. by John S. Brubacher, New York, Harper & Brothers, 1944.

Church and State in Education, William Clayton Bower, Chicago, University of Chicago Press, 1944.

Church, College and Nation, G. R. Elliott, Louisville, The Cloister Press, 1945.

The New Education and Religion, J. Paul Williams, New York, Association Press, 1945.

Religion in Public Education, V. T. Thayer, New York, The Viking Press, 1947.

Religion and Education Under the Constitution, J. M. O'Neill, New York, Harper & Brothers, 1949.

The American Tradition in Religion and Education, R. Freeman Butts, Boston, Beacon Press, 1950.

Moral Values and Secular Education, Robert E. Mason, New York, Columbia University Press, 1950.

* Arranged in chronological order, by titles, for easy reference. Those wishing additional items are referred to the Bibliography in The Function of the Public Schools in Dealing with Religion.

The Place of Religion in Public Schools, Virgil Henry, New York, Harper & Brothers, 1950.

Religious Values in Education, Ward Madden, New York, Harper & Brothers, 1951.

American Education and Religion: The Problem of Religion in the Schools, ed. by F. Ernest Johnson, New York, Harper & Brothers, 1952.

The Function of the Public Schools in Dealing with Religion (a report on the Exploratory Study made by the Committee on Religion and Education), Washington, American Council on Education, 1953.

OF CONCERN FOR RELIGION IN HIGHER EDUCATION

The College Seeks Religion, Merrimon Cuninggim, New Haven, Yale University Press, 1947.

College Reading and Religion (a survey of college reading materials, sponsored by The Edward W. Hazen Foundation and the Committee on Religion and Education of the American Council on Education), New Haven, Yale University Press, 1948.

The Religion of College Teachers, R. H. Edwin Epsy, New York, Association Press, 1951.

The Teaching of Religion in American Higher Education, ed. by Christian Gauss, New York, Ronald Press, 1951.

Liberal Learning and Religion, ed. by Amos N. Wilder, New York, Harper & Brothers, 1951.

College Teaching and Christian Values, ed. by Paul M. Limbert, New York, Association Press, 1951.

Character Building and Higher Education, Ordway Tead, New York, The Macmillan Company, 1953.

The critic impressed with this array of organizations and reported studies may well ask why such numerous efforts, adequately financed, directed with strong leadership, purposeful and inclusive in their planning, should not have been more successful. The reader, critical or uncritical, may also wonder why.

Perhaps the fullest answer lies in the ability of human nature to resist its own best self, as the Church through the centuries has come to understand. And yet that answer alone does not completely satisfy.

Chapter Two. Can Education Be Meaningfully Christian?

But what he should do with his chemistry or languages when he has acquired them, whether and why injustice and cruelty and fraud are bad and their opposites are good, whether faith in God is a snare and a delusion or is the only basis on which human life can be lived without disaster—all these things the student must find out for himself as best he may, for a university education can do nothing to help him. If you want a bomb the chemistry department will teach you how to make it, if you want a cathedral the department of architecture will teach you how to build it, if you want a healthy body the departments of physiology and medicine will teach you how to tend it. But when you ask whether and why you should want bombs or cathedrals or healthy bodies, the university, on this view, must be content to be dumb and impotent. It can give help and guidance in all things subsidiary but not in the attainment of the one thing needful. In living their lives the younger are left "the sport of every random gust." But for the educator this is abdication.[1]

SIR WALTER MOBERLY

A COLLEGE in the Middle West was preparing to celebrate its accumulation of one hundred years of history. A feature of that celebration was to be the erection of a centennial plaza at the entrance to the campus. The faculty committee charged with the wording on the stone casing took thought for its responsibility. There should be the name of the college, its dates, and an appropriate quotation. The committee was divided, however, on the question whether or not the college should be labeled simply a College of Liberal Arts and Sciences, or more specifically a Christian College of Liberal Arts and Sciences.

The debate spread far beyond the committee. It involved the faculty and the alumni, the trustees, and, of course, the students. The college in question was a church-related college. It was without legal restrictions in the matter of religion. The decision was, therefore, a family decision.

There were two basic questions to be faced: What do you mean by a Christian college? Or, in other words, to what extent, and how, can education be meaningfully Christian? When the answer was found to that question, the faculty committee then needed to face the second question: Do we want to be labeled to the world as a Christian institution?

Through extended discussion and the participation of energetic minds, the decision was made. The centennial plaza was erected, and those who visit the campus today come past an entrance plaza where on stone are engraved the words:

DENISON UNIVERSITY

A CHRISTIAN COLLEGE OF LIBERAL ARTS AND SCIENCES

The readers of Sir Walter Moberly's richly analytical book, *The Crisis in the University,* will recall that Sir Walter faced the question, Can Education be Christian? and brought forth the conclusion that it was not possible, in these days of our English-speaking civilization. "In the present state of the world Christians themselves ought not to want an all-Christian university,"[2] he wrote. I am persuaded that any thoughtful reader following Sir Walter's arguments will be convinced of their rightness, according to Sir Walter's definitions; for in asking whether it is possible for the universities of England to be founded on Christian faith and doctrine, Sir Walter is meaning an authentic, demanding, doctrinal Christianity. "A belief in truth and goodness, and a sustained effort to attain them," are to him but "an offshoot of Christianity" in sharp distinction from the true Christian life, which consists "not in keeping commandments, however stringent, nor in following principles, however lofty, nor even in the imitation of Christ. It is a life in grace—that is of prayer and sacrament, of daily and hourly dependence on power from on high, a life lived within the context of the worshipping community and based on faith in the great acts of God in Christ recounted in the Bible— Incarnation, Redemption, Resurrection."[3]

Sir Walter argues that if we are to return to this great tradition of the past, then theology will once again become the master science which holds together and gives meaning and direction to all the other studies. If it is the Christian tradition that is to be made basic in the educational program, then "the organic structure of our universities, the selection of their teachers, the assumptions underlying their social life, will be shaped by this supreme aim." But it cannot be, he concludes, alluring and powerfully appealing though the dream be, for the reason that it is impracticable; the intellectual climate will not sustain this tradition; and the individual members of the university community, who give it their full allegiance, are in a distinct minority. For his support he quotes from the Harvard Report, *General Education in a Free Society*: "Whatever one's views, religion is not now for most colleges a practicable source of intellectual unity."[4]

Not only is it impracticable, it would be also inequitable, Sir Walter continues, since it would be imposing the wish and the will of a minority upon the larger number. And being inequitable, it would be disastrous; for no matter how well intended, such a Christian program would become a sham. It would cloak the real genius of the Christian faith and would present a still more dangerous temptation to foster religious sentiment as a means to an end, and "such exploitations of the Christian religion for ends other than its own would be the ultimate profanity."[5]

These arguments are not to be dismissed lightly. They are profound and realistic. They are based, however, on an essential difference of emphasis between British and American Christianity—a difference which in the United States many believe to be shifting in favor of the British position. Sir Walter and the extensive church group that he represents grant Christian doctrine a centrality which is foreign to much American thinking. To Sir Walter a man is a Christian because he believes certain specified statements of Christian dogma; his is a voluntary wholehearted acceptance of a doctrinal position, with all of its consequences upon the man's thinking and living.

Our American churches, rightly or wrongly, are inclined—with notable exceptions—to put less emphasis upon creedal statements. To them the spirit of Christ is the pivotal center for the experience of a man coming into relations with his God. To them a man is a Christian who earnestly desires to follow Jesus Christ, accepting Him, in the words of the baptismal formula, as his Saviour and Lord, and submitting his will to the higher will of God. The Christian experience is the experience of the supreme commitment of a man, in love and loyalty to Jesus as God's incarnation of Himself in human existence. This is Christian doctrine, to be certain, and the thoughtful person coming to the Christian experience will scrutinize all of the doctrinal implications. But for the average Christian, the theological interpretations of the way of Christian salvation are secondary to the honest seeking of man for the controlling of his life by the spirit of Christ, with all of its implications for his thinking and living.

In part this is a difference of degree, for to Christians of both lands Christian doctrine and Christian spirit are each fundamental concerns; however, in part it is a difference of belief which item shall serve as the major focal point of Christian faith and action: the doctrine or the spirit.

Many American educators are in agreement with Sir Walter that education cannot put Christian doctrine at the core of its institutional life; and that even the church-controlled colleges would find it difficult to do so without serious reservation, first because of their conditioning by the educational climate of America and second because of their obligation to serve a constituency, in most cases, larger than their own church. However, many of these same educators would raise the question whether it is not possible for an educational institution to declare with honest intent its purpose to control its organized life by Christian principles of justice and love, and to exalt the contagious personality of Jesus Christ as the vision of greatness. In such a situation Christian doctrine would not be the unifying item of the curriculum, but in a significant way the spirit of Christ would be made the controlling purpose of the institution.

The individual Christian never fully reaches the goal toward which he presses; neither will the college. But it is the ever-renewed will to press toward the goal, as well as an ever-clarifying sense of the direction in which the goal lies, rather than the act of arriving which is the essence of Christian living. Similarly, might the college qualify which is Christian by intent?

The measure of that intent would of necessity differ according to the nature of the institution. The state-supported institution can have many manifestations of Christian spirit within its great organizational body, but inasmuch as it cannot be unreserved in its commitment to the Christian spirit—for the arguments Sir Walter offers —it cannot be Christian in any controlling fashion. For the church-related college or the independent college, there is the freedom to make this choice if the will to choose is theirs.

Can education be meaningfully Christian? Many will answer, "No"; if by Christian you mean a centrality of doctrine. Many will answer, "Yes"; if by Christian you mean a sincerity of intent and a relentless struggle under God's guidance for the personal and institutional integrity which embodies the spirit of Christ.

But this can be only the first step in the answer.

THE ANTAGONISM OF THE GLIMPSE OF TRUTH

It is temptingly easy to give assent to the generalization of Christian education without being fully aware of some of the antagonisms that must first be resolved. The most apparent of these is the possible antagonism between a free and unhampered search for truth and a well-intended but illiberal program of indoctrination. Christian education to be strong educationally demands free search.

We say, in the name of academic freedom, that the scholar must be without fetters to seek an enlargement of truth in his field, that he must be unlimited in his right to discuss all points of view, and that, while he teaches truth as he now comprehends it, the door of his understanding must never be closed against possible new truths as they may be discovered or disclosed. Is Christian education willing to endorse this unlimited freedom for the scholar and the teacher; and still more pertinent, is Christian education willing to offer the same unlimited freedom in the area of religion?

It is not difficult to give the scholar his freedom in such fields as chemistry and physics, or in those subjects which do not impinge directly on our daily living or our conventional thinking. It is not so easy, however, to give that freedom in other areas such as the field of contemporary political science and economics, for here the battle lines are drawn and many a campus has become a battleground. Here knights in armor—sometimes tin, sometimes steel—join in fearsome combat.

And in the area of Christian faith and action, are we ready to offer the same invitation to new truth as we are to new truth in biochemistry or astrophysics? Are we, as Christians, definitely seeking new truths for fuller enlightenment of that which we now accept as Christian truth? Or do we hold tenaciously to Christian truth as once for all and finally delivered to the saints—the saints being the giants of the past not the future? The record of the history of the Christian Church is not entirely a happy one when we try to draw from it conclusions for Christian education.

Galileo became the archheretic when he sought to substitute a global universe for the three-story house in which man at that time lived. Darwin and his fellow researchers brought down upon their heads the contumely of the Church when they offered their new ideas on the origins of life. Modern psychology and psychiatry have been, until recent days, looked upon by the religious leaders as opponents rather than allies, and only in limited situations are they now welcomed cordially for their rich insights into the mind of man and its working. Freedom of search and a welcoming spirit toward new truths have not been sturdy qualities in the life of the Church or its leaders, and in line with this tradition there are many repre-

sentatives of the Church who see the opportunity of Christian education largely as an invitation to indoctrination.

* * *

THE HOLY SPIRIT OF TRUTH

*When Homer Rainey, former President of Stephens Col-
lege, spoke, in 1950, to a group of faculty men at the University of Minnesota, he shared with them a new insight
which had come for him on the Holy Spirit.*

*"A college professor some time ago confessed to me that
even at his present stage of maturity, whenever the term
'The Holy Ghost' was mentioned, there still popped into his
mind a vague concept of some sort of figure moving around
with a sheet over it. A new insight into the meaning of this
term came more or less accidentally as I was rereading por-
tions of the New Testament. I ran across a statement Jesus
made about the Holy Spirit, and in this reference, he referred
to it as 'The Spirit of Truth.' Somehow I had never caught
that meaning before. The moment I saw it, it came as a new
light to me, with a great, new spiritual significance. I was led
to pursue the matter further, and I found that every time
Jesus referred to it, He always designated it specifically as
'The Spirit of Truth.' He told His disciples that upon His
departure there would be sent to them the Holy Spirit of God,
which he said was the Spirit of Truth and that it would guide
them into all truth. As I say, that concept has great meaning
and significance to me, and it ties the highest in education
and the highest in religion inseparably together."*[6]

* * *

"Indoctrination" in itself, however, is not necessarily a word to
fear. Indoctrination can be kindly and also useful. Obviously we
should not go through life holding the door open on all of our conclusions. There are axioms whose truth we do not need to question,
but if the need for questioning arises we shall not resist. Until there
is persistent protest that two plus two do not equal four, we may
continue to hold this as truth.

We need, moreover, to recognize clearly that by no means is
indoctrination limited to the field of religious thinking. Wherever
men have convictions—and men have deep, impressive, persuasive, and
frequently audible convictions on economics and politics, on social

and race relations—then the probability arises that they will seek to impress their judgment upon others, with the unspoken assumption that here is final truth: wisdom has spoken, and at least one of wisdom's children knows the best answers.

In discussing the function of education, the phrase is often used: the transmission of our American cultural and spiritual heritage. We mean that our teachers are expected to inculcate in our children an abiding respect for political democracy as the form of government, tried and tested in our American experience. We mean that they are expected to create a respect for the theory of the equality of individuals, as expounded in the Declaration of Independence. In these and in other regards, we expect teaching with conviction that will lead to persuasion. In simple words, we expect indoctrination, and in those areas where public opinion is strongly crystallized we accept indoctrination as legitimate.

Convictions in religion as in politics are the nourishers of moral fiber. Having convictions, we shall speak them and speak them to convince. If by chance we be teachers, we shall teach those convictions—and here one needs to choose words with care—we shall teach them *provided* they are convictions substantiated by the evidence of good scholarship, judged true by men competent to judge, and provided that we teach with them the point of view of the eternal search for fuller understanding of what we believe to be true.

This is a real antagonism both for the individual Christian, and also for the body of Christendom speaking in behalf of Christian education; for education at its best speaks without reservation or equivocation, saying that the search for truth must be unhampered, unlimited, and continuous. If either the Christian teacher or the Christian Church rises in protest or moves to shield the zone of religious understanding from the beams of this ceaseless searchlight, then it will give the lie to the theory that Christian education is a possibility.

The antagonism, however, is not to be interpreted as a conflict between a flabby, convictionless point of view holding all truth in continuous suspension and a kindly, reasonable indoctrination. It is an antagonism between the very spirit of truth-seeking and an indoctrination that closes and seals the door to all comers, and against further enlightenment.

Jacques Maritain, when asked if his allegiance to the Roman Catholic Church did not close certain doors to complete philosophic and religious inquiry, is reported to have made unequivocal answer:

He said that he was a loyal Catholic, but that his religious faith in no way limited or impaired his freedom of scholastic inquiry.

Howard Lowry has faced squarely the identical issue in *The Mind's Adventure*: "The committed Christian surrenders a certain freedom of action," he writes. "But he does not lose his freedom of inquiry. The allegiance he gives is to One in whose service there is 'perfect freedom.' This includes the right to reason, to investigation, to critical judgments. The Christian can hold with Socrates that the unexamined life is not worth living. But he insists that the examination be complete—that man be studied in a perspective that includes his highest aspirations and insights."[7]

Will the Christian Church have the courage to state its position with equal frankness? Such a candid commitment to truth is desperately needed for the future of Christian education.[8]

THE ANTAGONISM OF THE DEFINITIONS OF EDUCATION

A second antagonism to be faced and resolved is that among the major educational attitudes toward religion commonly held in America today. The more common of these refuses to allow religion any place in the educational process. Those who hold to this theory contend that religion is a personal matter, a voluntary choice of the individual, an item of life of fifth or seventh importance, and without direct connection with the training of the mind. Because they see it exclusively in personal terms, and because they count it of small consequence, they find no reason to interpret the part which religion has played in the founding of nations, or the conception of liberty, or the fostering of good will between men and peoples. Those who espouse this interpretation of education know the history of the Church largely in terms of its error, its benighted hostility to new truth, its savage protection of itself against heresy and heretics; and knowing only this aspect of the Church's history they look upon it with disfavor and contempt. To such as these, the idea of Christian education is fundamentally preposterous, unthinkable, and undesirable.

* * *

CHAPEL CHIMES

I cherish a letter which came to me during my years of college administration. It was written by an apprentice seaman who was in our Navy V-12 unit:

While wrapping a present for my mother, a handkerchief for my aunt, a pair of slippers for my cousin, and addressing my Christmas cards, I was suddenly confronted with this question: "What shall I give the President of the institution of which I am now a part—neckties, hose, handkerchiefs, a book?" I came to the conclusion that perhaps a letter of appreciation would be appropriate.

I came to our campus six months ago, not knowing what to expect. Truthfully speaking, I would not have come to the college in ordinary times, but on my first night here, I took a different attitude while strolling around the campus. I walked by the fraternity houses, the administration building, the science laboratory, and on toward Swasey Chapel. I stood admiring the chapel for quite some time, then I walked slowly away, thinking of home, of the things I was now beginning to appreciate. I don't know why, but there is about the chapel something that makes me think of home and of the happy moments of my life. From that very hour, I knew I would never be lonely, as long as Swasey towered above the campus.

Even now, when I retire at night, I can see the bright light shining from the tower; as I look at it from my window it is a symbol of something just a little higher than I can comprehend. It serves as a beacon to better manhood and a deeper appreciation of the opportunities that confront me.

That first evening last July, as I stood humbly before the massive pillars, the bells began to play. I can hear them yet—"Oh, Jesus I Have Promised," they were pealing. You will never know how impressive it was to one who in a strange place was feeling a little bewildered.

* * *

There is, however, another group that would exclude religion from any place in the curricular or organizational life of a school, not because of its scorn for religion but because of its literal understanding of our American principle of the separation of Church and State. Following the popular interpretation, this great doctrine is conceived as a divorce of religion from all organized public life, misdefining the Church as religion, and the State as life itself. These men and women are by no means necessarily hostile to religion. On Sunday at eleven o'clock, or during out-of-office hours, they may be deeply spiritually minded, but they hold that concept of education which controls so much of our public-school system, namely, that in the classroom there can be no place for religion. They will argue that it is right to present the pie of our American culture to the hungry schoolboy, with the slice of religion left out.

This same theory is frequently held in our state-supported colleges and in many graduate schools. Indeed, it has become not so much a principle to be advocated and defended as an axiom not even open to debate; many educators will have no sympathy whatever with the thesis that an integration of Christianity and education is possible which is fair and equitable, both to Christianity and to education.

There are, however, those men and women who hold that education is complete only if there is an honest, fruitful integration of religion in the entire educational process of learning. They would spurn any simile of icing on the cake, or the fifth wheel to be used in case of necessity, or the penthouse built on top of the essential structure. All of these figures of speech are foreign to their thinking. For them the concern for the spirit of man and its growth to maturity is as much an integral part of education as the concern for man as a citizen, or man as a social creature, or man in his mental outreach. They make no argument for less education and more religion; they argue only for more complete education.

Here is an antagonism clearly to be recognized and presumably to be accepted, since any early resolution seems unlikely. The events of recent years have raised doubts in an increasing number of minds and brought questions as to the effectiveness of our religionless education if it produces only generations which have no concern for ethics or values, leaving aside for the moment the question of religious faith. The Christian educator will face this antagonism with full recognition of the strength of his opponent. The Christian educator is doing battle these days with a publicly popular tradition, generally misinterpreted but nevertheless strongly entrenched. Yet the minority of doubters is growing, and there are times when the wall of separation seems an unholy barrier rather than a welcomed protection. The Christian educator is tilting his lance against the teaching of some of the great graduate schools of the country. His presence in battle is testimony to the proposition that with faithfulness, both to the best in education and to the spirit of Christianity, Christian education can be made a reality, and that without it there is danger that our American system of the school and the college will breed clever men and women without concern for the needs of their fellows, intelligent pagans, happy in their self-centered contentment. "Fear only educated men," Justice Robert H. Jackson once remarked.

THE ANTAGONISM OF THE NATURES OF RELIGION

Whereas the first two are antagonisms which Christian education faces with forceful ideas outside of itself, the third antagonism is an antagonism within Christian education itself. This third conflict is a struggle between a narrow sectarianism, seeking to dominate the educational process with which it is allied, and broad, inclusive Christianity.

With the discussion of the integration of religion and education, it is the specter of sectarianism, hovering threateningly, which dismays the suspicious. Too often that specter is a church-written form of education which emphasizes denominational differences and stresses unduly the minutiae of doctrines, the details of sectarian worship and the exclusive rightness of the sect, at the expense of those great affirmations which Christians hold in common. It is easy enough for the religionist to fear the secularist and his God-absent theory of life, and the fear has its grounds for being. But the religionist will be wise enough to recognize that the sectarian churchman and the secularist are both to be feared when their hands are laid in dominance on education.

Lest the picture be distorted, let it be said with fervent thanks that our church-related colleges have rendered superb service. They have produced many great minds and many great hearts. They have trained for the country numberless leaders in which the great heart and the great mind were gloriously combined.

These colleges, moreover, founded by churchmen with deep loyalty to the Church and to Christian faith, were often given, even in pioneer days, an ecumenical flavor which belied the narrow limitations of the adjective *denominational*. "No sectarian teaching shall be offered"—many a college charter so reads. Founded in faith these colleges were, but the faith that was to undergird the teaching of the classroom was to be broad and tolerant and searching.

They called them Methodist colleges, Baptist colleges, and Mennonite colleges because of the churches that gave them birth and fostered them during their years of growth. But that did not mean that the teacher in the classroom taught Methodist mathematics or Baptist physics. Nor did it mean that a sectarian brand of theology was offered in the courses in religion. Those church-related colleges founded in the nineteenth century drew their sustenance from the broad basis of Christian faith and understanding. It was a partnership of educational breadth and religious depth which helped men and women to grow in wisdom and moral stature, and in the ability to give good will to their fellow men and loyalty to their God.

* * *

Just What Do You Mean by Integrity?

The student questioned the chapel speaker, and the campus visitor replied, "Let me illustrate with a story. On a college campus that I know, the active members of a certain fraternity were making their plans to go to a nearby town where a pornographic motion picture was to be shown privately. It was the kind of film that could not be publicly shown, for the procurer and exhibitor were transgressing the law in making it available. It was agreed that all of the active members who wanted to (and apparently most of them wanted to) would go. Then the question was raised, 'How about our pledges, are they included?' The young man who had been elected pledgemaster rose and faced his brothers. 'You have every right, if you want to, to see a filthy picture. However, you have elected me pledgemaster, and as pledgemaster I say to you that our pledges are not going. If you decide otherwise, you can find a new pledgemaster.'

"There was no desire to find a new pledgemaster and somehow the stand which the young leader had taken dimmed the enthusiasm of some of the brothers for the entertainment planned. The group went but without the pledges or the pledgemaster, and also without some who figured they would rather be on the side of the pledgemaster. . . . For me, that's an example of integrity."

* * *

The denominational college as we have it in America today follows no single pattern. At its best it has forsaken any remnants of sectarianism which the name "denominational college" might suggest. In the majority of cases the college is denominational in name only;

the label suggests a tradition and a church loyalty and a financial support too often more in the past than in the present.

At its weakest the denominational college represents a narrow point of view, which does disservice both to education and to religion. It seeks a compelling homogeneity of student and faculty that would appear to deny the value of the educational friction which comes when differing minds rub hard against each other. It, again at its worst, exalts the sectarian flavoring above the educational process itself. It is well satisfied with the end results of conformity instead of mental strength, with unquestioned compliance with convention instead of a vigorous intelligent morality.

When one writes of Christian education, too many readers conjure up this wraith of the denominational college at its weakest and rightly hesitate to give assent. Therein lies the third antagonism, an antagonism within Christian education itself. It is a conflict between a broad, tolerant, yet vigorously minded religious point of view and a narrow restricting sectarianism.

Can education ever be essentially, genuinely, meaningfully Christian? The answer will depend in part upon the response to these three fundamental antagonisms. If Christian education is to become a wise, robust reality, the antagonism between the eager welcome to truth in all fields and the dogma of kindly but limiting indoctrination must be resolved in favor of unrestricted search. The antagonism between the point of view that the educational process is without interest in religion and the faith by which man lives—a kind of amoral operation with ethics and value sitting outside the door of the operating room—and the ideal of education as concerned for the whole man, the nature of his basic loyalties as well as his ability to punctuate correctly, his concept of man and of God as well as his understanding of the capitalistic system, must be resolved in favor of the larger concept. And the third antagonism, within Christian education itself, between a limited, parochial approach to religious truth and a broad interdenominational yet vigorously Christian approach must be resolved on the side of ecumenicity. Only with a hearty and unreserved acceptance of these alternatives can the educational process ever stand within the possibility of being Christian.

Is the hope unreal that the privately endowed church-related college, together with the independent college which has broken from church allegiance but still counts itself religious, might prove to be the working center of an inclusive Christianity? Is the dream fantastic that these colleges might blaze a new and a glowing trail in the whole process of God-centered education?

Definitions clarified, however, and antagonisms resolved are of themselves not enough to give the answer to our question: Basically, fundamentally, can education be Christian? Agreement on definition may serve as a general road map. The clearing of antagonisms may remove the road blocks that impede passage. But the conditions of travel are still to be determined and the goal of the traveling set. If education can be Christian and if those responsible for education desire it to be Christian, what are the conditions for this achievement? Here are three suggestions:

THE QUALITATIVE STANDARDS OF SECULAR EDUCATION MUST BE MET

If education be thoroughly, meaningfully Christian, it must first meet all the qualitative and quantitative standards for academic excellence which have been sought and won in battle by the might of secular education. Christian education cannot overlook the tremendous contribution which secular education has made to the life and culture of the American people. The standards for judging academic competence which are now generally accepted in our country could never have been reached except for the prolonged and vigilant efforts of the colleges and the leaders of the colleges who are deeply concerned for educational quality. The individual church-founded school might have achieved its own high criteria of excellence, but no such system of general accreditation as that which we now have through our state and regional associations would have come without the steady drive of the secularist for education which is quality education, and for teachers who are trained to teach the students who are equipped to learn.

* * *

EDUCATION IS VISION

Playgoers will remember The Corn is Green *as a beautiful play in which Ethel Barrymore essayed the role of schoolteacher. An ignorant, pugnacious Welsh mine boy is brought under the teaching of a spinster teacher with light in her eyes. His ability proves such that the teacher dreams that some day he will go up to Oxford and have the best that English*

*education can offer. Morgan Evans goes to Oxford to try his
scholarship examinations. It is his first view of the world
outside of his Welsh mining hills. When he comes back, he
pours his delight into the ears of his proud teacher: "I have
been to Oxford and come back. . . . I have come back—from
the world! Since the day I was born, I have been a prisoner
behind a stone wall, and now somebody has given me a leg-up
to have a look at the other side. . . . They can't drag me back
again, they cannot. They must give me a push and send me
over!"*[9]

* * *

Not infrequently the church college advertises that it emphasizes
character as the first essential in its list of educational qualities. I
have no strong distaste for character. At times I can work up quite
an enthusiasm for character, but I get fearful when someone cries
that character is the first consideration of education. Would it be a
good idea to graduate for character rather than for academic achievement? "By virtue of the faculty's inability to discover any evidence
of grave dishonesty or inexcusable immorality in this man . . . we
hereby confer . . ." etc.

What do we mean by character, on the college campus, for
example? Is it something to be achieved apart from academic endeavor, from conscientious preparation of assignments, from consistent and wise work habits, from an intellectual curiosity and an
intellectual honesty which go hand in hand? Many seem to think so.
One sometimes has the weird notion that character is largely the
absence of vicious vices—a kind of moral zero point where the cons
and the pros cancel out each other. Or is character something aggres-
sively affirmative and positively creative?

I know of one institution which, as far as one can judge from its
public advertising, counts its greatest strength in the number of men
and women who are going into full-time Christian service. I am
happy whenever good men and women choose to enter full-time
Christian service, but I have been seriously worried of late whether
the education experienced at that particular college, both for those
men and women going into full-time Christian service and those not,
is academically of a quality which justifies the institution being called
a college. The fear rises in my mind that they are substituting
homiletics for a sound exploration into ideas, and righteousness for
mental achievement.

The Christian college like the non-Christian college has the obligation of honesty, and that honesty needs to be extended to self-inquiry and self-criticism—and there are times when one may wonder if it ought not to be extended even to the point of self-effacement and extinction. There may come the time in the history of a college when by commonly accepted academic standards it ceases to be an educational institution. The storms of fortune and misfortune may beat upon the ivy walls and the ivory tower until, whether or not they fall, they fail to qualify as sturdy architecture of education. But institutions, like men, find dying hard. Alumni who refuse to give a penny cry piteously and sentimentally for the maintenance of feeble life. Trustees, untrained as surgeons, are hesitant to use the knife. Students and faculty members plead "for tradition's sake."

If it be a church-related college, the church speaks arguments that might come from a recording: "It's the only college our church has in an area of a hundred miles." (The answer that there are three other church-related colleges within the area is deemed irrelevant and disloyal.) "It has existed since the days our state was colonized." "It's the only home the alumni have." "Maybe better days are ahead."

Essentially, however, it becomes a question of integrity: Shall the Church be responsible for maintaining an institution which by accepted academic standards is not decently educational and, therefore, non-Christian?

The Christian college cannot be all things to all men as the state university is—or thinks it is. The small college of limited endowment, endeavoring to make honest demonstration of Christian education, must recognize its limitations and, if necessary, acknowledge them in public. There is no disgrace in being limited. There is disgrace in dishonestly refusing to recognize and to acknowledge those limitations.

If a college has only six departments, but six departments well cared for by men who are trained in those fields, let the college representatives touring the high schools in search of uncommitted students refuse the temptation of beguiling the unwary who want training in kindergarten work into taking a secondary-school certificate—"It's all teaching, you know"—or of tempting the senior who wants to be a Hollywood star with the argument that his college offers a course in astronomy. The temptation is strong when it is evident that the monthly salary check may not be received unless there can be a dozen more students added to the enrollment. But

better six strong departments than twelve rickety academic chairs
occupied timorously by instructors whose learning and training are
inadequate according to any legitimate demand of educational
standards.

Then the library, with its number of books and the training of its
staff members, the need for decency in the standards of maintenance
of the whole institution, the routine of the registrar's office, the
attention to efficient and competent counseling, the trustworthiness
of its business operations—these and many more are all items of
academic administration where qualitative standards have been set by
secular education. They are standards that must be met by both the
secular and the Christian institution.

What I am saying has an echo of platitude, and yet the emphasis
is still needed. Religious sentiment is not a substitute for the graduate-school grind. If education be Christian, the institution must
meet all the standards for quality and competence demanded of all
institutions—this and then the Something More.

AT THE HEART OF THE PROBLEM STAND MEN

It is that Something More that is the challenge as well as the
exasperation of the Christian educator. To a reasonable extent, the
academic competence of a college can be evaluated—measured in
terms of library books, laboratory equipment, men and women
dangling graduate degrees—but the Something More does not lend
itself to objective measurement. It is influence which, like the wind,
bloweth where it listeth. It is personal example which shines for those
eyes which are open to shining. It is deep-seated purpose; it is wise,
well-planned intent; it is rightly ambitious desire. Neither purpose
nor intent stands still when you hold a yardstick to them. However,
from these very words—influence, personal example, purpose, intent,
desire—it becomes clear that we are talking about qualities which are
embodied in human personality. The Something More is not in
terms of buildings or courses or programs that can be put down upon
paper. It rests in the measure of men and women.

*If education be Christian, the achievement will come largely
through the men and women of the college staff who consciously and
intelligently give their best selves for the furthering of the high purpose of the institution.* I am not using "college staff" as a synonym
for the faculty. I would, of course, include the faculty and I would
put it first. But perhaps we overestimate sometimes the influence of

the faculty man upon the immature student, for in spite of our picks and shovels and bulldozers, the earthen redoubt which divides faculty from students still stands. Perhaps we underestimate the influence of the maintenance man with whom the student may have daily conversation, the kindly matron who serves as head resident *in loco parentis*, or the smiling secretary with whom the student chats while he waits for a formidable session with the dean.

* * *

"MA" KELLER

She was a house supervisor in a college dormitory, serving as campus mother to sixty college women. It was they who called her "Ma" Keller. She died a year ago. She died of a brain tumor, going quickly, as she would have wished.

In an emergency, she served as dean of women for the college, and then, recognizing her inexpertness in this position, suggested that she would be happy to stay on as house mother in one of the women's dormitories. If she thought the change was a demotion, she never spoke her thought. If the step down was hard to take, none of her friends knew it.

"Ma" Keller was not taught in the latest and best techniques of counseling. Hers was a friendly room and hers a friendly ear, and many a student poured out her difficulties, her problems, her loneliness, and her fears for "Ma" Keller to hear. Out of the wisdom that was hers, out of the experiences of her own family, "Ma" Keller made her replies.

The tides of favor rise and fall in a women's dormitory. Restlessness sweeps the hall like a plague and as quickly passes. Through it all "Ma" Keller moved serenely, not unaware of what was going on. She knew and accepted it in a buoyant faith that in the end, wisdom and goodness would win.

Her faith was an essential part of her living. For her, religion was never a cloak to be worn and discarded, or a decoration to be displayed at the holiday seasons; Christianity was life's sustaining power. Perhaps the greatest sacrifice she made for her work was the choice of staying in her hall on Sunday mornings, when she felt the girls might need her, instead of going to church where her heart wanted to be.

It was at the beginning of her second year that she came into the president's office with a request. All her life she had tithed. She was asking if she might send him each month a tithe of the never-large salary which was hers from the college, to be used for the students as he saw fit.

Each month for nine years the envelope came, with its folded bills and loose change—exact to the penny—and usually a note. Sometimes there was a verse of Scripture, sometimes a word of the joy that came with the giving. As faithfully as he knew how, he made use of the money in accordance with her wishes: sometimes for the student who needed a little more for the periodic tuition bill, sometimes for books, occasionally for chapel speakers, once for a party dress for a girl for whom a party dress was a life essential.

There was one time when "Ma" Keller asked that the fund be used for labor on her garden. She saw no sacrilege in using her tithe for the beautifying of God's earth. She loved bright flowers, and they grew for her in spite of rocks and sterile soil. With her own hands, she cleared a hillside and planted jonquils and daffodils. Year by year, she had pushed back the yard behind the dormitory, reclaiming it from wild weeds and belligerent undergrowth.

She was always in full sympathy with the academic objectives of the college, but as house mother and friend she wanted her women to have something beyond the knowledge of textbooks. Once she said that the thing she desired most for them was that they should be women with an educated heart. How many achieved her goal, no one will ever know. If they failed, it was not because they lacked a pattern. Through her kindly living day by day in her small, crowded house mother's suite, "Ma" Keller gave them that.

* * *

A college is a fellowship. A college, particularly a small college, partakes of the nature of the family, including not only the students and the faculty but all who are associated with the life of the campus. From that family fellowship come the actions and the reactions that determine so much of the living.

That is why the major responsibility of the top administrator must be the choosing and the training—and the continual refreshing—of the men and women who make up that fellowship. The wise administrators who rank their official responsibilities put at the top of their list the obligation to discover and court and woo strong faculty candidates; and then to be present at the marriage service when they and the bride of the college say their vows. Nothing else is of comparable importance unless it be to protect the liberty of operation for these men and women in the years following the wedding.

The administrators also know, although they do precious little about it, that they must provide some kind of in-service training for the inexperienced who come to them. One common administrative blindness is the unawareness that faculty men grow stale; that good men and women may become weary of well-doing and falter under the constant repetitions and the common frustrations of campus life. Every college president has had the experience of appointing a man who gave promise of being an extraordinarily fine teacher only to see him gradually lose the zest and the spark. Somewhere in that busy administrator's program must be a concern for the frequent refreshing, the periodic restrengthening, of the staff member.

The teacher must teach. But academic competence is not the whole story. He must be the kind of person who both by instruction and example will teach such important lessons as the dignity of the individual, the respect for the rights of others, the desire for cooperation in social enterprises. He must be the kind of person who, in addition to his competence as a teacher, can command as a person the respect and, it is not too much to add, the affection of the students.

Administrators know that it is easy to list these qualifications and they know, too, how hard it is to locate them and to tie them by contact. There is urgent need for an appeal to young men and women, equipped by intellect and personality for teaching, to consider entering education as their life work. It is an appeal that should be made on the grounds of Christian service; that they may bring to their job of teaching the gift of dedication to a Christian calling. And even while this appeal is being broadcast, every possible effort should be made through the local community and the states to arouse public opinion against the inadequate salaries which we pay our teachers. We cannot content ourselves alone with urging our best minds and hearts to go into teaching, expecting them to accept as a missionary condition the financial limitations which the job will put upon their living, without at the same time doing our utmost to see that a decent recognition is given by the community and the American public to the men and women charged with the terrible responsibility of teaching.

Of one thing we can be certain: both today and tomorrow, if education be Christian, the achievement will come in large measure through the men and women of quality who are given places on our campus staffs and then given, also, the freedom to be their best selves in their assignment.

CAMPUS LIFE CAN TEMPT UPWARD

In the strange alchemy, however, of a college campus, the Something More than secular standards of competence and the daily endeavors of well-trained, spiritually minded men and women is necessary. *If education be truly Christian, the total impact of the college on the student must have its effect directly or indirectly for the larger allegiance of that student to the God of his highest understanding and His will, and to a more brotherly relation between the student and his fellow man.*

There may not be many institutions seeking to apply under such rigid terms, but, nevertheless, the terms are implicit. Just as it is simple for the easygoing, surface-living individual to content himself with a Sunday-morning-eleven-o'clock Christianity, so it is likewise simple for the college when questioned on the validity of its Christian character to offer the easy earmarks of chapel, department of religion, monthly vespers, Christian Emphasis Week—and be angry if these are counted less than fully satisfying answers.

* * *

There Is Such a Thing as Gratitude

One of the pleasant memories which I cherish as an administrator is that of the day when a letter came to my desk enclosing a check for $100. It was from a young businessman in his thirties, just getting started again after his war years in the Navy. I knew he was buying a home on the installment plan. I knew also that he was doing his level best to make good for the sake of his wife and their two small sons. The letter caused me to think back to the day when the writer was a college freshman, struggling desperately to keep himself in college by any kind of honest work, for his family was entirely unable to help him. It was in that year that he made his first profession of Christian faith and took membership in the college church.

One of the paragraphs in his letter read:

"I am sending the check to you in trust . . . when you find a chap who seems worthy of a little help, who has been to you with tears in his eyes because he thinks he can't continue in school, then please use this. You will do me a favor if you

will withhold my name. Perhaps some day I may be privileged
to know something from you about the guy you give it to."

* * *

The total impact of a campus on an individual is a complicated and
multiple affair. To be sure, it contains the influence of a chapel service and the work of a department of religion, if the student has come
within its shadow, and the possible implications of a special week
when the college takes thought for the things of the spirit; but it
contains, also, the associations of the dormitory living, and they
depend on the kind of leaders brought into the dormitories and the
kind of leisure provided. It depends, too, on the ideals of the fraternity
and sorority life and still more on the practice, good or bad, or just
morally neutral, behind those ideals and sometimes without any relation to those ideals; it depends on the miracle of personality when
student meets faculty and the sparks of contact that jump; it depends
upon the healthiness of the social life and the adequacy of its care
for all; it depends—that total impact of the institution—on so many
things, and by no means least on the tone which the college leaders
over a period of years give to the campus.

Every college possesses a voice. It is more than the stentorian voices
of the trustees or the public utterances of the president. It is more
than the voice of the student body at pep rallies or the utterances
repeatable and nonrepeatable of the football coach. It is not even
the voices of the faculty either in classroom pronouncements or in the
intimacy of the faculty lounge. The alumni think the voice of
the college is their voice, but again they are mistaken. Some wish the
campus voice were the chapel chimes with their call to duty and
memory.

The voice of the campus, however, includes all these, but is more
than any one. It speaks louder and in more lasting tones than any
of the other voices. The voice of the campus says certain things are
important—and those are the things that the students of that campus
strive for. The voice of the campus, at least by silence and neglect,
says certain things are unimportant—and those are the things that
the students on that campus and the faculty and the administration,
too, leave to be cared for in the leisure hour that never comes.

The voice speaks in behalf of Christian ideals and Christian living
on some campuses, and on others it speaks against them.

They are right who argue that on any basis of dogma and doctrine, on any condition that theology be made the cornerstone of the curriculum, modern educational thought prohibts an institution from being genuinely, intrinsically Christian. If a man is Christian, however, who has earnest intent to make the spirit of Jesus the commanding mood of his life, giving first loyalty to his God, recognizing as first duty the doing of His will, constantly under the obligation to be his finest and wisest and best self, then may it not be said likewise of an institution where intent is clear and desire strong, and Christian ideals are presented as temptations upward, that it too may rightfully be known by the adjective *Christian*? But if it be Christian, it will be so partially because the total impact of the institution on the student has the effect both directly and indirectly of presenting an invitation which the student is free to accept or to reject —an invitation to high loyalty to the Father-God and to His Son, Jesus Christ. No Christian institution dare fail to present this opportunity to its students. How can it be Christian unless it invites its students to be Christian? Too often the invitation has gone by default: but as Sir Walter Moberly reminds us, "the challenge should be fairly and squarely presented."[10]

In Christopher Fry's play, *A Sleep of Prisoners*, written for the Festival of Britain, 1951, the characters speak these lines:

ADAMS: Who are you?
MEADOWS: Man.
ADAMS: Under what command?
MEADOWS: God's.
ADAMS: May we come through?
MEADOWS: If you have the patience and the love.[11]

Can education be meaningfully, fundamentally Christian? The answer is yes, education can be Christian. But the conditions are onerous. The way is narrow. And the number of the educational pilgrims is not large.

Chapter Three. "And Gladly Wolde He Lerne"—We Hope

> Maturity is achieved when a person accepts life as full of tension; when he does not torment himself with childish guilt feelings, but avoids tragic adult sins; when he knows how to postpone immediate pleasures for the sake of some long-term values; when he makes peace with the unarguable fact that he is not omnipotent, nor is anyone else on earth, but that all men must share each other's frailties and draw from each other's powers. Our generation must be inspired to search for that maturity which will manifest itself in the qualities of tenacity, dependability, co-operativeness and the inner drive to work and sacrifice for a nobler future for mankind.[1]
>
> JOSHUA LOTH LIEBMAN

A SOFT bed for the lazybones; a sorority affiliation for the socially ambitious; an open door to intellectual adventures for the academic explorer; an alumnus label for the Peter Pan who anticipates with unconcealed glee the annual reunions, where he can wear a paper cap and blow on a child's whistle; the meager but never relinquished prospect of a mate for the social wallflower; freedom— and fun—for the adolescent to whom studies come without great difficulty; an invitation to mature fellowship for the man with ideas; and a command to "rise and shine," academically speaking, to the young person who is hungering and thirsting for the best that life has to offer—college means many things to many people. The American college would do its job in superior fashion if it were possible for it to ignore the budgetary implications of enrollment—a consummation devoutly to be wished—and to decide what it genuinely wants to be to the students to whom it seeks to minister.

John and Eva are there with a determination to know the right people so that they may join the right groups, to learn to say the right things with the hope that in time they may, in a far larger way, come to know the right people and join the right groups and learn to say the right things—although it should be added footnote-wise, that their use of the word *right* is without moral significance. Perhaps, however, that will come later with greater maturity.

Bill and Judy are there, delightful, likable, easygoing, and always ready for fun. They try to study enough to get by without wasted effort. They live by their ethical code, but it is the ethical code of an untroubled group, and fulfillment comes without heavy demand. Charming companions, well dressed, ready to fill in a bridge quartet or to make up a hand in Canasta, helpful with spontaneous chatting in a conversational void, they make perfect fair-weather companions, and if one were critical, the vein of criticism would be that they are without deep loyalties or commanding commitments. Maybe, however, loyalties and commitments lie ahead with greater responsibilities.

Fred and Jane are there, shy, self-conscious, ever fearful that they will blunder. They feel themselves on the outside, and more than anything else they would like to have the assurance of belonging, of being a part of a group, welcomed. Sometimes, in their effort to please, they talk too much, sometimes they reach too far, and sometimes they expose their vulnerability in ways they little dream. If they could forget themselves in a human need greater than their own, it would be life's largest blessing for them and the surest way to a fuller, mature individuality.

Ralph and Mary are there, deeply earnest about life, sometimes losing their share of fun in their absorption in "problems." Loyal to great causes and great persons, they count their years an investment which they must make wisely; they are committed to make their period of preparation a genuine search for significance. Maturity is rapidly coming their way, although they, likewise, have much still to learn.

Paul and Sarah are there, studying hard and finding large satisfaction in their work, motivated by a Christian purpose, which holds the present as an invitation to the future and, therefore, to be wisely used. They are trying hard to make for themselves normal lives with a fair proportion of work and play and love and worship. Sarah asked Paul once in a moment of serious conversation what he thought a Christian was. Paul paraphrased Sherwood Eddy for answer. "He's something more than a man who is satisfied to accept a formula or a shibboleth in a transaction which seems to be an escape from reality. I think a Christian is one who tries to bring into his own life day by day the values which he finds in Jesus Christ, as he comes to understand him through study and discipleship."[2] There's a long road ahead for Paul and Sarah, but they've made a strong start.

Among the group also, whatever their names may be, there are a few undesirables—the rotten apples in the barrel. They would destroy for the sheer exuberance of destruction. They care nothing for maturity; indeed the only kind of maturity they recognize is physical maturity, which will come to them with the mere accumulation of years, and without effort on their own part.

How shall one generalize? "Is it possible to paint a portrait of an entire generation? Each generation has a million faces and a million voices."[3]

Any generalization is essentially false, for it divides the millions of American students into groups in which they only temporarily belong. The freshman is a kind of United States within himself; some days, with honesty, he might write his name as John Wisconsin or Bill Arizona and some days, with equal honesty, as Fred Kentucky or Ralph Ohio.

* * *

It Doesn't Look Heavy

It doesn't look heavy, a high-school diploma: only a bit of paper (it isn't really sheepskin), a few drops of ink, a bit of colored ribbon from Woolworth's. It doesn't weigh much; nevertheless, a high-school diploma is heavy. It is heavy with expectations.

There is the expectation of teachers that the diploma bearer will be willing to use the dictionary and the encyclopedia, the expectation that he will think clean and clear and straight and frequently.

There is the expectation of both teachers and parents that he will be teachable, and being teachable is essentially wanting to grow in wisdom and understanding.

There are the citizens who expect him to be a good citizen, informed about the world with its variety of governments but loyal to America.

There are the neighbors who expect him to be dependable, able to carry routine for a succession of days.

And there are those friends who expect him to have a special ability of understanding and caring for people, any people, all people.

The high-school diploma is a heavy bit of luggage when the proud graduate sets out for college.

* * *

There is, however, one fundamental difference among college students—the difference in the depth and the extent and the kind of their basic loyalties. There is the breezy, comfortable pagan who lives easily within his lesser loyalties until the day of emergency, and then the response that he makes is the lonely cry of the inadequate. When campus temptations bear down upon him, sometimes he recognizes them for what they are, and sometimes not. But always he sees them through the glass of self-interest. The most important question to ask of any situation is, What's in it for me?

There is, on the same campus, the Christian student. He is one who has cultivated the loyalty to the highest it is given him to know. This is not just a casual "I believe" statement, nor yet merely an organizational affiliation, meaningful though such affiliation can be. Rather, it is a life commitment to a God whom he touches through the person of Jesus Christ, and a daily renewed commitment to live his life in intelligent service to mankind. This student knows the temptations of the campus for what they are, and even when he yields to them, he is careful not to build his alibis. He can be counted on never to commit the unpardonable sin of calling evil good or good evil.

And in between are all gradations of self-centered and God-centered lives, just as they are found in any community.

Labels, however, are not a matter of prime importance. Many a pagan student would refuse to recognize the paganism of his lesser loyalties. Many a Christian student, likewise, might be doubtful about the appropriateness of his title, wearing it hesitantly as a strait jacket of free thought or worrying over it as a possible stumbling block to campus fellowship. But the distinctions are there, as in their own ways and at their own paces the American students press on to maturity, most of them hoping to escape the calamity of being an "almost-but-not-quite" person.

They press on, hoping to avoid that devastating weakness of which Frederic Prokosch wrote in his "Elegy," yet knowing it to be a malignancy common in American student life:

> Like dolls they wander by,
> Paralyzed by an ignorance of what they seek,
> Driven by an inner rage. Yet nothing but dry
> Habitual, piping sounds fall when they speak.
> Lonesome? Idle? Unhappy? Yes, but above all weak.[4]

They hope, also, to achieve that participation in living which Justice Oliver Wendell Holmes had in mind when he said: "Life is action and passion. I think it is required of a man that he should share the action and passion of his time at peril of being judged not to have lived."[5]

Today they press, hoping especially to grasp a large measure of that freedom which the college administrator has promised either at the opening college convocation or on baccalaureate Sunday, ignorant often of the price tag of discipline which that freedom carries. In all probability, the president illustrated his address by giving the classical rootage of the word "liberal": is not the college of liberal arts intended to "free" the minds and the spirits of men? But so often the college administrator seems to limit the area of freedom which he is offering to his hearers. It is freedom from ignorance, he exclaims, and nobody will disagree. It is freedom to use the promises of the Bill of Rights, and again he will have unanimous consent from his American audiences. But not always does he go on to point out that that freedom can come only in terms of a spiritual maturity, a psychic wholeness which accepts life as full of tensions. He might wisely include the word which Gerald Heard used in addressing an assembly of students at Washington University: "The purpose of life is liberation—liberation to act without fear or favor, or reward, or punishment. . . . As long as you can be bought by office or by money or by pain, you are not a free man."

The differences among American students do not fall clearly and easily either in terms of geographical sectioning or the kinds of institutions they attend. There is about the students in our colleges of agriculture and home economics, however, an earthy wholesomeness that one does not discover elsewhere. It is probably true also that our engineering schools and other like vocational institutions have a sense of urgency and job commitment which are not to be found in the liberal-arts colleges.

But the extremes of high and low loyalties, of devoted commitment and careless indifference, are to be found on every campus, and the problem which the administrator of the church-related college faces is not essentially different from that which the presidents of the state universities struggle with—that is, as far as the nature of the student body of the institution goes. The temptations of the student world and the spiritual dangers which press upon the campus dwellers do not differ widely whether that institution be East or West, church-supported or independent. Indeed, one might venture a guess that, in a large measure, young America which does not go to college is struggling—struggling if there be combativeness in him—with closely similar situations.

SOME TEMPTATIONS OF CAMPUS LIFE

1. There is for both the habitants of the college and the noncollege world the pressure of immediacy exaggerated in our times by international events. One is tempted to believe that there will be no tomorrow. Contemporary life, with its world entanglements, its calls to military service, its war temperatures—for there can be fever in a cold as well as a hot war—has done much to increase the exasperating uncertainty with which young America is at present forced to live. The teacher and the administrator are fully aware of the intellectual climate and emotional turmoil which this pressure of immediacy has brought. They will urge, as indeed they must, that life's decisions be made irrespective of the delayed career or the broken plans which many a young American man—and in consequence, many a young American woman—faces. Yet in their hearts, they know how difficult it is to accept the wise advice they offer. The situation itself demands of the student a maturity greater than his physical age. The wise will reach for it and grasp it, but the young person still dewy from adolescence, who sees adulthood as an unattractive encumbrance of age and responsibility, may fall the easy victim to this temptation. Depending on the solidarity of his faith, which should teach him to live gracefully and wisely within uncertainty, the Christian student will surmount or succumb to the heresy that the sun may not rise tomorrow. In any case, he cannot hold himself entirely aloof from it.

2. Growing out of that pressure of immediacy is an apparently increasing absorption in the trivia of college life—a temptation which Hollywood and comic books and TV have done much to encourage. The evil of trivia is the absorption in the unimportant: sheer wastage of time, the excessive hours spent in planning social affairs, the extravagances (financial and otherwise) of certain aspects of fraternity and sorority life, the multiplication of inconsequential activities, the insignificances of certain features of the campus religious endeavors.

It would, of course, be unrealistic and nonsensical to bar trivia from normal life. Trivia have their place, but they do not deserve to be crowned King and Queen. Neither is trivia an adequate preparation for crisis. Edith Lovejoy Pierce's "Main Street, U.S.A." is frequently the mood of the campus.

> Balance your cup
> And crowd another biscuit on your plate.
> A thousand starving shadows
> Push against the gate.
> Sleep quietly
> On your mattress smooth and soft and flat.
> An earthquake splits the house,
> But what of that?
> The sky is turning dark:
> We're going to have a squall.
> Open your umbrella,
> For the atom bomb will fall.
> Starch the bedroom curtains,
> Shine the silver tray,
> Put on a little make-up—
> Here comes the Judgment Day.[6]

The college student might, however, be snared into revealing his ignorance by his question, "What do you mean, Judgment Day?"

* * *

FORMULA FOR FAILURE

1. Failure will come a little more easily to the student who was unsuccessful in learning to study in high school; but even good habits, with effort, can be sloughed off, and the know-how of learning forgotten. It is amazing how much college freshmen can forget.

2. The important thing in college is to have a good time. Keep in mind that fun comes first, and never let class assignments interfere.

3. It will help if you delay in locating the bookstore for a fortnight, and then wait another week before picking up your textbooks. If you delay long enough, there is always the chance that the stock will be exhausted. Obviously, you can't study if you have no text.

4. If your heart is set on failure, you have probably told yourself that nothing much happens in the first few meetings of the class. Here is a chance to rest from the exhaustion of travel. Again, if you insist on attending classes, at least occa-

sionally, you can spare yourself the ignominy of an excessive amount of time spent in the academic atmosphere by sitting in the rear and arriving late, after the instructor has begun.

5. Lest you feel the hypocrite by going to class at all, try looking bored and scrupulously avoid asking any questions. If you find it hard to resist the campus talk of teachers wanting to be friendly, remind yourself of the high-school truism that the man or woman behind the desk is a constitutional and inevitable enemy.

6. Romance will help, sometimes considerably. Psychologically, it is interesting how the fact of a man being in love during his freshman year makes for success in failing academically; and not infrequently, he can aid his beloved to pull down low grades too.

7. If you are one of those students who has never been away from home before, college will give you every possible chance to prove your independence. By independence freshmen usually mean getting in late at night and staying abed in the morning.

8. The library may present a problem, particularly if you like the looks of books. Remember that "required reading" is contrary to American freedom for the individual and necessarily cramps your style. Read as much as you wish, but avoid as you would an invitation to Phi Beta Kappa those books which bear upon your courses.

9. Even though the college town may be dry, if you are determined to drink, you can usually find bars and beer parlors. In spite of the law forbidding the sale of liquor to minors, you can probably get the stuff if you grow a week's beard and look haggard.

10. Put your whole heart into your determination; concentrate on it; give yourself 100 per cent to it. D would be a mark of failure. Only F or O signifies success.

Ten simple rules. No conscientious student, determined to flunk out, need henceforth worry lest he be unable in the course of the academic year to succeed in achieving a most complete and abysmal failure.

* * *

The temptation to college trivia is by no means, however, a modern invention. American students have cherished it far above their European cousins, and the American public has abetted them in their delusion of prolonged adolescence. The struggle of the colleges to be looked upon as institutions of learning, as places where young America can learn the art and the heritage, the work and the joys of adulthood has been an uphill battle, and that it has been in some appreciable measure won is a tribute to the integrity of the colleges and their leadership.

The invasion of the veterans, in the late Forties, was a boon, not only financially but intellectually, to the college. Here were men and women in contrast to boys and girls. Here were new students who were eager to get into the job of their life. Many of them had traveled far more widely than their instructors, and many of them had had experiences with foreign peoples and with the tangles of human relations that could add much to class discussions. The eighteen-year-olds coming during that last half of the decade of the Forties, fresh from high school and for the most part without immediate call for military service, found themselves drawn out of their earlier misconceptions of college as a place where you raised hell and gave time to study only if there was nothing better to do. The sheer daily example of these battle-ribboned colleagues (although the ribbons were never in evidence) had its effect.

It is true that the G.I. turned Joe College brought to the campus his own particular Army and Navy variety of worldliness, and it may be doubted if the college campus will ever be quite the same again. Nevertheless, his contribution in building an atmosphere of seriousness and academic application will, likewise, it is to be hoped, have some degree of permanency.

The Christian student facing this tempting absorption in the trivia of college life will put the temptation down, not with long face and pious words, but with an anticipation of the joy of achievement which can come with more mature occupations.

3. Growing out of the pressure of immediacy and yet long antedating it, cousin, also, to the absorption in the trivia of college life, is the campus tendency to entertain a distaste for the intellectual. The average student, like the average adult, is tempted to avoid the struggle of minds, to escape when possible the mental effort of coming to grips with the great problems of our day. The temptation is by no means confined to campus life; every American community and institution knows it or its counterpart. One can learn much about a campus by a careful judgment of the average student response to the local chapter of Phi Beta Kappa. The sophomoric assumption,

"I too could have made it but it wasn't worth the effort," tells something about the speaker, and any repeated attempt to explain away the success of membership by generalizations of dishonesty, or warped and inhuman absorption in the textbook, or apple polishing under any of its pseudonyms, will speak its own truth about the campus's lack of interest in hard intellectual struggle.

On the college campus one finds this revolt against brains particularly in the idea that the intellectual is but one aspect of the many developments which the four campus years should bring. There is, of course, a core of truth in the statement, but so often the student enamored of this idea, either because of intellectual laziness or because of mediocre ability, rationalizes until he has put the intellectual at the bottom of his list of possible sources of new maturity, and in consequence it is the most neglected of the lot.

Physically, college may be for him a growing experience; socially, it may bring new competence; vocationally, he may have a clearer idea of his direction; spiritually there may be fresh, cleansing understanding; but unless something has happened to his mental equipment, unless there has come an eager desire to grapple with hard ideas, to seek truth through a morass of half-truths, unless he can achieve a larger ability to think clearly and logically and to know fact from fiction, he may have done those things which he ought to have done, but he has left undone that thing most essential to the success of the college experience.

The Christian student, strong in his idealism, may be subtle victim of this temptation, feeling he should substitute community service for classroom success, or church activity for hours over the textbook. If he can realize that his own strength in the future lies in his intellectual progress during college years, he may be wise enough to put first things first and build for a strong future.

4. There is a fourth moral hazard common to campuses and college students: the danger of an easy self-complacency. Sometimes it is a smugness growing out of a sense of superiority. This temptation will differ from campus to campus and also from student generation to student generation, depending in part upon the heterogeneity of the student body, and the seriousness of purpose and the "sense of mission"—horrible phrase—that the majority of the students hold. Yet, "We are the world's elite" is too often the frame of mind in which one finds the young, half-educated American.

It is this attitude to which industrial leaders have been most hostile. Their criticism, together with the increased competition of college-trained men for posts in the world of industry, has frequently brought a more humble spirit as the young collegian faced his future and put his foot on the first rung of the work ladder.

It is inexperience linked with this sense of superiority which has caused many students to reach for a freedom beyond that which community living permits. For example, the college student—and his parents, too—expect the dean to make certain that in any conflict with the civil authorities he, the student, is given special protection above that which his working brother would receive. It is inexperience and this self-complacency which cause the student to believe that he is entitled to a kind of special respect from the press —here, the successful parent is doubly concerned—when his misconduct and alert reporting give the newspaper information which he regrets, remembering too late that "Father will be terribly angry." In such cases the college authorities for institutional reasons are inclined to abet the student in seeking a protection from undesirable publicity of the sort which the ordinary American in misconduct receives.

The Christian student, with all of his proneness to this hazard, will guard himself, recognizing that advantages bring their own responsibilities and that experiences which raise him above the level of American young people need continuous translating into obligations, the better and more wisely to serve.

5. There is a fifth danger which, I am persuaded, any close observer of American college life for the last twenty years will recognize: the growing tendency to vulgarity and bad taste. It too springs out of inexperience. It is, moreover, a reflection of the larger American vulgarity and bad taste which appear to have increased in the interim between the wars and the more recent years, and may still be on the increase in many circles of our national day-by-day existence.

* * *

Mildred McAfee Horton quotes a Japanese educator as saying to the group of Americans who visited Japan shortly after the Armistice: "We do want our Japanese girls to have the freedom to think as your American girls have, but we do hope—excuse us—that our girls will continue to be polite."

* * *

Submerged in American campus life, one often can rest unaware of this; but traveling in foreign lands, one is immediately confronted with the judgment of sane, cultured Europeans and Asians who fear the contagion of American vulgarity. They see it in many of our imported movies; they find it in many of our American jokes, particularly the *double-entendre*. They are troubled by many of our most popular comedians, whose humor they cannot always understand. And they find it, unfortunately amply illustrated, in the conduct of many Americans whose pocketbooks make travel a possibility.

To point out the commonness of this national characteristic of vulgarity is not to exonerate the college. It does, however, bring into perspective the necessary struggle of the college to mold rather than meekly to reflect American public opinion. The college must be more than a mirror for American social life; it is its obligation to give direction. Meanwhile, the ambitious student editor frequently sees as his goal the out-*esquiring* of *Esquire* and the sorority president, captured by the idea of freedom, opens the doors into experience both for herself and her sisters which the thoughtful, mature American will count as bad taste or something more objectionable.

STUDENT EXPECTATIONS BOTH GREAT AND SMALL

It would be inaccurate to suggest that college freshmen come to the campus without expectations. Their pockets are filled with them, their luggage crammed, their minds stuffed. Some expectations are realistic and some are fantastic. Some will be fulfilled, some will be quickly discarded as unworthy, and some will be discarded as too difficult of accomplishment.

A study of Christian education may wisely raise the question: What are reasonable expectations for the student and more especially for the Christian-minded student to hold toward his college and his college years?

In the process of admissions, the college makes known its expectations of those students who are coming to enroll under its banner. In no equally tangible way does the student have the invitation to express his expectations of the college where he is himself enrolling. There was a day when it was scarcely thought that a student had the right of private expectation; that was a judgment that belonged to our academic yesteryears.

In his book *How to Educate Human Beings*, Edward A. Fitzpatrick, president of Mount Mary College, gives at length a student

Bill of Rights.[7] It is an excellent presentation of the new status which the student holds in the college community. Written here is a listing of his rights as a campus citizen. Many a student body under competent student leadership will do well to press for a comparable document on its own campus, and in turn give its support to a national student Bill of Rights.

These are rights, however, which have little connection with the question of religious faith and religious freedom. It is with a student's expectation in this particular realm that the question of expectations is raised. If a Christian student chooses to matriculate in an avowedly Christian institution or even an institution which professes general concern for the religious development of its students, it is inevitable that he shall hold certain definite expectations, reasonable or unreasonable.

THE ENCOURAGEMENT TO BE A CHRISTIAN

His first expectation may well be the freedom and the encouragement to be a Christian according to his own best understanding of Christian faith. The student must always be given the right to reject Christianity—there is usually no problem of infringement here. The student must also be given the right to accept and to practice Christianity. It is this second freedom which is less secure on the American campus—if it can be understood not as freedom legally interpreted but freedom with encouragement—in part because of the inadequate presentation of the Christian faith, and in part because of the peripheral attention so often given to religion and religious activities.

A faculty frankly antagonistic to the things of the spirit is not common; but common is the faculty whose first loyalties are given to the secular standards of academic objectivity. Often unaware, such a group creates an atmosphere of resistance to Christian faith which, by its very frowning, curtails the student's likelihood of choice. Moreover, there is in the characteristic of youth itself, the fear and feeling that somehow religion may be asking him to believe something that is not true: "something that he must take wholly upon faith, without the privilege of asking questions about it and applying the same sort of rigid intellectual tests that he applies to every other area of life and thought."[8]

The question, therefore, becomes more than the simple question of the right to accept or to reject. It is a larger question of understanding and of compassion and of growth. It is a question of the campus atmosphere accepting as rational and significant the Christian commitment.

But the critic, reading these pages, will at once object: "Is there not freedom to practice religious faith even in an atmosphere of hostility or indifference? Has not the Christian ever developed muscles by climbing? With his advent into college circles, can the student not be expected to stand upon his own integrity religiously as well as otherwise and to meet hostility and ridicule and contempt as they may come?"

The answer is, of course, that this is true for the young student, as he carries his religious faith into an unsympathetic world. But we are facing now his expectations of a college which is either frankly Christian or publicly proclaims its concern for the religious development of its students. Even here, to be sure, there may be pockets of flaming opposition. Nevertheless, has he not the right to expect from such an institution, not alone the freedom to accept the Christian faith, but a friendly encouragement to live it? And this encouragement must be genuinely, wholeheartedly given.

A hatred of pretense has ever been a dominant quality of youth. College students are quick to detect sham; they are unanimous in their condemnation. Their admiration, on the other hand, is readily given to genuineness wherever they may find it. It was this hard core of reality which F. R. Leavis had in mind when he wrote, "The only value remaining to us in the collapse of values is sincerity."[9]

If the college undertakes to foster the religious development of its student body, it must, of necessity, present some kind of comprehensive understanding of what it believes religion to be. It is religion in its inclusive aspects of both individual and community, of both rationale and attitudes, that the academic institution is committed to present. The young person with his nose for sham will easily detect any defect in the sincerity of the presentation.

In *The Mind's Adventure*, Dr. Lowry has endeavored to set forth the inclusive Christianity which the church-related college may offer as a norm. It is a paragraph of searching, crystallizing faith.

Christianity will make its way in men's imaginations if it reveals itself as more than a set of rules. Without losing its ethical character or its moral power, it can show that its secret is more than the secret of renunciation. It suffers, among young people especially, from the suggestion it too often gives of spiritual pride, tight-lipped respectability, or a tidy goodness that lacks humor, sympathy, and understanding, and any human sense of how life can knock and batter at the bodies and souls of men. It is, as has been said, morality lighted up with something else—with a life-bestowing bond of man to a power beyond himself. It is the morality of a heart and will regenerated in a new relationship. For faith, in Newman's superb insight, is "a habit of the soul," a practical keeping alive of such a sustained and full communion with God that every instinct of the spirit, in all daily tasks and experience, is in perpetual reference to Him. This becomes a working principle of living in which "life, law, joy, impulse are one thing."[10]

THE FRIENDLY COUNSEL OF THE FACULTY

A second expectation which the young Christian student may hold of the institution of his choice is that the faculty and the administration will give him aid in his own honest search for religious understanding. When the student approaches an instructor for help, he has a right to expect a thoughtful reply. The instructor will fail his high calling if he does not offer patience and cooperativeness and unshockability. It is the student's right, because he is a student, to question in sincerity the basic assumptions of life and death. Faith is made strong through such questioning, and truth comes often in the honest endeavor to press beyond doubt.

There is, of course, no guarantee that the religious faith of a senior will duplicate the religious faith of a freshman; indeed, if in four years' time no new breadth or depth has come, the situation would appear to be one not of growth but of stalemate. The family and the Church must recognize the possibility—even the probability—that under the influence of both the mature and the immature minds which the campus provides for fellowship, there will come changes which may or may not be acceptable. The point remains, however, that the student in question is trying to satisfy himself, in line with his own integrity, as to what truth is. He has every right to expect both sympathy and full aid from the faculty in that search.

* * *

COLOSSAL EDUCATIONAL FAILURE

Inadequate understanding of education is not uncommon. One finds it frequently in conferences with parents. I recall the interview I had with a mother and her son during freshman days.

"Here he is, sir, take good care of him. Bill is a good boy. There is only one promise I want you to make to me, and that is that you will return him to his father and me at the end of the year just as he is today. Make sure, please that he doesn't get any crazy ideas in his head. Make sure that he doesn't have any new desires or impulses. We want him back just the way he is."

An honest answer to that mother might have been: "Madam, that might be possible, but if so, think what a colossal educational failure!"

* * *

There is no concealed suggestion here that the faculty man or woman is expected to pass on an "official" view of religion contrary to or differing from his own experience-tested faith. The Christian will share his own Christian philosophy of life, and the pagan is free to share his paganism. It is to be hoped, however, that in our church-related colleges and in many of our state institutions that give consideration to the religious influences of the campus, the seeking student surely can be provided "with an intelligible alternative to secularism, a Christian map of the world, however provisional."

Sir Walter Moberly goes on to add, "Failing that, they are left, at best, with a Christian top-dressing on a thoroughly secularized understanding of history, literature, or natural science, on the lines on which these are commonly studied in universities."[11]

The charge has been made that "the college attempts to inculcate in young males the apron-string virtues of passivity, dependence, and docility."[12] If the charge has validity, the situation is serious. When a man enters college, he has put aside the need for intellectual protection that may have shadowed his high-school days. He is ready now, as an adult, to face the uncertainties and the controversies of life. Too often have colleges and their faculties excluded from appropriate discussions those ultimate questions of existence, those far goals of education, ruling them out of bounds, and thereby depriving the student of his best opportunity to explore in good companionship.

For this kind of exploration in fellowship there is needed on the faculty team the kind of teacher which the National Education Association praised in its brochure *The Education of Free Men in American Democracy*. Besides being an excellent technician, "he [the teacher in a democracy] must be a person to command the respect, evoke the enthusiasm, and even enlist the affection of the pupil."[13]

It is to be hoped that the Christian college, through its enrollment of a Christian faculty, may be able to help the student to piece together this "Christian map of the world." It is likewise to be desired that the state universities, through their faculties of Catholics, Protestants, and Jews many of whom will have deep concern for the religious presuppositions of living, will share freely and in good earnest their own religious convictions and the grounds for their persuasion. In this way, the student may come to have some understanding, not alone of his treasure of faith but of its religious implication for his daily living.

From this fellowship with the faculty, there should come comprehension of what is going on in the world today; something also of the Christian responsibility for that world, and the place that the student as one individual is expected some day to take in that larger scene, first as a citizen of his own country, and then as a citizen of the world.

Perhaps the pedagogues are right when they say that virtue cannot be taught, but surely, in this kind of campus fellowship of faith, "virtue can be loved."[14]

A STUDENT FELLOWSHIP OF KINDRED MINDS

The Christian student, moreover, has a right to expect that he will find on the campus a student fellowship of like minds and hearts. This is not to be interpreted as a suggestion that the admissions office should choose only those students that come from the same economic bracket, or list the same denominational affiliation, or come from homes of the same political coloring. That kind of homogeneity can be intellectually deadening. It does mean, however, that the church-related college, free to choose its student members, holds the responsibility to see that there is in the student body a majority of earnest, industrious, ambitious students; and still more, it means that the college will, over the decades, build a tradition to attract that kind of young person.

The new world of the college campus can be disconcerting to the freshman who comes from a protected home or a protected church. Even when the adjustment has been made to a new and larger freedom, the problems of the campus still must be mastered: the problem of trustworthiness in all of the intricate campus relationships, from that of honesty in the classroom to honesty within oneself;

the problem of race, and color of skin; the problem of the rights of minorities, which may never have been met before in quite the way they present themselves on the college campus; the problem of faculty-student relationships, and how one climbs over the old high-school barrier of believing the teacher to be in the camp of the enemy; the problem of the fraternity and the sorority, which seem to shuttle between being beneficial to religious growth and being detrimental, according to the quality of the leadership which is theirs. The average college freshman, with the imperfect maturity of his late teen years, stands in grave need of a student fellowship of friendly minds and companionable hearts, which will support him as he seeks for the answers of integrity to these common perplexities.

There will be the bull session, which at its best can be a truly educational forum, and at its worst an exchange of ignorance. The bull session can aid the freshman to scrutinize with critical care the ideas and ideals which are bandied about. He learns to overcome some of his fear of being laughed at for asking the naïve question. He learns also to test some of his own presuppositions against the experience and the presuppositions of others whose lives he finds himself admiring.

* * *

POETRY CONTEST

Ann, a sophomore at one of our great American universities, had written a poem to be entered in a national competition for the best student poem. It was an analysis of the full man, and Ann had listed forgiveness as one of the necessary qualities.

A local poet of some repute, who was sitting with the committee charged with the choice of the winning poem, called her into conference. He liked the poem, the idea was good; but the reference to forgiveness—forgiveness was a Christian concept. And the committee would like the poem better if she saw fit to omit this idea.

Ann's poem still contains the lines regarding forgiveness. It did not win the prize.

* * *

It is this warm fellowship and this eager searching of comrade-minds that bring growth to the freshman as he struggles with those eternal problems of the measures of personal success, the validity of moral standards, the problem of communism, the question of the existence of significance—and the eternal fact of God.

ARROWS OF DIRECTION FOR THE YEARS AHEAD

The Christian student has the rightful expectation that his years of study will bring him a reinforced sense of direction and a new purposefulness of life. Howard Thurman, in his collection of magnificent religious poems entitled *The Greatest of These*, has the haunting phrase: "To die without benefit of Cause."[15] The right kind of education is intended to save the student from the futility of such death, but this salvation will come only as he himself seeks for the Cause with his whole mind and heart.

It was this which the leaders of the Ford Foundation had in mind when they wrote:

School should be the most important influence outside of the home for the molding of whole persons. Yet individual purpose, character, and values, the bases of which are laid in the home, are often inadequately developed by institutions which could, by precept and deeper teaching, assume a major share in supporting them most successfully.

Education must meet the needs of the human spirit. It must assist persons to develop a satisfactory personal philosophy and sense of values; to cultivate taste for literature, music, and the arts; and to grow in ability to analyze problems and arrive at thoughtful conclusions. Only thus will graduates of our schools and colleges attain the wisdom necessary to live integrated and purposeful lives.[16]

The two most common patterns of adolescence are docility and rebellion. Both are demonstrated day by day on the American college campus. Both must be identified and responded to by faculty counselors and student leaders. It is usually in one of these two moods that the student faces that great gift of the college experience, "the freedom to choose a vital center for his life on the basis of intelligence and understanding in an atmosphere of good will and freedom."[17]

Few students, however, make the choice of their vital center in a single dramatic moment. Often it is a matter of predisposition, built over months of effort, both conscious and unconscious. Often it comes from a subtle and silent weighing of the rival claims for the position of center in a man's life. There is the noisy claim of personal profits, exploited by so much of our contemporary living, including the movie and the cheap press, which Sir Richard Livingstone has called "the substitute for religion" in our day.[18] There is the sense of duty, but duty, lonely, isolated in a kind of philosophic void. There is the center of human service, of devotion to the needs of mankind. There is also the Christian center of God. The student may go from one rival claimant to the other, testing, experimenting, resolving; and eventually he must choose. For a refusal to choose casts the die to one of the competitors.

Is it to drag into undue prominence the faculty-student encounter to suggest that here again the faculty holds a responsibility in its hands? One of the sadnesses of so many of our American campuses is the lack of interest of the faculty member in the individual student and, in turn, the lack of expectation of the individual student that the faculty member should have any concern for him, outside of his obligation to read badly scrawled test papers and assign an appropriate grade.

One thinks of those lines of misunderstanding from T. S. Eliot's *The Cocktail Party*, applicable to many a college campus in their description of the failure of the faculty and the student body to come to human understandings.

> They make noises,
>   and think they are talking to each other;
> They make faces,
>   and think they understand each other.[19]

The wise, responsible instructor goes back again and again to the phrase of Alfred North Whitehead, reminding himself of the obligation of education to provide the student with the habitual vision of greatness. That vision comes, in part, from the lives and examples of the faculty. It comes also in part both intentionally and unintentionally from the lives and the examples of students. And it comes also from the biographies of the giant minds and the giant spirits of past days. And from that habitual vision of greatness, both present and past, along with the fulfillment of the daily assignment, along with the routine of the weeks that pass one much like the other, there should come that new sense of direction and that new purposefulness of life which can make work a sacrament, and the right job a Christian vocation.

CHANNELS FOR SOCIAL ACTION

The Christian student has the right to hold an additional expectation, namely, that among the activities of the college he shall find reasonable opportunity for the expression of his Christian social concern. Campus living is community living, and within the confines of the college walls are most of the problems of community life. There is the opportunity to express Christian citizenship, so needed in the days ahead when the student has taken his place in the larger community. Moreover, these are days when the college community is recognizing its obligation to the society of which it is a part. College administrations are encouraging the exchange of services, so that the campus group and the noncampus group may come to know the life of the other and, through understanding, learn compassion.

Many a campus today has its excellent program of deputation groups, whereby not only are church services in rural centers cared for, but often students arrange to go to a community for a week end. By living in the homes of the community, by fostering a recreational program on Saturday evening, as well as the religious program for Sunday morning, students give and also receive in generous measure. Many a college campus today likewise has a substantial listing of religious and sociological projects, in which the student may participate; and on many campuses, the participation is generous and enthusiastic.

* * *

The Wheat Trailer

One of the interesting stories of social activities to come from a college campus is the story of the Wheat Trailer. It started when Stringfellow Barr spoke at Macalester College and urged the students to do something about the bill then pending in Congress that was to provide wheat for India. At a luncheon following the convocation the student leaders pressed Dr. Barr for suggestions for action. He in turn replied, "Why not take some wheat to Washington?" Stirred by the idea, the student leaders got permission to take a collection from the students following chapel the next day and something in excess of $200 was raised. The money was spent for wheat, which was shipped to Washington in 100-pound bags.

> *Then came the idea of the Student Caravan carrying a token gift of wheat. Twenty students were selected to go as representatives of Macalester College. Nine days were allowed for travel and a twenty-four-hour stay in Washington. The students cared for their own expenses on the trip and the college provided the gas and oil for the cars.*
>
> *Other colleges joined along the way. At the University of Wisconsin the Indian students provided hospitality for the Caravan. On May 7, 1951, the contribution of 700 pounds of wheat was delivered to the Indian Embassy and Madame Pandit made personal acknowledgment.*

* * *

The college man and woman are still latent idealists. Concealed often by a false sophistication, pressed down on occasion by the absorption in one's own personal living, that idealism, nevertheless, comes bobbing to the surface at strange and unexpected moments.

Theodore O. Wedel has called it a "pragmatic" idealism. "Ideals —these are with us in abundance! Ideals for social betterment, ideals for government, ideals for world peace, ideals for happy marriage, ideals for personal happiness, cosmetic ideals, sartorial ideals, ideals of service, ideals of beauty, truth, and even goodness. If ideals could be defined as a substitute for God, our secularist culture would be intensely religious. Humanist idealism is, in fact, our reigning American faith. It is the great rival to authentic Christianity in our western, still democratic world. Our universities and colleges are its cathedrals."[20]

Dr. Wedel is correct that the idealism one finds on a college campus is by no means always a Christian idealism. There may be a Christian toleration in the ideal, but often it is divorced from the substance of Christian faith and Christian doctrine. He overlooks, however, the fact that pragmatic idealism can be a fertile soil for Christian seed. Although it is frequently a humanistic idealism, it nevertheless becomes the meeting point for the Christian student seeking the expression for his Christian social concerns, and the student who knows only a desire to be helpful to his less fortunate brother.

The Christian student, however, will not need to leave the campus to find a major area for the expression of his social concern. Presumably the campus is a democratic community; and as such, there is within the college democracy urgent need for the working out of plans for campus government, ideally containing both faculty and students. He may be able to bring persuasion so that the plans embody in high degree the Christian respect for human personality and regard for both minority and majority groups.

The academician is sometimes jealous of the hours which the student gives to community service. The churchman sometimes criticizes it as an effort to find a substitute for faith. The campus visitor occasionally questions its motivation, when it becomes too closely tied with fraternity prestige and activity points. Nevertheless, while each critic has a valid point of criticism, sight must not be lost of the importance for the student of a legitimate expression of his own desire to participate creatively in the larger community group.

* * *

No Greater Compliment

The words and the voice come from a day long ago, but the voice is still with me, and the words clear. It was in a study room in a fraternity house. I was a sophomore working on my classroom assignments at my desk. My roommate, who has since become a distinguished clergyman in the East, was at his desk. One of the pledges of the house, a freshman, came in, and asked for help from my roommate on his assignment in mathematics. They worked together; I was aware of their conversation, although it did not interfere with my own study.

Patiently, my roommate showed the freshman where his reasoning had led him astray, and together, step by step, they worked through the problems. Then the freshman, timidly and hesitantly, raised a question of moral choice, which he had to face. Pressure was on him to do that which he did not believe he should do; out of the strength of his own conviction, my roommate counseled him.

The freshman rose to leave, and as he turned to the door he paid my roommate a great compliment. "Thank you. I guess I am just stupid and weak. But knowing you makes being a Christian on this campus just a little bit easier."

* * *

In his volume *Strengthening the Spiritual Life*, Nels Ferré has written: "Christianity is not worth the breath it takes to say the creed unless it can produce individuals who have found in concrete living a new community commitment in every dimension. A rabid sectarian, a racialist, a sectionalist, a nationalist shows by his fruits that his heart is full of something that is not Christianity."[21]

"Gladly wolde he lerne"—we hope so. The learning experiences will not all be in the classroom nor the lessons always found in textbooks. In that respect college is like life.

Chapter Four. "The Terrible Responsibility of the Teacher"

Like the direction of the wind the direction of the life of a people is the result of many forces. But if education alone cannot do what must be done, neither can it alone neglect what must be done. At the very least it can assert the difference between means and ends, and value each. It can attempt to discover among the ideas which have vitality in our times those, like the conception of human dignity and value, which seem to stand for the time and to speak its mind and to look toward its future. It can oppose with all the weight of its authority and tradition any practice of life, whatever the name it goes by, which finds its justification in things—in the use of things or the possession of things—to the exclusion of man. It can abandon its efforts, based upon a misapplication of the methods of the natural sciences, to maintain an abstract and disinterested neutrality even on issues affecting man and his destiny. It can accept again the moral responsibility to decide and teach —not merely select and report. It can accept in brief the terrible responsibility of the teacher. For without the acceptance of that responsibility, teaching—teaching at least for life—is impossible.[1]

ARCHIBALD MacLEISH

IN T. S. Eliot's play, *The Cocktail Party*, there is a bit of searching dialogue between Edward and his wife, Lavinia. The expressions of their hostility may be taken as the relationship too often existing between the secular teacher and his Christian colleague.

Edward, who in this case would represent the secular teacher, cries at Lavinia,

> One of the most infuriating things about you
> Has always been your perfect assurance
> That you understood me better than I understood myself.

And Lavinia, who in our allegory may be taken as the representative of the Christian teacher, replies:

> And the most infuriating thing about you
> Has always been your placid assumption
> That I wasn't worth the trouble of understanding.[2]

At the danger of repetition, let it be reasserted that the Christian teacher stands upon the same foundation of academic integrity and academic standards and academic quality as his non-Christian colleague. The majority of the time-tested dicta regarding successful teaching will apply to both men. The Christian teacher must answer to, and be subject to, a higher and a broader judgment than his secular colleague, but never will he be responsive to less.

In the circles of religion there is always the persistent and hideous danger that the effort will be made to substitute good character for good scholarship. Many a church college has lost its moral right to be recognized as a Christian institution by its flimsy willingness to substitute good influence for the qualities of sound, effective, competent teaching, and to allow piety and denominational conformity to stand in lieu of academic excellence and rigorous performance. Few administrators of church colleges have not at some time been confronted by the troublesome "good man" who can see no reason for undergoing the laborious regimen of graduate study when he, by his own pronouncement, confesses to be "called by the Lord to teach."

THE SEARCH FOR THE TEACHER

When the administrator of a church-related college needs a new teacher, he embarks on his search for "the teacher-plus." The secularist, in examining that "plus," thinks of it as something quite irrelevant to the arts of teaching, but in that he is wrong. The president or dean, charged with the responsibility for appointments in a Christian college, wants as a basic minimum the man who by training and experience gives promise of being the competent teacher. When he has found this assurance, then he must start evaluating the "plus." Is he a man who is keenly interested in his students as human beings? The administrator rightly doubts if the teacher of undergraduates can be wholly successful without that deep concern for the learning process as it operates in the minds and hearts of his learners. The administrator likewise wants a man of exemplary life, for the very nature of the closely knit character of the small campus (the critic may call it the "fish-bowl quality") can make the philandering husband or the wife beater an unhappy and improper appointment. The academic leader will also be looking for a man who will take his part as a normal citizen in the life of the community, sharing the responsibilities and providing the kind of leadership which the educated man is expected, at least theoretically, to supply.

* * *

SEVEN MEASURES

Julius Seelye Bixler, president of Colby College, outlines seven attributes of a good college teacher:

First of all and most obviously, he must know his stuff and be a master at his chosen field with a record in it of pioneering achievement.

Second, he must know it philosophically with an eye to its relation to other fields and to the larger outlines of the world of learning.

Third, he must know it enthusiastically so that his students will be brought to share his passion for knowledge.

Fourth, he must know it religiously—that is to say, with a sense for the mystery and the pathos of human existence and in particular for the tragic choices the present student generation confronts.

Fifth, he must know his students and their difficulties and must have an awareness of the modern methods of learning which help to overcome them.

Sixth, as a creative artist he should have some feeling for the dramatic unity of the teaching hour and should be able to avoid both the pedantry of the too formal lecture and the wayward listlessness of the too informal discussion.

Seventh and hardest, he must know himself and his weaknesses, especially his proneness to seek adulation for himself instead of stimulating originality in others.

"A great teacher" says Henry Adams, "affects eternity. He never knows where his influence stops." Dr. Bixler adds, "Of a poor teacher, alas, the same is true."[3]

* * *

If the critic shouts in derision that none of these items is concerned with the art of teaching, again let it be said that he is wrong —wrong at least in the eyes of the church-related and the independent college. This type of institution holds fast to a sturdy ideal which has permeated all of our public education for decades, that the teacher should by example represent the kind of living that education at its best stands for—the considerate counselor concerned with the growth of a student, the family man making his home life representative of the best, and the informed citizen willing to take his part in the life of his community.

There are those who say that the administrator in the tax-supported school, either voluntarily or by compulsion of the profession, must wipe from the blackboard of his mind all considerations regarding the "plus," and insist that all that he is concerned with is academic competence. Indeed this may be the critic whom Sir Walter Moberly quotes: "What is wanted of the university teacher is not that he should be a good husband and father, an active citizen or a pillar of his church. It is the scholar's distinctive equipment and conscience, a critical sense trained to the finest discrimination, a thorough mastery of his subject, together with the gift of lucid teaching and of stimulating his pupils."[4] The Christian administrator is constrained to ask why his colleague in the tax-supported institution cannot have all this, and in addition the "plus," assuming that fallible humanity can be found containing all these qualities.

Certainly many who are teachers-plus in marked degree have given their lives to the classroom in the tax-supported college and university, and one judges that they are there through no trivial chance or by happy accident. A diligent administrator set his pattern and followed it; and yet the assumption is commonly made that in the state-controlled institutions academic competence is not alone the first ground for appointment, as indeed it should be, but the only ground.

A DIALOGUE OF OPPOSING POINTS OF VIEW

In a recent faculty conference in Wisconsin there was a revealing exchange between two men representing the two points of view suggested here. The chairman of a major department in one of the great universities said: "In engaging a new man for my department I have only one concern, and that is his educational training, his academic competence. I am allowed to make no inquiry as to the color of his skin, the nature of his political loyalty, the presence or absence of a church affiliation, his relations with his family, or his past record as a citizen. None of these items is pertinent to the one question of whether or not he is qualified for membership in a department of a great university."

And the exponent of the "plus" theory said in reply: "But do you actually have no concern whatever for these most revealing facets of a man's life, even though you call them extraneous? Do they not disclose to you something of the nature of the man as he will stand in the classroom before his students? Do you not, as the administrator charged with appointment, of necessity need to know these items even though you will not, by the very nature of your post, make your choice on secondary matters?

"It may be that you want definitely a Negro member for your department of sociology, or that under the circumstances you do not want a Negro, but is it not pertinent to know the color of his skin? It may be that the conservatism or the liberalism of the applicant's economic and political views are not relevant, but if you are administering a department in the social studies, is there not good reason to be informed of them in advance? And if by chance your department is heavily loaded on either side, would there not be adequate reason for choosing a man with his liberalism or his conservatism in mind? Granted at once that, for a great state university, you have no right to choose a man *primarily* on the basis of his religious affiliation; but do you not have a right, as well as an obligation to make certain that whatever he be, Catholic, Jew, or Protestant, secularist or atheist, he takes religion seriously, that is, seriously enough to understand it, and if it is his choice to combat it, to combat it by legitimate means and not by scorn and contempt? Are you not interested in his attitude toward communism? Is teaching as completely divorced from humanity as you appear to make it?"

The man who was speaking concluded with these words: "Even in a state university, is there not relevance between these aspects of the man's life and thinking and his ability to go before a group of undergraduates and present his subject matter honestly, intelligently, persuasively? Under hostile pressure, terrorized by the bugaboo of church v. state, white v. black, conservative v. radical, have we not allowed ourselves to be forced into a corner where we are deprived of the right to make the choices of appointment in a wise and efficient manner? Curiously, and to my mind most ignorantly, the assumption is that the administrator will use the material *against* the candidate, where in many cases it is this 'plus' information which may be the occasion for the appointment."

His opponent shook his head unpersuaded: "Nothing except the soundness of his educational training and the success of his previous teaching can be recognized." Perhaps it was wishful thinking on my part, but I thought there was a shade of sadness in his voice.

Whenever academic competence is made the sole and exclusive criterion of a candidate for a teaching post, there is always the danger that personal abnormalities may color the complexion of the teacher. No friend of education wants to belittle the importance of sound academic training, sturdy academic experience, and all that goes into complete competence in the classroom, in the laboratory, in the research office. These are items which must always be given first consideration in the appointment of a teacher. But the disagreement, it appears, comes in terms of the secondary qualifications, and he who would speak on behalf of religious insight in the teacher would demand that these not be overlooked, whereas his opponent dictatorially rules them out of court.

"PERSONAL GIFTS AND INTELLECTUAL ARTS"

In Columbia's *A College Program in Action*, issued in 1946, there is reference to "the personal gifts and the intellectual arts of a first-rate teacher." The report goes on to say the undergraduate teacher "should be a competent scholar, but his scholarship should be the correlative of his talent and passion for teaching."[5] This is sound educational theory and moves in the direction of recognizing those items which, in addition to academic competence, have a large part in the making of a great, or even an acceptable, teacher.

* * *

"SOMEONE . . . TO WHOM SHE COULD GO"

I was having luncheon with a group of faculty and students who were making their plans for a Religion in Life Week. One of the young women in the group spoke up: "It seems to me dreadfully important that during one's college career every student have a chance to feel that there is someone on the faculty or the administrative staff to whom she can go if she has a pressing problem."

One of the faculty men made answer: "Every student has his counselor."

"But that isn't what I mean," she replied. "I want somebody I feel is willing to listen to me with a certain amount of genuine friendship. My counselor has the job of approving my academic schedule, and he does that, but he never makes me feel that he cares what happens to me, provided I take the courses that will allow me to graduate when that time comes."

"How would you do it?" another student asked. "It doesn't seem to me that any kind of organization is possible, because

*you want something that amounts to personal ties, and they
can't be organized."*

"No, I think you're right," the first student said. "I don't
think it can be organized in quite that way, but I still wish it
were possible for every student to feel that there was a least
one faculty man or woman to whom he could go without
hesitation or embarrassment and unload the stuff that's on
his heart."

* * *

These are days when increasing attention is paid to counseling, and
when most teachers are expected, either officially or unofficially, to
include student counseling among their responsibilities. At its lowest
denominator, student counseling can be simply the approval or disapproval of academic schedules. At its best—and it is fair to assume
that the good teacher wants counseling to be at its best—it is an
exchange of human experience on a basis of mutual trust and
confidence. The fruits of sound scholarship, the understandings that
come from successful teaching, the scholar's integrity—all of these
have a place in the art of counseling, but here again that "something more" assumes a still greater importance. The counselors, as
Howard Lowry has wisely written, "must be men who know that
beyond the world of information there lies a world of value and deep
loyalties—that men were born to hate some things and to love
others; that there are causes and affections to which men of good
will may conceivably be bound forever. And it helps if they really
care about young people."[6]

Moreover, somewhere in that "significant plus" must be reckoned
the importance of the academic family: not just the classroom with
its formal instruction, nor even the counseling chamber with its attention to individual problems, but the household of persons wherein
the lessons of the classroom are given daily and pertinent application.
Too often there is validity in the complaint so commonly heard on
the college campus that "the professor is incomprehensible inside of
class and invisible outside." There is legitimate desire on the part
of many students to know their teachers as men of flesh and blood.
There is envy for the tiny minority who are welcomed into the
friendliness of the instructor's home. It is easy to laugh at the *re-
ductio ad absurdum* that the argument runs into when one confronts
the tremendous hordes of students at some of our great metropolitan

colleges and recognizes the severe limitations of the hospitable home. Granted, reluctantly, that there are many institutions in which the academic family cannot be accessible to the student; nevertheless, the ideal is valid, and we have here one of the indisputable strengths of the small college. There it is possible for faculty to know students, and for students to be entertained in the faculty home—and the pity is that so few of the faculty in the small college are willing to grasp this educational opportunity as it waits for them on their doorstep.

In emphasizing what the Hazen and the Danforth Foundations have done in encouraging their Associates on several hundred campuses to make use of their annual grants for student entertaining, Albert C. Outler has paid this tribute to the academic family:

The religious perspective in higher education begins in the academic home, in an atmosphere created in the normal community of persons where friends are welcomed, and where the fellowship is reasonably amiable and productive. The miracles of time and space are demanded of faculty men and women as they bring students into their homes, welcoming them for themselves, concerned for their growth in spite of their small whims, and in spite of their own crowded personal schedules. The home which is open to the student can afford him a revealing experience of seeing mature people seeking to perfect their inter-personal relationships. The faculty home is where the canons of excellence are regarded and partially at least observed.[7]

THE TEACHER MUST NOT RESIGN FROM HIS CITIZENSHIP

Furthermore there is the activity of the teacher as citizen. Heaven forbid that this should be thought by any to be a warning against the occasional professor who follows his freedom into modes of thinking and action which are counted detrimental to the welfare of the community. His situation is relatively infrequent, whereas far more serious is the professor who makes his citizenship a matter of words. Rather than a question of disloyalty, it is a question of inactivity, and the community is a poorer place because of his membership, in that he gives to his students the dramatization of an educated man disassociating himself from the responsibilities of normal group life.

It is significant that it was a group of professors from the State University of Iowa who took a public stand on this question:

The ultimate effect of what is achieved, or not achieved, in the classroom is of immeasurable consequence so far as society is concerned, because every student goes forth to be a citizen. The teacher helps to determine whether that student will be a burglar or a missionary, the maladjusted enemy or the friend of his fellow men. *Social vision and perspective are therefore prime requisites if an instructor is to be successful in terms of the objectives of general education. A good teacher, as in the days when teaching began, cannot help being interested in ethics, in social progress, religion, justice, beauty, freedom, physical nature, in all that man was, is, and may be.*[8]

In facing the future of education, the teacher must decide whether education has a responsibility for helping to inaugurate social change, or whether its sole function is the transmission of the accepted values of the group. If his choice is the former—and it would appear to be a reflection on his intellectual competence if it is not —then he must accept his responsibility for "stimulating, and judging, and representing his community." As a leader, he will recognize that he dare not yield passively to the pressures of the citizenry. He must defend the community from the university, but in addition he must defend the university from the community. "The leader counts for just as many people as he fully leads," Dr. Outler has remarked, and the word is true of the faculty man as citizen.

"The terrible responsibility of the teacher" is not an idle phrase. The teacher, to be worthy of his vocation, is more than the lecturer behind the desk transmitting facts—or even facts interpreted. The independent college has been eagerly responsive to these additional qualities which give extra strength to good teaching. And the administrators of our great state institutions will not forever be indifferent. Meanwhile for the Christian teacher, because of the lostness and wistfulness of his students, the responsibility becomes the more terrible.

FOUR STEPS OF GRADATION

The assumption underlying this chapter is that the Christian teacher is more than the Christian who happens to have found his vocation in the classroom or the counseling chamber. The Christian teacher is more than the man of academic competence, according to all the best secular standards, who happens to be a faithful church member.

The Christian teacher is one who fulfills all the demands of secular academic excellence, and who brings to these demands a Christian perspective. There is a Christian insight in the decisions which he makes as an academician. There is a Christian maturity which infuses his teaching and counseling. As a Christian teacher he brings to his task qualities in addition to those which are required of his secular colleague.

There appear to be four definite stages of gradation between the teacher who is a Christian and the fully matured Christian teacher.

For the first group, the adjective is a label with little more meaning than the same label carries when applied to our culture or our nation. By only the most pallid interpretation is our culture Christian, our nation Christian—or is he Christian. In this group stands the confused, theologically vague, unchurched man or woman who uses the label "Christian" apparently as the antonym for unrighteous. In no obvious way is he different from the good, conscientious secularist practicing the absence of God. Some will quickly question his right to be included in this group, and the coloration is indeed pale. It is only because of his own grasping for the label *Christian*, which he counts a "title of fellowship," that he gains this place.

When I was a young administrator, still inexperienced in my search for Christian teachers, I interviewed a highly recommended young man for a post. It was with trepidation that I approached the question of his church affiliation. His reply was somewhat overwhelming, although condescending. "Have no fear whatever regarding that," he replied to my question. "My uncle was moderator of the Presbyterian Church." But apparently the moderator-uncle had been assigned the religious responsibilities of the family, for the young man in question, acceptable secular teacher though he proved to be, saw no reason whatever for exceeding the demands of secular academic excellence. He never was seen at a church service and, although never openly critical of religion, he saw fit to make clear that in his busy, purposeful life there was no place nor need for Christian faith.

The second group comprises the faithful, nominal Sunday Christians, whose religion is confined largely to the hour from eleven to twelve on Sunday morning. They are persons of character, esteemed in the community, and with good reason for they are active in humanitarian projects; but the criteria of excellence which they hold for themselves as teachers are definitely those set by the secular graduate schools. They would question the assumption that there should be any difference in their teaching from that of their secularist confreres on the same staff.

Among these, however, are those—in reality a third group—who have their occasional uncertainties. There is the stirring of conscience within, and the vague wish that somehow they could see their field in religious perspective. But they know not what it is they desire. The members of the third group are those who fit the pattern of Group Two, but who are uneasy about the fit. There is the gnawing feeling that something more is expected of them. They are certain that many of their professional colleagues would disapprove if they were to make the effort. They are aware that their own knowledge of religion is limited. There is a disconcerting ignorance where to start. And so they never start.

* * *

At Wardha

The All-India Village Industries Association is located at Wardha, C. P. This is one of the organizational activities inaugurated by Gandhi and directed at present by the distinguished Hindu leader, Shri G. Ramachandran.

In the gardens of the Association, there stands a rough piece of sculpture. It is the figure of an emaciated Christ, taken from the cross and lying in the laps of the women.

Nearby is a board, on which is written: "Satyagrahi Mandir" (The temple of the adherents of the non-violence movement). Gramsevaks (village-workers) who obtain their training in the various departments housed in this Udyog Bhavan (workers' haven) are expected to be imbued with the spirit of the true Satyagrahi. They should go out to serve the villages, dedicating all they have to such service in the pursuit of their ideal. They should be prepared to lay down even their lives, if need be.

To symbolize this spirit of vicarious suffering and sacrifice that should be the goal of all Satyagrahis, this sculpture is erected, depicting Jesus being taken down from the cross on which He was crucified by the leaders of His day because with His life of purity and unrelenting championship of truth, He proved an unbearable critic of the evil customs and traditions prevalent at the time He laid down His life to fulfill His ideals.

* * *

The fourth group is made up of those teachers who come to their academic duties with Christian insight and quest. They bring to their classroom a beginning, at least, of the effort at integrating Christian faith and their own subject matter. They are struggling to achieve the relationship between their Christian faith and their task as a teacher. While growing into increasing maturity, they are in truth Christian teachers.

BETTER THAN AND DIFFERENT FROM

To press the contrast between the Christian teacher and his secular colleague still further, let it be said that the Christian teacher should be better than, and different from, his secular neighbor. And if one asks quizzically, "Different—how? Better—wherein?" the answer is that the difference will come in part in degree, and in part because of the additional expectations held of the Christian teacher and the additional demands made on him.

"Better and different"—let the application be tested in these five qualities of good teaching:

THE DEPTH OF RESPECT FOR TRUTH

The good teacher comes to his vocation with a deep respect for truth, and an utter honesty in his search. The axiom holds for all teachers, both Christian and secular. If there be any who question if the Christian, by his very commitment of religious faith, is not barred from the completely objective and impartial search for truth to which the scholar gives himself, let the Christian make answer in the words of John Baillie: "God must take all the risks of honest inquiry."[9] He might have added, "not only must but can." If truth so disclosed refutes Christian faith, then Christian faith must be revised to conform to this truth, for truth is of God. The Christian comes to his search with all the ardor of the scientist, and with a conviction that his act of searching is an act of religious commitment.

In conversation with Julius Seelye Bixler, Albert Schweitzer once said, "I think the most important quality in a person concerned with religion is absolute devotion to the truth." But the skeptic will still raise a questioning eyebrow. "Are there not conservative groups, and persons of integrity within those groups, who would not for the moment yield the absolutes of Christian faith to any man-discovered truth?" One will not deny that there are, but one can assert that insofar as there be this limitation in the teacher's devotion to truth, he denies his relationship with the God of Truth.

The Christian teacher should be more eager in his search for and more committed in his devotion to truth than his secular colleague, for the discovery of truth is the progressive laying open of the mind of God.

THE RIGHT OF DIGNITY IN THE HUMAN PERSON

The good teacher will come to his classroom and his counseling chamber with a deep respect for human personality. And again the skeptic may raise the question, In what regard is the Christian teacher superior to the humanist whose respect for human personality is broad and rich and deep? The answer will be that the Christian teacher can bring to his classroom a religious insight, born of the Christian view of man, that should make his respect for human personality stronger and more meaningful than that of the devoted humanist. Both may bring unqualified patience—that sine qua non of the good teacher. Both may be willing to give generously of the hours of the day to the student who comes with honest inquiry. Both may be willing to partition their leisure to allow for the interruptions, both justified and unjustified. Both may be quite willing to offer the friendship which the instructor can give to the limited few of his classroom. But the difference will come in the conceptual understanding of human nature and the Christian's additional respect for man as a creature of God, destined for His high purposes, and accountable to His judgments.

Jacques Barzun comments bluntly, "Friendship between an instructor and a student is impossible."[10] It is not unlikely that Professor Barzun defines friendship in such high terms that the experience so described becomes unlikely across a gulf of immaturity. Or it may be that he feels the incipient unfairness of the situation, where a few of a class can enjoy the relation of friendship with an instructor which the very nature of time and endurance may bar to others. But many a teacher will testify that his friendships with students have been a source of great happiness to him, and some of those same teachers will bear witness to the inspiration that came to them, as students, when an instructor singled them out for this precious gift.

The teacher, in offering friendship, is thereby likely to remove himself from that semi-blindness which sees the student not as a human being but as an academic dilemma. Is it fair to say that a teacher with mellow religious maturity never sees the student of his classroom exclusively as a problem to be solved, or even a distress signal to be responded to? With genuine respect for personality, the teacher looks with level eye, and his greater maturity and greater experience see in the boy or girl before him not simply immaturity and inexperience, but a creation of God capable of growth and service. The humanist can see him only as a fellow human being, needy and lonely in a needy and lonely and purposeless world.

"AND MOSES WIST NOT THAT . . . HIS FACE SHONE"

The good teacher is recognized by the quality of insight which he brings to his teaching, and the sheen of his commitment, which even the dullness of a classroom cannot totally dim. The one most commanding quality of a Christian teacher is this commitment, including as it must a commitment to academic excellence. When it is real, nothing can conceal it.

Nevertheless we must remember that a commitment may be for either good or evil ends. The Communist who holds a teaching appointment likely has a commitment to his task as great as, or greater than, that of the Christian teacher.

For the Christian, the commitment comes in a sense of vocation. In his hands lies an opportunity supremely worth taking, a job to be done, beyond which there is no greater. Dexter Keezer tells how, when applying for the job of teaching, he was asked by a supercilious administrator: "And what, my dear young man, is your call to teaching?" Dr. Keezer, with his refreshing frankness and his response of genuineness to the stuffy administrator, replied, "I am not quite sure, but I think it may be the call of three months' vacation every year."[11] In reality, for Dr. Keezer, and for the thousands of other committed teachers, the three months' vacation is but the opportunity to prepare oneself to do in superior fashion the work at hand.

* * *

The very true beginning of wisdom is the desire for discipline; and the care of discipline is love.—HEBREW WISDOM.

* * *

Gerald Heard once coined the phrase, "Gainfully Employed v. Giftfully Employed." It is a distinction that the good teacher recognizes as realistic, for he with Christian insight will make continuing search for the larger fullness of life which must be his if his gift hands are not to be empty. The teacher with insight knows, as Gerald Heard has said, that much will be given by intuition, and that the instructor will inspire the student to say, "I, too, can paint a masterpiece." One needs that eternal spirit of youth to deal day by day successfully with youth: that is in part the outcome of a commitment of loyalty, to be, as every good teacher yearns to be, perpetually and academically "unwhiskered,"[12] no matter what the quantity of hair may be on one's chin.

THE NEED FOR PHILOSOPHICAL ORIENTATION

The good teacher will likewise make every effort to relate his subject matter philosophically to the total universe. For the Christian teacher, that relation will be against the Christian over-all view of the cosmos as a creation of an eternal Heavenly Father, peopled by individuals to whom God has given the inestimable gift of the freedom of choice between good and evil. The barriers of departmentalism have confined many a teacher from going beyond the prescribed limits of the subject matter assigned to his group, and in consequence many a student has never seen the intimate relationships, historically and chronologically, between the academic islands of economics and sociology, and history and literature. Even within the humanities, the academic era of excessive departmentalism has brought ignorance of the common expressions of the great movements in art and music, as well as literature. We have taught the islands but overlooked the bridges.

Within departmentalism, the tendency toward high specialization has made the teacher loath to relate his subject matter even to the allied subject matter of the larger department. And with his zeal of specialization, so often there comes the endeavor to "force or massage too much factual content into a course." "The mania of wishing to teach more than students can learn should be ruthlessly suppressed," commented the Iowa teachers in *Toward General Education*.[13]

One possible escape from this dilemma of a "spread of knowledge so broad that no single mind can command more than a small specialized portion of it" is that a larger number of our good teachers will "venture to embark on a synthesis of facts and theories albeit with secondhand and incomplete knowledge of some of them—and at the risk of making fools"[14] of themselves.

When the opportunity comes for the teacher to make this kind of contribution toward general education, he will do it gladly and with humility, acknowledging the vastness of the effort. And he will do it, recognizing the opportunity to aid the student to grasp those entangling interrelations of people and events which have their place in one's philosophical map of the world.

WITH RELIGIOUS PERSPECTIVES

The Christian teacher finds himself more specially differentiated from his secular colleague by his endeavor to see his academic discipline religiously, that is, in the context and within the relationships of Christian faith and understanding, and the goal of the Christian community. In all probability this is the main dividing point between the Christian and the non-Christian teacher, the Christian classroom and the secular classroom. And this difference can be a major difference, indeed.

Let it be said again that we are not talking of classroom sermons. There is no place in strong academic teaching for the moralistic asides. Sectarian propaganda is as much out of place in the classroom as any other kind of propaganda. At no time is the suggestion warranted that the teacher scatter inappropriate, unrelated comments on morality and religion.

When this caution, however, has been reiterated, we can return again to the thesis of this volume—that the Christian teacher is one who is able to present the subject matter of his discipline within a religious frame of reference. If the American public honestly desires the education of their young people to bring to them a larger understanding of moral and spiritual values than our education of the past years has succeeded in doing, and if it genuinely wants student America to understand and to continue one of the major traditions of our American nation, namely, the tradition of religious integrity and freedom, teachers must be found who are themselves deeply committed to the Judaic or the Christian faith. That in all probability means that we shall need definitely to make changes in the pattern of training for those who are to be teachers. At the present time our secular patterns of graduate study encourage the teacher to be wholly secular, and in turn the student so taught becomes the teacher so teaching. Somewhere the chain must be broken and a pattern found which will include the high standards of our present academic world; and in addition, an emphasis on values and ideals and religious perspectives which is not now an integral part of any considerable portion of American education.

* * *

THE WELL OF TROUBLED WATER—A PARABLE

[This parable was written after a student reported that while she received a great deal from a course, she still found herself much confused in her religious thinking. A question which all teachers of courses in Bible and religion should answer is: Should not the water be troubled and give life during the same course?]

Again the Kingdom of Heaven is like unto a pool of precious water in a dry land, which a man inherited from his fathers.

And the owner called his servants and said unto them, Behold, here is priceless water which is mine. Now, lest it become polluted and foul, let us make a well thereof that I and my children, my cattle and the stranger within our gates may drink and live.

So he commanded them to bring good stone, to go deep, and to build around it a wall of hewn stone, making of it a well, like unto the well which Jacob gave to his people.

After some time, the steward of that man came unto him and said: The well which thou badest us make, sir, is ready. Come, I pray thee, and behold it.

And when he came with haste to see, the well was, indeed, a goodly well, built as his steward had said. But, lo, the water therein was troubled and cloudy, and he cried out, Alas, the precious pool my fathers gave me is corrupted and useless. Would that I had left it undisturbed, for now I know not where to turn for water.

And he went away sorrowful.

Now it happened after many days that he passed by that way and turned aside again to see the well of his disappointment. And, behold, when he looked, the water was clear as crystal, and when he drank thereof, it was cool and sweet to taste.

And his servant said unto him, Master, when thou badest us make the well, we could obey thy word only by meddling with the water, until it became troubled and cloudy. But when my lord left the well and went his way, the water settled and became as now thou seest it, clear and goodly.

And the owner said unto him, Go quickly and call all my friends and neighbors, that they may come and rejoice with me, for this my well was cloudy and now is clear, it was troubled and now it giveth life.[15]

* * *

The need for such teachers, wise, tolerant, patient, understanding, is our major need in education today. Systems rise and fall on the shoulders of teachers, and for teachers the magic word is quality. With no love for loud-speakers or mass education, Dexter M. Keezer could write: ". . . good sense coming out of a loud-speaker is much better in the long run than a highly individualized application of hokum."[16] We need also to remind ourselves that we have no reason to hold that teacher making his fullest and best effort to anything like a 100 per cent return from his students. No teacher is able to secure that response. Jacques Barzun comments in *Teacher in America:* "It is also wise to bear in mind that any one teacher need only affect 10 per cent of the enrolled student body to be worth his price."[17]

There are two conditions of educational success: the competent teacher and the hungry student. The competent teacher may often cause the complacent student to become aware of his inadequacy and encourage a hungering and thirsting after knowledge. But human nature runs a wide gamut, and success may be long postponed— and sometimes never come. Often the great teacher is the one who touches deeply rather than widely; the future will depend upon the number of people who can inspire men to believe that they can make a creative response to a given difficult situation.

THE HOW OF RELIGIOUS PERSPECTIVES

But how? How does the Christian teacher present his discipline within a religious frame of reference? It must be freely acknowledged that the answer is still in the kindergarten stage. Our fullest answers will be incomplete until we have made prolonged scholarly research into the correlation not alone of religion and education, but of religion and the specific disciplines.

Earnestly desiring during my years of college administration that the teaching in our institution should be done within religious perspectives, I took occasion one year to call upon three members of the faculty and to put to them specifically this question: "You call yourself a Christian teacher. In what way is your teaching different from what it would be if you were not a Christian?"

Perhaps my question took them by surprise. But in each case I was given a prompt answer which later on was partially amplified as further thought was given to the question.

Those answers may serve as partial illustration of the opportunity for the teacher appropriately, and without abuse of scholarship, to present his classroom material within religious perspectives.

FROM THE MATHEMATICIAN

There was on the campus a beloved professor of mathematics who for years had been training undergraduates for successful careers in the field. I was aware that his students were receiving something more than excellent training in mathematics. With it came a philosophical overview of life itself and an awareness of the tremendous implications of mathematics for the kind of world of which we are a part. I knew also that it was his custom to open each class hour with a short simple talk on some item of mathematical interest.

In answer to my question he gave me a manuscript of one of his talks. "Perhaps this will be a partial answer to your question." I share it with the reader.

I have here a book. Note that I can pass my hands completely around it; there seems to be nothing mysterious about it. For your sakes I have chosen a mathematics book. Now it rests on the desk top; but I am going to push it as far away from me as I can—just as some of you would like to do. It is now close to the edge of the desk, dangerously close. Do not be alarmed, however, for by a magic trick I have the situation under perfect control. I shall push the book completely from the desk, and it will remain suspended in mid-air. It— Oh, oh! I forgot to say the magic word. What happened? You tell me, "It fell to the floor." I convinced you the earth has no strings tied to the book; did the earth reach up and take hold of it and pull? "Silly," you say.

I see by the look in your eyes that you can barely withhold your eagerness to enlighten me. You, Ed, are saying that this is the pull of gravity; you, Pat, that it is a force which amounts to thirty-two pounds per second; you, Don, are reciting Newton's Law. Others of you are ready for action; you would measure the distance from the desk top to the floor; you would then use your mathematics to determine the time of fall, the velocity, the work done, and the like.

Restrain yourselves and listen. For this moment those are not my questions. Rather they are: What is the source of that unseen power— that power so great and so enduring that with it, through countless ages, the sun swings the earth and all of the mightier planets in majestic circles about her? How does it operate through distances even up to untold millions of miles? Why does it operate at all? What and how and why? You are not so ready now with answers.

Be not dismayed—you are not alone in this ignorance. Review the studies of the world's great scientists; follow them as they climb, figuratively speaking, upon the shoulders of their predecessors that they may reach higher; then note that each, in turn, lifts for a still higher reach those who come after. Follow them from Newton to Einstein; you will review significant experiments; you will pursue weighty mathematics; you will think ponderous thoughts; but you will have only half of the answer; you will still be asking: What, how, and why?

I should like to have you think of mathematics and science not as great achievements of the minds of men, but as God's act of revealing Himself through His universe to man—revealing Himself to the extent that man can take that revelation for the time being. I like to think of mathematics as one means by which God leads man into His secrets of creation, and that there rests upon those who can use that means the responsibility of constantly delving further into the wonders of His universe, of attempting to think God's thoughts after Him—or, may we suggest, *with* Him.

Go back with me to the fallen book, back to the invisible power that pulled it to the floor. Will you dare to think with me a great thought —a thought that, in the light of the foregoing, is fully appropriate in a classroom of mathematics? What if this mysterious power of gravity is only God's voice saying, "Let there be," and God's hand on the universe still holding secure His creation—in truth, God still creating?

FROM A TEACHER OF LITERATURE

I had heard one of our most competent teachers state in a public address that the teacher in the Christian college must come to the classroom with basic Christian assumptions in his hands—not alone because he teaches in a Christian college, for that suggests hypocrisy, but because he as a Christian teacher has the freedom of the classroom in a Christian college. I approached her and asked for a specific example. Here is her reply:

In the Humanities one has a wealth of first-class material. Much of it is profoundly Christian in its concept. It seems to me that one needs principally to let such material speak for itself.

Don't think I'm suggesting that one would choose only Christian materials. That would be poor teaching. Much of our world literature and music and art is deeply Christian, and much is thoroughly pagan. One makes choice from all schools, but the Christian sources will often speak the louder by contrast with the non-Christian. And to my mind, it is entirely legitimate to point this out to the student.

For example, in our freshman English course we have a section on plays. We read among others *Medea, Agamemnon*; then later we come on to some modern plays such as Maxwell Anderson's *Winterset*. I point out to my class that *Medea* and *Agamemnon* are two of the great revenge plays of all time. Revenge is their major—in fact, it is their only—theme. When you come to *Winterset*, you have a modern revenge play, Mio driven to revenge the death of his father. But *Winterset* is a revenge-love play. There is in it the additional feature of redemption of a man through love. That seems to me to be a significant contrast between non-Christian and Christian literature. In the latter there is the assumption, as there is not in the former, of the possibility of human redemption.

Take Mio's words to Miriamne in the third act:

> Miriamne, if you love me
> teach me a treason to what I am, and have been,
> till I learn to live like a man! I think I'm waking
> from a long trauma of hate and fear and death
> that's hemmed me from my birth—and glimpse a life
> to be lived in hope—but it's young in me yet, I can't
> get free or forgive. But teach me how to live
> and forget to hate.[18]

Or, if you're teaching Ibsen, I don't see how you can avoid pointing out the contrast in such plays as *Peer Gynt* and *Brand*. In Peer you have the personification of self-interest and self-concentration. In Brand you have the man who has sacrificed all for the priestly goal of divine companionship—property, mother, and child.

In the fields of the fine arts, as we treat them in our course in the Humanities, the student cannot escape the conclusion that Christianity has been the mother of much of the greatest in art: take your Sistine Chapel—or literature, Dante, for example—or music, such as the *Messiah*. And the class—at least, I find it so—reaches out to ask what this tremendously creative force is that has produced all of this greatness.

And mentioning the Sistine Chapel, when we come to that, we like to contrast the attitude of the Greeks toward the human body, as shown in their sculpture, and Michelangelo, who believed that the human body was less a source of beauty in itself than it was a bearer of spiritual meanings. Here you get into a contrast of cultural ideas, one non-Christian, the other Christian.

The teacher of the humanities certainly has all the freedom in the world to use the Bible and sacred literature for reading-substance in the courses.

Let me give you one more specific example. Take the theme of compassion. Obviously, the teacher of the humanities doesn't go forth and announce, "Today we teach compassion." But for myself I would question if the teacher of humanities has been completely successful if the year's study hasn't brought to the student a deeper understanding of compassion.

Take the Russian play, *The Lower Depths*, by Gorky. It's an excellent example of dramatic naturalism, and yet with the repeating note of compassion. Or take the famous painting of the *Old Man with a Child* by Ghirlandaio. One of my students asked his father if he liked the picture, and the father made the easy reply that he did not and that he could see no place in art for so ugly a thing as the old man's bulbous nose. The boy's reply was this: "You're looking at the wrong thing. It isn't the nose that's important. It's the look of trust in the child's eyes; he isn't even seeing the nose."

I don't see how you can teach the Humanities, by its very substance, without coming closer to some of the basic faiths of the Christian religion.

FROM THE SOCIAL SCIENTIST

There was on our faculty at the time of my question a young man who was outlining and teaching an experimental core course in the joint fields of economics and sociology. The name of the course still stands as Economic and Social Trends. It is a course in general education on the freshman-sophomore level, offered frankly and without apology against the "value judgments" of the Christian faith.

A labor-management dispute at a tire company in a nearby city had gained national headlines. The management of the company claimed that it could continue to operate at a profit only if the seven hundred workers would take a wage cut of 10 to 35 per cent. This the employees, through their union leaders, said they would not do, believing the statement of management to be unfair and untrue. Students in the class asked the instructor's help in "getting the facts" so that they might judge which side was right, labor or management. The instructor presented the class with these three major problems:

"There is the problem of fact which is the primary concern of the social sciences. What is happening in the labor management controversy?

"There is the problem of value which is the primary concern of ethics. What ought to happen in the labor-management controversy? What ends or values ought to be realized in the solution of the controversy?

"There is the problem of religion. What is the will of my Creator in this situation? Or, for the Christian, what does the God revealed in Christ will should happen in the labor-management controversy?"

The Intercollegian carried at a later date an article by the instructor describing his approach to this specific struggle of management and labor:

> For myself I consider these three areas (social science, ethics, and religion) so interrelated that I believe colleges must provide courses which seek to integrate across departmental lines and develop professors who are constantly striving to show the limitations of the specialities and the implications of other fields to their own.
>
> The student wants the tools of inquiry developed in the social sciences to give him the facts in the controversy. But knowledge of ethics can help him get all the relevant facts. . . . Increasingly, from the insights of ethics and religion about the nature of man, social scientists have learned that workers in factories are not purely economic creatures. They have the moral and religious drives to discover some meaning in the work they do. . . . They are political men who want some share in those decisions of the plant that affect their working lives. . . .
>
> This interdependence of ethics and social science is not a one-way process. For example, ethics will help the student to understand what goal he wishes to realize in the . . . dispute, but the facts revealed through the methods of social inquiry will indicate the possibility and methods of achieving various goals. When in life (or in the organization of our college courses) we attempt to separate ethics and social science, we cut the nerve of social change. . . .
>
> Both as a Christian and as an observer of human behavior, I believe that no profound and intense ethic has existed for long unless it has been rooted in a religious faith. For the insight of religion into the nature of the Supreme Being, the Lawgiver or Creator of the Universe, transforms man's whole attitude toward the values he seeks to realize or the obligations he seeks to fulfill. The desire to seek justice in a social controversy . . . is made much more intense by the realization that not I alone, but God, my Creator, wills justice in the situation. . . .
>
> As a social scientist, I know no pride in keeping ethics and religion out of my classroom. I am obligated to make clear the values which I seek to realize in society in order better to control my own bias and to make clear the meaning of my data. I must press my students to make clear their own premises of investigation and action and to seek beyond science the ultimate meaning and motivation for their life work.[19]

THE ANCHOR OF OBJECTIVITY

To all of this and particularly to illustrations of the variety offered by the mathematician, the teacher of literature, and the social scientist, the educational imperialist will raise his voice on behalf of scholarly objectivity. "Does not the good teacher," he will argue, "withdraw himself from his subject matter and without regard to his own prejudices [he would include convictions] and opinions [he would include value judgments] present quite impersonally that subject matter to the student?" The answer which many teachers must give on the basis of experience is a kindly denial.

The imperialist continues: "Objectivity is the anchor of the teaching profession. Without it the individual instructor may veer far from his course and drift into waters which are wholly irrelevant to the subject matter he is commissioned to teach."

There is truth, but not whole truth, in the critic's words. It was to withstand the flagrant misuse of the classroom as a pulpit for topics, religious and nonreligious, which are quite without relevancy to the subject matter of the department, that the theory of scholarly objectivity became an accepted doctrine of the profession. It came, also, in the endeavor by the scientists to enthrone reason as king. It would be unjust to fail to recognize that this dogma has played a significant and constructive role in education, and at no cost must be totally abandoned.

Curiously and paradoxically, some of the most flagrant abuse of objectivity has come from those who spoke in its name. "A teacher can set forth, with some sympathy and enthusiasm, a materialistic philosophy in many a field of learning—some poet of negation and his lyrical rapture over zero; the decadent art and thought of some perverted genius—all this to be sucked up as gospel or rejected, according to the wit and taste of the student. But almost never is it questioned as regards its academic propriety."[20]

Shall scholarly objectivity be likened to an anchor? There are moments in the academic world when an anchor is a highly necessary piece of equipment. It helps one to stay where one is. But when the ship is under sail the anchor is stowed.

There are two answers to be made to those who would seek a *total* scholarly objectivity: first, it is impossible; and second, it is undesirable. These advocates of objectivity seem unaware that in the very choice of materials for a classroom hour, the instructor must make decision which invariably contains elements of personal judgment. By the inclusion of certain facts and the omission of others, made necessary by the inelasticity of the academic hour, he is transgressing against a total objectivity. By the espousing of a point of view in preference to other points of view, he is guilty; and again time often fails to allow for the presentation of all points of view, even if such were commendable teaching. As long as teaching is in the hands of teachers, total objectivity is impossible.

Since teaching must remain in the hands of teachers, who in turn are breathing, aspiring, differing human beings, the cult of the ultra-impersonal is undesirable. As those of us who have gone through the educational mill look back upon the millers of our day and make choice of those who milled well as against those who milled badly, is it not invariably true that our choice of the best millers includes those men and women who brought to the classroom, first, an unquestioned command of their subject matter; and second, a sharing of some of the wisdom and insights from their own rich experience of living?

The sailor treasures his anchor for the day of storm, but the good sailor does not sail dragging his anchor behind him.

Whenever anyone raises the cry of objectivity as a supposed rebuttal to those who would allow an instructor to present his material with appropriate philosophical setting, I am reminded of a situation which I met in connection with a visit to a small town in Indiana. A community was under a pall of sadness, for one of the most popular of the young boys in town had been drowned. The father of the boy had his small yacht, and the son, a youngster of ten, had his own sailboat. One morning the boy had come to his mother, begging for permission to take the anchor from his father's boat that he might make use of it on his own. The mother had resisted, saying that the father would be angry if anything should happen to the anchor. Then finally she yielded to the boy's persisting, but only on condition that he would promise to make certain that the anchor was returned to the father's boat; the boy in all the seriousness of adolescence made his promise that he would not come back without the anchor.

As he set sail in his small catboat he tied the anchor rope about his wrist. The squall came; the boat was tipped over; the boy, a good swimmer, was unable to swim with the rope entangling him; and in the confusion of the upset he was unable to untie the knot. In a tragic way the boy's promise was kept.

The arguments of persuasion, thoroughly logical and permissible in the church, the labor union, the political platform, are not appropriate to the classroom. The best teaching will be done by teachers trained as scholars, impartial in their approach to truth, and yet,

nevertheless, willing to share with their students on appropriate occasions the reason for the faith that is in them, particularly when the
student asks, "Professor, what do you believe?"

Anchors have their use. And the anchor of objectivity has saved
many a weak teacher from misplaced homiletics in the classroom. But
when its ropes are tied around the teacher's hands, they may become
fetters of sterile impersonality and academic death.

Today we have the newly organized Faculty Christian Fellowship.
What is important is that there shall come a sense of relatedness
among the men and women throughout America who see the necessity, as well as the opportunity, of making teaching a Christian
vocation. It will never be their thought to proselyte for their own
church or their own limited grasp of faith. At no time will there be
any effort among them to command a word agreement to any of the
doctrinal or dogmatic tenets of the Christian faith—and that is not
to suggest on their part indifference to those mighty doctrines. It
will, however, be their honest purpose to serve faithfully the student
of their classroom, and the counselee in the office. It will be their
hope that this ministry of teaching may be fulfilled in such a way
that the student will be helped in his discovery of himself, in his
adjustment to life, to his relation to his fellow man, and in his loyalty
to the God who made him and to whom he is accountable.

Such a fellowship—whether within or outside the Faculty Christian
Fellowship—will be to many teachers a source of strength and inspiration. Such a fellowship, with its high academic standard, will also
be an encouragement to continued intellectual growth. Such a fellowship will aid the teacher to keep clear and clean the purpose of his
profession—to serve not minds alone but men.

Chapter Five. Some Problems of Creative Leadership

Nestled underneath a sheaf of old papers,
Carefully protected from prying eyes and softly treading cats,
I found five moist-eyed mice.
A surging impulse of destruction gushed into every muscle,
And all the thirst of a thousand aeons of the Will to Kill
Paralyzed my new-born dream that life was sacred.
And yet, I paused!
Deliberation, the armored foe of action, caused me to pause!
Who am I that I should crush in one fell swoop
The throbbing pulse of life caught in these tiny forms?
Are they not life?
To let them live would be
To run the risk of pestilence, disease and death.
How to destroy and yet not feel
The curse of power—
And not atone in all the subtle ways?—
    There—a slight increase in carelessness,
    Here—a bit more callous,
    Again—less mindful of another's plight
    Where no persistent duty claims me. . . .
To Power, stark and Omnipotent in its narrow
Sphere of time and circumstance,
What are ethics, morality, tenderness, religion? . . .
To grant man power and hazard the trust
That he would make life safe for aught but that which keeps it
Fat and strong:
This was God's great gamble
When into man He blew the breath of Life![1]

HOWARD THURMAN

SOMEWHERE in every administrative problem there beats a
human heart. Every executive, in his absorption with budgets and
supervisory boards and grandiose building plans, encounters the
danger of losing the feel of people, the care for faces. For there are
faces behind those budget figures—faculty faces and janitors' faces—
and the boards are made up of men and women, and the plans are
without meaning unless human beings are through them given a
fuller chance at educational opportunity. It is blasphemy to see people
only as perambulating problems.

There is a story of a foreign student who had come from his home-
land direct to one of our smaller American colleges. The students
and the faculty were kind; he was delighted with the reception given
him. His dreams for study in America were being fulfilled above his
highest expectation. His first impulse was to offer his thanks. In
European fashion it seemed appropriate that the thanks should be
tendered to the head of the institution. It was with some timidity
that he knocked upon the president's door and was ushered in. In
course of time the president came to him. "Sir," the boy said, "I am
here to thank you for the opportunity of being at your college. Everyone is very kind. I am very happy."

"That's fine, my young friend," the president said. "Now tell me
what you have come for."

"Oh, sir, I have come only to express to you my joy at being one
of your students."

"Tut, tut," the president answered, "surely something more than
that brought you here. You have a problem of some kind, you are in
some difficulty—money, homesickness, a girl? Tell me what your
trouble is."

By this time the student was retreating toward the door; the president followed him. "Don't be afraid, tell me what's on your mind.
What really brought you here?"

The boy had the door partly opened. "Sir, I came only to tell you
how happy I was to be on the campus." And before the door could
be closed the president made his last appeal. "Well, when your
courage comes back and you can find words, don't be afraid; come
back and tell me what your problem is."

Guy E. Snavely is reported to have given this sage advice at the
inauguration of a young and unsuspecting college president: "Your
main responsibilities, my friend, are three: get all the students you
need; get all the faculty you need; get all the money you need. Then
go off on a fishing trip."

There is a sequel to the story. The young man took the wise counsel to heart. When he had found all the students the college needed,
and all the faculty the college needed, and all the money the college
needed, he took his fishing equipment and tottered away on a fishing
trip, his first since the day of his inauguration. But to his astonish-
ment and disappointment the stream that he had frequently fished
as a dean was totally dry. The bed of the stream lay bare in the sun,
and the few pools of water were dark and brackish.

The bank of a dry stream, however, can be a perfect setting for meditation on the persistent problems of creative leadership, although it is to be hoped that the administrator in question had not postponed until then his facing unafraid such questions as: How do you offer vigorous, seasoned leadership rightly compounded of experience and faith and hope, and in accordance with the best democratic procedures? How does the college president or the dean delegate power, and yet at the same time offer leadership to integrate and synthetize the multitude of judgments so that there is a unity in the institution? How does he offer the leadership to provide wise and continuous discussion of the purposes of the university, and still keep the university or the college basically united, following a charted course, and concerned with distant but tremendously important goals?

* * *

From Top to Bottom

John Jacob Niles, the gentle philosopher and charming singer of old folk songs, lives in a lovely home outside of Lexington, Kentucky. In his beautiful living room there is a large table. Running around the end of the table is the hand-carved motto of the mountain, "Goodness and Strength Trickle Down from the Top."

It is a motto which has special application for college administrators.

* * *

Assuming that he, this college president on a fishing excursion, counts himself, and in truth is, a Christian administrator, how does he bring that Christian insight to the problems which are his, of making concern for character and the interior life a fundamental part of the institution? Recognizing that the same answer cannot be applied to all institutions, how does he, with his own particular local situation, fix the place of religion in the organized and unorganized campus life for which he and his staff are responsible? To the list should be added the problems Sir Walter Moberly raises: "What can Christian insight contribute to enable the university to be the university?" Sir Walter comments: "The vital question is not whether the university does or does not include certain directly religious activities. It is concerned with the university's *raison d'être* and with the whole of its life and work."[2]

And when these and a multitude of other questions have been answered, let him then face that persisting question of life that comes in some fashion to all men: How does he, entrusted on the one side with the symbols of power, and plagued on the other with the temptations of its abuse, maintain his own inner personal integrity?

THE WHITE PLUME

The greater his loyalty to his institution's material needs, the more insidious the temptation to compromise. This donor might be induced to make large contributions if he could be persuaded that "free enterprise" is taught with the certitude that attaches itself to arithmetic; yet the administrator knows that if the industrialist fully understands the academic process of total survey and the freedom of the classroom to explore and discuss and to choose—that freedom so precious and so vulnerable—he will be in violent disagreement. Dare the administrator be silent and profit by misunderstanding?

This widow, who has accumulated years, prejudices, and dollars, is thinking of a possible bequest to the college, but she must be continually reassured that the doctrines of her church are properly exalted—and the morals of the student body kept properly high. There are many items of campus life that can be honestly reported to her and there is no wrong—or is there—in hoping that other items may not reach her sensitive ears.

This trustee believes only in limited academic freedom for the faculty; this alumnus is organizing his fellow alumni surreptitiously to offer financial aid to the star quarterback; this church leader is concerned with the liberal-in-quotation-marks teaching of the department of religion; this almunae auxiliary is troubled by the nature of the plays the college theater is producing.

It is not that the administrator expects his official life to partake of a millpond calm. He anticipates vigorous discussions of all policies. He rightly knows that each day will bring its opposition, both reasonable and unreasonable. But so much of the opposition stems from a misunderstanding of the fundamental purpose of education and a mistrust of the essential freedom of discussion. Shall he move to correct that misunderstanding, knowing that he will inevitably offend and possibly alienate financial support? Or shall he do his utmost quietly to protect the academic freedoms, and by silence or gentle misinterpretation allow the critic to think what he may? Or shall he —base and horrible thought!—move to curtail those essential freedoms, justifying his treason by the pecuniary needs of the institution? Wherein lies honesty—and necessity? Where does excessive tact become hypocrisy? And silence untruthfulness? And this choice of front to match another's prejudices a denial of one's inherent honesty?

Yielding to intimidation is such an easily accessible form of cowardice, especially to the administrator, charged with large problems, concerned with men and women both mature and immature, and attempting to devise a program that shall be worthy of public respect and, fervently to be hoped, public support. Yielding can be so temptingly easy, when intimidation masquerades as "wise caution" or "what the public wants."

By the nature of his responsibility, the college administrator faces a daily trial of integrity greater than most men, until he may well wonder, at times, who he is and what he believes and where he stands in the great controversial questions of his day. It is not that he has lied, but he has gently deceived; and where words might provoke, he has chosen to be silent. Wisely? At least a gift was given, and the college profited.

* * *

A CERTAIN COLLEGE PRESIDENT

A certain college president of an institution of national prestige finds himself and his board faced with the necessity of choice. A wealthy man has made promise to the university of a bequest, the amount of which will contain at least six ciphers. But if that bequest is written, it will carry with it a condition that the institution shall go on record as agreeing never in its future to admit students of non-Caucasian races. The purpose of the condition is to refuse admission for all time to qualified Negro students who might seek entrance to the university.

The president is aware that the institution needs the money, needs it desperately. The president is also aware that there are in his clientele individuals and groups of individuals who are already pressing for a more liberal policy in terms of admission. He himself is heartily in favor of a more liberal policy, but the conservatism which comes with power has possessed his soul and he has persuaded himself that the time is not ripe for any radical step.

It is the responsibility of the trustees to make answer to the prospective donor, but the trustees will look to the pres-

ident for leadership, and he must make recommendation. In his own mind the debate simmers down to the pecuniary necessities of the institution v. a principle of eternal right. Meanwhile he fancies the argument that a strengthened institution would be justification for the ignoring of principle. Is not his first duty to protect the college and to make it strong? Or—and this comes as a delayed second thought—is it his responsibility, first, to uphold principle? He toys with the casuistry that he must favor the welfare of the majority, even though a minority suffer.

Some day, while he is still sitting so uncomfortably and hazardously on a moral fence, the words of the past will come to him, "What shall it profit a man, [or an institution] if he shall gain the whole world and lose his own soul?"

* * *

Perhaps every administrator ought to take an hour a day wherein he is himself—wholly, not partially, himself—wherein he can examine his motives without fear or fraud; wherein he accepts with forthright openness the pressures to which he intends to yield. Perhaps every Christian administrator ought to spend two hours a day in this review, the second hour being devoted to a rededication to the truth and the courage and the integrity which he finds embodied in the Master he is committed to serve. The second hour will not make the gift less needed; conceivably, however, it may make the price too high.

The hour of devotion will contain its prayer for the wisdom to use Christian insight in the specific administrative problems which are his. There is embarrassing familiarity with the educational situation which Sir Walter Moberly describes.

Today many university teachers and administrators are Christians. But few, if any, of us are *Christian teachers* or *Christian administrators*. That is, we have failed so far to bring any distinctive Christian insight to the problems of university training and governance with which, in our professional capacity, we are constantly concerned. On such issues as those of freedom and planning, scholarship and citizenship, a carefully balanced and predetermined curriculum or a free choice of subjects by the individual student, an austere scholastic standard or the throwing open of university training to the widest possible number, the respective claims of teaching and research, and a hundred others— on all these the Christian professor or lecturer may well have a personal view. But he probably holds it on grounds which would be exactly the same if he did not happen to be a Christian, and his fellow-Christians on the staff are as likely as anyone else to be at variance with him. On the main questions of university policy, Christian teachers or students, as such, are not aligned in any particular way.[3]

SOME SNARES OF THE ADMINISTRATOR

The administrator, like Christian in *Pilgrim's Progress*, walks the avenue of temptation. The Last Judgment is, for him, as for all human beings, somewhere in a distant future; but the judgment day for him, more than for most human beings, is continually upon him— with the alumni, the faculty, the students, the trustees, and the public, each sitting as judge in his own court and, unhappily, not always concerned for the same major issues. More dispiriting, however, than any of these trials, is that wherein he sits as judge himself of his own action.

Dr. Edgar Goodspeed has written of the Last Judgment, "The point of the story is not this colossal phantasmagoria of the universal judgment of all mankind but the moral demand that will inevitably be the basis of such a judgment."[4] It is that same moral demand which is upon the administrator as he sits in review of his own puny efforts.

The administrator is aware, sometimes dimly, of the temptation to misuse the power which lies in his hands. Power is a means to an end. When the acquisition of power brings its own satisfaction, a worthy means has been distorted to an unworthy end, and evil results. He knows himself to be faced constantly with the temptation to relish the feel of power. And there is, too, the snare of misusing it without sufficient regard for the rights of the individual.

He will be wise if he keeps his guard against the temptation to blow up his personal whims and preoccupations until they look like mighty plans of impressive dimensions. A prejudice can be made to look like an aspiration if one gazes at it continuously, and in isolation. Perhaps that is why the administrator of creative leadership needs so constantly to subject himself to the unremitting and uncompromising criticism of men whose judgment he dares to trust. More than most men, he needs to fear compliant agreement, for it may simply confirm him in his incomplete and prejudiced thinking.

* * *

"... OF COURSE I WILL GO"

Eleanor Roosevelt tells of a visit of King George to a CCC camp in our country. The commandant of the camp, recog-

nizing that the King was weary, offered to excuse him from
the visit to the barracks. The King was quick in his response:
"If they expect me to go, of course I will go."[5]

* * *

One of the snares the administrator must, at all costs, avoid is the snare of excessive busyness. Of all men, he must find time for dreaming. Perhaps the major justification for the college president who spends a goodly portion of his time rushing from alumni club to alumni club to acquaint his academic family with the tremendous successes and also the tremendous needs of the beloved college is that the journeying allows him hours on trains and planes. Since no new preparation is needed for the next address, there is the possibility that he will see in perspective the individual problems of the home campus, and work to devise over-all strategy, so difficult an achievement when one finds oneself in the midst of the struggle. "He was a man of many but little endeavors": a sad but fitting epitaph for the administrators who pour forth their energy and give themselves untiringly but unwisely, never coming into sight of the important.

Perhaps a still more dangerous snare for the creative administrator is the danger of mistaking prominence and noise and shiny brass for significance. Half-truths are not transformed into truths by shouting. Neither is that institution greatest which receives the largest amount of publicity. In his *Russian Journal*, John Steinbeck wrote of the unimportance of exteriors: ". . . the shining metal of our [American] planes does not really make them fly any better. I once knew a man whose wife claimed that the car ran better whenever it had been washed."[6]

That college is deserving of maximum appreciation which has fashioned its building program in recent decades, according to standards of simple adequacy rather than the luxury and the extravagance of many academic buildings. Wherein lies significance on a campus: that it shall have dormitories and fraternity houses of size and elegance exceeding anything which the student is likely to know in the years ahead? That there shall be a swimming pool, largest of all college swimming pools, and, as one institution boasts, "flooded with colored lights, to reflect the moods of the bathers"? Or that a faculty of keen minds and warm hearts shall be continuously reinspired to make the process of learning an exciting adventure for students who themselves are hungry for the understanding and maturity that can come from that adventure? Therein lies significance—but therein also lies Utopia.

THE BURDEN OF LEADERSHIP

With the administrator is the responsibility of leadership, although the effective channeling of that leadership must come through other hands. That leadership must be creative without being dictatorial, constructive with full use of democratic procedures, forceful without the misuse of power.

The college president will, by the very nature of his office, set the tone of the institution, and his wishes, although he may never be fully aware of this, may sometimes carry a persuasion that goes with other men's commands.

In a terrifying degree, the strength of the religious program of the institution will depend upon his approval or disapproval. In tangible ways, he will control: through the budget, his agreement to suggested new policies or the change of old, his choice of staff leaders. In less tangible ways he will strongly influence: through the support which he gives to the appointed religious leadership on the campus, his expression of interest and faith in the voluntary religious activities, and his own loyalty to his church. More than any other man, his attendance, or his absence, will be noted and commented on. Who shall say how many Harvard students and faculty men took note and were persuaded by the presence Sunday by Sunday of President and Mrs. Lowell in their side pew of old Appleton Chapel, and by President Lowell's regular reading of the Scripture?

There is no more testing trial of courage for the Christian administrator in the state institution than his willingness to press for the strongest and most inclusive religious life for his institution within the legal limits of state and federal law and the deepest desires of his cosmopolitan constituency. Twenty-five per cent of our tax-supported institutions accept credit for courses in religion. Courses about religion are not interpreted as breaches in the legal wall of separation between the Church and the State, although not infrequently the alibi of legality is used by the administrator who chooses not to give support to such a department. Denominational foundations and the Student Christian Movement, in its various manifestations, have long been welcomed on state campuses where the administration was friendly to their prospering.

Homer P. Rainey, who has had administrative experience in both church-related colleges and tax-supported institutions, has made this comment: "It [the university] can let its students know that it believes that religion is relevant to human life and society and that it is its obligation to study and teach about it, just as it does all of the other areas of human experience. . . . If religion matters to the university, it will sooner or later matter to the students who come here."[7]

* * *

HAPPY RECOLLECTION

One of the happy recollections of two decades of college administration is the memory of a day when I was visited by a student committee. Student committees had come before, frequently to ask for something, sometimes to complain about something. It is the habit of student committees to feel that the college administration is the easy and frequently the sole source of blame. "The administrator should do something about it." It is a basic assumption of student thought.

The committee members settled themselves and began, "We have come to ask a favor." My natural response was "Again." But their next words caused me to regret the implied cynicism of my thinking. "We students are concerned that there are not more DP students on our campus. We want to do something about it. We have had a committee working for some weeks and we have checked with our fraternities. They are willing to underwrite the board and lodging of two DP men if we can secure them through the regular channels. We would expect, of course, that they would fulfill all of the entrance requirements of the college.

"When from their records that may be available two DP men are given assurance of entrance, we will then guarantee their travel expenses in this country and their board and lodging for a year. Would the college be willing to care for their tuition on scholarship?"

The answer was, of course, a hearty and enthusiastic "Yes." Then came the deserved word of appreciation that the request had come not at the beginning of the committee's endeavor but at the end after it had gone as far as it could with its own solution of the problem.

* * *

THE CHOICE OF VITAL CENTER

There are three major questions the administrator must wrestle with, not once but a thousand times. The administrator will not escape the inevitability of these questions by virtue of being Christian, Jew, Buddhist, secularist, pagan; although the nature of his religious convictions and the place he accords religion in life will greatly influence his answer. Only if he is weak and incompetent will he fail to recognize the confronting issue, and then the escape will come through cowardly evasion.

The first major issue is the administrator's choice of the vital center around which the academic life shall be organized. Not all of his campus colleagues will recognize the need for such a focal point; for some, the emergency of the moment, the demands of each passing hour, will bring their own questions and their own answers. But the more thoughtful, those more fully oriented in the mystery of learning, will ask for points of reference, aside from emergency and fleeting hours. Together they stand with the administrator in recognized need of some vital center in the educational process to which they can refer the pressing questions of curriculum, personnel, inevitable change.

This is not to suggest that with every new administration an institution is oriented to a new focal point which the president produces on the occasion of his inauguration. The institution, unless it be one of our wandering-star colleges, unplaced in the educational heavens, has long since come to accept its philosophical center. It is to be presumed that in choosing a new leader, the trustees will search for a man who has himself given the question serious thought, and has found his philosophy of education to accord with that of the institution which he is being invited to serve.

In history, there was the time when theology was the cornerstone of the curricular arch. An academic life could be judged in terms of that absolute. That day is passed, and in even the church-related institutions the place of centrality is seldom accorded "the science of God."

More recently, with the popularization of humanism has come the theory of the individual as the focal point for education—his needs, desires, opportunities, potentialities. No one will deny that any educational program must be constantly studied in terms of those to whom it ministers, and yet there is a gnawing dissatisfaction with any effort to make of human need an absolute.

* * *

IDENTIFICATION

Sholem Asch in his small volume, One Destiny, *has told a story of creative leadership. When the Nazis published a decree in Denmark during the Second World War requiring all Jews to appear with a yellow patch on their sleeves, the Danish King put on the yellow arm band marked with the Star of David and identified himself with a persecuted minority.*[8]

* * *

Science also presented its claim to be the focal point of the educational process, and many a scientist was in vigorous agreement; but the day has passed when science is seen as the sum total of human knowledge, or the scientific method as a single instrument for the ascertaining of truth. With all our modern respect for science, we now recognize that it is neither omnipotent nor omniscient. The growing edge of knowledge and insight belongs at the present time to the social sciences, with sociology aiming to be both a wisdom and a science. Sociology and anthropology, literature and a new criticism, philosophy and religion: these are becoming the competitors among the disciplines for the vital center of the academic life.[9] And yet, these are but segments of a whole, partial, and themselves incomplete.

Any choice of educational center must assimilate science and the other disciplines. It must accommodate theology as far as theology is an academic discipline. It will serve as ready reference to all human need, but the human need itself will not have that centrality.

Where shall the administrator find that inevitable center, that focal point? For the Christian administrator and the Christian college, the educational center should be—must be—God. Education deserves to be God-centered. As men differ in their understanding of God, so the educational center will move within the orbit of those differences. But to all men, whatever name their vocabulary holds for God, that name represents the highest-known good, the clearest-known truth, the deepest-known love. With all our variety of experiences and ignorances, God is still the symbol of man's farthest reach in knowing and in being—whatever else He may be to the believer. In the other educational centers, which have been tried and discarded, man was giving centrality to that which, at the moment, seemed to him of ultimate significance: God, if you will, in terms of theology, God in terms of science, God in terms of human need. Man always will continue to interpret the verbal representation of his highest reach, but as that interpretation may shift, he must always come back to the ultimate pivotal center which is God.

This will not mean any effort to re-enthrone theology as the queen of the sciences, for God's truth is seen in chemistry, physics, history, art, as well as in theology. It will mean, however, a continuing referral of the disciplines to the educational center so that God—according to whatever interpretation shall be given: for the Christian, the Father of our Lord and Saviour, Jesus Christ; for the Moslem, Allah; for the secularist, man's highest good; for the pagan, an exalted self—God will be revealed in the disciplines of the curriculum.

In *The Crisis in the University*, Sir Walter Moberly quotes a paragraph from Edward Pusey, which Henry Van Dusen suggests "spells out the implication of this basic principle" that Newman once declared: God has "relations of His own towards the subject-matter of each particular science which the book of knowledge unfolds."[10]

All things must speak of God, refer to God, or they are atheistic. History, without God, is a chaos without design or end or aim. Political Economy, without God, would be a selfish teaching about the acquisition of wealth, making the larger portion of mankind animate machines for its production; Physics, without God, would be but a dull enquiry into certain meaningless phenomena; Ethics, without God, would be a varying rule without principle, or substance, or centre, or ruling hand; Metaphysics, without God, would make man his own temporary god, to be resolved, after his brief hour here, into the nothingness out of which he proceeded. All sciences . . . will tend to exclude the thought of God if they are not cultivated with reference to Him. History will become an account of man's passions and brute strength, instead of the ordering of God's providence for His creatures' good; Physics will materialize man, and Metaphysics God.[11]

THE DEMOCRATIC USES OF AUTHORITY

The second major question with which the administrator must wrestle is the question how to use authority democratically. Religious authoritarianism at best is not much better than a nonreligious authoritarianism. When authority exalts itself, even in the name of wisdom, there is immediate loss to the democratic tradition.

At the present time, and in America at least, Christian education is under the necessity of being democratic education, and the Christian administrator of attempting to be the democratic administrator. Wise, tolerant, successful administration does not belie Charles W. Eliot's dictum that an institution is the lengthened shadow of a great leader. But the shadow ought not to be lonely in the absence of other companioning shadows. The leader will not be great if he fails to recognize how many hands carry the burden.

Democratic education has not infrequently been confused with free education. "American education is founded on the notion," Robert Maynard Hutchins commented ironically in his plea for a national system of competitive scholarships, "that democracy is achieved if low fees or none are charged and there is no discrimination among students in terms of their intellectual ability. We assume that we have democratic education if we do not charge for it and if we make clear that every citizen is entitled, as a matter of right, to as much free education as every other citizen." Then he adds, "This assumption is false in all its parts."[12]

But the question of tuition fees remains to be answered with the other items of the student's financial need: the problem of student subsistence, and also, in many cases, the need of the family for the student's earning power for his four years of college. Therefore, "free education" becomes the education you have the money to buy, even when no fees are charged.

The program of student work, which in the past was so often exalted with high praise for the student who worked his way through college, is not the answer. If we have genuine intellectual competition in our colleges, and if we hold concern for the men of highest ability, we shall not allow them to endanger their future health or to minimize the benefits of their education by carrying heavy work loads which have no relation to the educational program and are in addition to the study schedule. Indeed we need to change our praise for this kind of thrift and industry to condemnation for the college that allows it.

The problem of student fees and the right within a democracy of the best minds to have access to the best education are, however, only distant relatives of democratic education. It is possible to have free or so-called democratic education which operates in an oligarchical way. The American campus has been strong in its preachment on democracy and frequently short on its practice. Preachment will become more convincing as we are able to turn practices into recognized democratic procedures.

Although Paul Hoffman is drawing upon his experience in the area of government and politics, his analysis is applicable to education: ". . . the conference table is the most unappreciated weapon in the arsenal of democracy. I am always moved when I think of how quietly and effectively ECA personnel overseas has exemplified this kind of political maturity which is simply respect for the dignity, the opinions and the concerns of others. I feel that this pattern of conduct gave the real meaning to our exports of food and machinery. And I am sure that our national experience in easing frictions among ourselves, the whole give-and-take flexibility which is the essence of our domestic politics, has provided us with an invaluable apprenticeship for our newer tasks in world politics."[13]

The college president and dean need to be a neat combination of prophet and priest. How the fallible human being can be both at the same time is the continuing perplexity of the offices. Democratic administration demands the choosing of competent assistants and a wise assignment of responsibility. Further, democratic administration demands the frequent use of action by committee, in spite of Jacques Barzun's quip that "addiction to meetings is the teacher's professional disease." The administrator must hold himself sensitive to the feelings of his faculty so that he stands ready to increase the authority granted to committees when there are rumblings of discontent; and he must be equally sensitive to the periodic desires of the faculty for a diminishing of committee authority when the pendulum swings in the opposite direction. In either case he must have an open ear and a skin sensitive to faculty weather conditions.

There is refreshing insight in the comment of Melvin E. Haggerty, written near the close of his years at the University of Minnesota: "The faculty meeting is not merely an agency for collective action. It is also a mirror that reflects the competence, the sincerity, the morale of the body of individuals responsible for the educational welfare of the institution."[14] The faculty meeting is an appropriate place to raise the wetted finger so that one may catch the drift of the wind.

The Christian administrator frequently is fully aware of the desirability of democratic procedures, but the pressures for quick accomplishment, and the demands upon his time which make his mere twenty-four hours a day a ridiculous insufficiency, tempt him to the short cut of dictatorial decision. The conference round table is time-consuming, it has its particular pattern of inefficiency; nevertheless, there is in it a safety and a security which carry their own vindication.

Many colleges have come to recognize the value of student representation on major faculty committees, and in practically every situation the experience has been that the responsibility is sobering and maturing. One of the most enriching experiences I had in college administration was that of working with a faculty-student council set up with strict regard for the equality of the groups represented. The faculty and administration were represented by the executive committee of the institution, the students by their six highest elective officers, plus a student-at-large. The meetings were held monthly and on call. It was the custom for the president of the student body and the president of the college to alternate in chairing the meetings. The agenda was open to all of the members and there was no item of campus life which could not find its place by request in the discussion.

Constitutionally, the council was without authority. Actually, its authority was great in that its decisions represented the thinking of responsible leaders, decisions that resulted in referral action either to the student senate or to the faculty, or, as in many cases, to both groups.

The council acted, many times, as a safety valve. The students were free to ask for information regarding dark issues that were the occasion for rumor, and the information was freely given. Also, its usefulness was attested by their willingness to bring irritating situations, often unrecognized by the administration, which, if left unattended, might have resulted in festering misunderstanding. In turn, the faculty representatives were able to gain a better understanding of student thought as they quizzed the student officers on campus opinion. But perhaps the largest value that came from it was the recognition on the part of students that the faculty and administration were willing to listen to considered student opinion; and in turn, the faculty had the experience of finding elected student leaders wise, alert, responsible.

THE ACADEMIC USES OF FREEDOM

The third problem of the administrator is the essential relationship between the academic institution and the community and national life of which it is a part. The day is past when any college is an island of isolation. The mores of the surrounding community are in a large measure the mores of the college campus. In styles of dress the college may be a world unto its own with such influence moving outward from the campus rather than inward. The noncollegiate male has condescended to put aside his headgear, although, fortunately, not many of the noncollegiate females have been persuaded to don bluejeans—or have they?

In other matters of fashion, however, fashion of thinking, fashion of prejudice, fashion of action, the campus apes the community. There is upon the administrator and the faculty an obligation to see that the academic communities shall be kept both continuous with and also discontinuous from the society of which they are a part. Albert Outler, who made that observation in a summer lecture, went on to amplify that the university of today is too continuous with and reflects far too much the market-place culture, the utilitarian concept of learning, and the racial segregation of the outside world. It was he who suggested that the academic community possesses the "defective mores of our generation, documented and irrationalized."

If the academic community is to cultivate its responsibility to be discontinuous from the mores of the outside society, it must give continuous thought to its concept of God-centered truth and its assurance that it is seeking for whole truth. It must also give adequate protection to those who are engaged in the search.

Whole truth is never popular with a society, for whole truth ignores the prejudices and the blindnesses which are at all times well loved, even though the particular prejudice or the particular kind of blindness may change. Too often Christianity and Christian education themselves have been contemptuous of whole truth.

Partly from fear and partly from a misunderstanding of the purposes of education, there are bound to be occasions when the American public is pressured into expressing its opposition to the freedom which education must enjoy if education is to be itself. That is why the relations between the administrator and the community of which the campus is a part are of fundamental importance. He must win community respect. If possible, he must win a measure of affection. Then when it becomes necessary for him, in his own integrity, to take a stand against the majority judgment, there is a possibility of his carrying the community's approval, even though not its agreement.

The administrator dare not be too far ahead of the crowd; neither dare he be behind it: but always in front, near enough to have constant communication, yet far enough ahead to exercise a creative leadership.

In a peculiar way, the administrator is the protector of educational freedom. To his hands is committed a portion of that freedom of education which is prerequisite to all freedom.

In his relations with the nonacademic public, he and the university which he represents have no larger obligation than to maintain and to protect and to use wisely this freedom of education. If, under his leadership, the trustees of the institution can be brought to see the necessity of this freedom and his faculty and students aided to use it wisely and creatively, then the administrator will have achieved what is indeed no small success—the making of the campus a center of demonstration in democratic freedom. And if by chance his institution bears the label "Christian," he and his college may be particularly aware that the Christian college is a possibility only within a free state. Smother the free state, and the Christian college quickly disappears; and in not too long a time, there will be no education worthy of the name.

* * *

Let It Be Reported to Their Credit

Boards of regents are sometimes known to change their mind. There is a kind of glory in the willingness of a high authoritative body to reverse its judgment when a mistake has evidently been made.

During the First World War, the regents of the University of Minnesota saw fit to expel Professor William Schaper from the faculty of the University. The charge was that of being pro-German. Rumors multiplied and whirled themselves into apparent fact. Popular feeling was aroused. It was with a sense of loyalty to America, and in the spirit of righteous patriotism, that the regents took this action.

Then with the passing of the years doubts arose whether the situation deserved the drastic treatment which had been heaped on an inoffensive professor. A few consciences were aroused; whereas loud public opinion had demanded the action, now a small trickle of opinion was suggesting reconsideration.

It was in 1938 that the regents reversed themselves. By that time Professor Schaper was reaching the age of retire-

ment at the University of Oklahoma, where he had gone, following a series of trying years of nonacademic endeavors. The regents of the University of Minnesota appointed Professor Schaper professor emeritus and voted him "a sum of money equivalent to the salary lost for the academic year of 1917-18."

It was a public recognition of an error of judgment. Mr. Gray, the official historian of the University, comments, "There was great rejoicing among liberals everywhere that a university with prestige enough to indulge, if it wished, in the luxury of nursing its mistakes had preferred to make acknowledgment of error and to repudiate the false principle involved."[15]

* * *

It is against the background of this freedom of education that academic administration on all levels must give attention to the continuing problem of faculty appointments. The candidates under consideration must be academically competent; in addition, it is important that they be men and women able and willing to use the freedom of education creatively. This does not call for men who will speak conventional truths in conventional words, and never offend public pleasure by departing from the conventional center of life. To instructors of this mind, freedom is the talent which the owner buried; and then, surprised, found himself deprived of his possession which he had valued in disuse rather than in use.

The administrator will seek out men for his staff whose vigorous originality of thought and whose strong, humanitarian sympathy will lead them into words and ways which may stir controversy, which even may offend. The conservative public is most often displeased when men speak on behalf of the "dangerous new." The administrator will, of course, by-pass the teacher candidate who delights to offend, who speaks wildly, not from conviction, but from a self-centeredness which takes sadistic pleasure in hurting. But the administrator dare not avoid vigorous originality and strong humanitarian sympathy, for these are the substance of which good teaching is made. He will need to defend them from the public critic. He will need often to explain and interpret as well as defend, and he will do so gladly, knowing that in these qualities lies the "something more" which can turn competent teaching into brilliant teaching.

* * *

Struggle with Discipline

The headmaster of one of the eastern preparatory schools is responsible for this story from his own experience.

Some boy had turned in a false fire alarm, and at considerable expense of time and effort the local fire department had responded. It saw no humor in the prank. Obviously something must be done lest the young man be made a school hero and an example to follow.

It was not too difficult to discover that the culprit was a senior leader in student government. But what should be the punishment? A reprimand was too easy; expulsion too hard.

The headmaster summoned the student council, including the young man. He explained the seriousness of the situation and the need for steps to prevent any possible recurrence. A talk to the students, he suggested, from one of their leaders might be good. He would choose the one to do it.

An assembly was called. When the headmaster had said his word of caution, he called upon the boy who had turned in the alarm to address the students. The boy gave a forceful talk on the evil of mistaken humor and returned to his seat. Then the headmaster called the culprit back to the platform. Producing a fireman's hat from the desk, he announced that his punishment would be to wear it for the rest of the day. Much crestfallen, the boy donned the helmet and took his place among his fellows, who did their best to suppress their snickers. The young leader was bowed in chagrin.

At the dining hall there was no obvious confusion, but a long, low whistle followed wherever the boy went and he was obviously embarrassed.

That afternoon the headmaster's secretary announced two callers. The first was the boy with the helmet. "I can't wear it any longer, sir. Do anything to me short of expelling me. But don't make me wear that awful thing. Please, sir. The boys will never stop kidding me."

The headmaster was convinced he had acted wisely.

The second was a youngster from one of the lower forms. "Sir, if—if I got my courage up and—and turned in a false alarm, would you let me wear the helmet . . . for a whole day?"

The struggle with discipline was not over!

* * *

In addition to the relationships with the nonacademic public, the administrator must give leadership to the training of his students to recognize and to use wisely the freedom of education. In the nature of human frailty, it is well for the students to know that there are limits of taste, beyond which they cannot go with impunity. Call it censorship, if you will, but it is censorship only in the extreme and final measure when the good name of the institution is at stake. For the student, whether he be leader or follower, the area of his freedom is large, and so it must be. The student editor, the student orator, the student leader, must have freedom even while they are being cautioned against misuse, yet in their misuse of that freedom the penalty must never be the curtailment of freedom for those who follow.

The public will bring its pressures on education's freedom; the pressures will come, largely, to "be careful, to pull in, to withdraw; to teach not more but less." Educators will hear themselves told as Dr. Hutchins has forewarned them, "that society requires of the institutions of higher education, not that they should increase the light, extend the area of knowledge, trust the people with the truth, but that they should deny the people the truth in certain directions, narrow the acreage of knowledge in certain fields, put out the light in certain quarters, darken it, confine it. The areas to be darkened, moreover, will be areas selected not with the needs of education in mind, and not with the needs of the people in mind, and not with the needs of the future in mind, but with a mind solely to the fears and the hatreds of the moment."[16]

But education's freedom has a quality of demand about it which by very possession requires that it be used. It is freedom to rehearse the achievements and the glories of our American democracy, and also freedom to speak of our failures and weaknesses. It is freedom to examine without let or hindrance the accomplishments of American capitalism, but also to examine the capitalistic system against the mandate of Christian brotherhood.

I have a constitutional distaste for required courses, but I sometimes wish that every American college student could be subject to a thorough course in political doctrine, with a careful study of socialism, fascism, communism, and democracy. I should like to be certain that students would hear the best that can be said for each of these systems. I should also like to be certain that they would hear the worst. Let them see the systems in action and learn how far theory comports with practice. One of the reasons why communism on paper is attractive to the idealistic young American is the depth of his ignorance as to how far removed theory is from daily living in the Soviet republics. He would come through such a course a more intelligent democrat—or lest I be misunderstood, a more intelligent believer in democracy. I hope he would come through it a more intelligent critic of the contemporary systems of political economy.

James B. Conant, former president of Harvard, committed himself to a similar suggestion when he wrote in *Education in a Divided World*: "The first requirement for maintaining a healthy attitude in our universities in these days, therefore, is to get the discussion of modern Marxism out into the open."[17]

I tremble at the assumption of so many of the critics of academic freedom that democracy cannot defend itself intellectually; that to learn anything of any opposing political doctrine is for the young American to be converted to that doctrine. Are our young people as childish and as unintelligent as that?

Leslie Weatherhead reminds us, "There was a time when the aristocracy would not employ a Methodist cook, for she would seek to convert the house maid and the kitchen maid, and the parlor maid, and the between-maid, and spend and be spent in the activity."[18]

Our colleges and universities are the bastions of freedom, freedom to inquire, freedom to investigate, freedom of conscience, freedom to speak—all of these thoroughly respectable democratic freedoms. We do not want communism promoted in our schools, but to fear the objective, dispassionate analysis of communism in our schools is to fear education itself.

If the survey of free thought and free speech on our American campuses, as offered by Kalman Seigel in his series in *The New York Times*,[19] was correct, then have our administrators failed in their obligation to the American public, to maintain and protect and use their educational freedoms? Mr. Seigel began his series with this ominous sentence, "A subtle, creeping paralysis of freedom of thought and speech is attacking college campuses in many parts of the country, limiting both students and faculty in the area traditionally reserved for the free exploration of knowledge and truth." And in the years since Mr. Seigel's study the paralysis has advanced, rather than retreated.

THE ADMINISTRATOR'S MAIN JOB

These are the three basic educational problems for the administrator: a pivotal center for education, the democratic uses of authority, and the responsibilities toward the community in safeguarding the freedom of education. One might conclude that when he has struggled hard and long with these, he is entitled to a second fishing expedition. And so he is. But when the administrator goes on a vacation, it is usually with the supply of books that he finds scant time to read and a mind full of campus perplexities.

For still uncared for is his main job as an administrator. Dr. Outler has framed the *raison d'être* for academic administration in these words: "I propose the implausible and impractical theory that the only real foundation and purpose of academic administration at any level, from trustees through chancellors and presidents on down through deans and department heads, the only function of this whole machinery in the university or college is to provide the optimum situation for learning and teaching and personal growth. This is all they are for. This is why you have administration."[20]

Dr. Outler is challenging the American administrator to establish the conditions under which a worthy, inspired faculty can gather and teach according to its highest purpose and deepest insights, so that a worthy, inspired student body can gather and learn, and in the learning process find its stumbling way into the intellectual and moral and spiritual maturity which is beckoning.

It was Sir Richard Livingstone who reminded us that "like religion, education quickly degenerates into a routine; then its meaning and its effects are lost."[21] Somehow a campus ought to be maintained as a center of the old revolutionary impulse which education once possessed, a corner of the mundane world where the dynamite of education's primitive passion is stored. But how do the administrators with the best of purposes and faculty leaders determined to do their utmost keep a campus a place of intellectual exploration and independence of mind? How does one generate that electric curiosity about what is going on in the world and the why and the wherefore of it? How can one provide the kind of stirring intellectual experience which has a thousand times more carry-over value for the students willing and able to take it with them into later life than the sports with which "carry-over value" is popularly associated.

"Optimum situation for learning and teaching," Dr. Outler said.

Long tenure among faculty members is an academic blessing if those enjoying long tenure have maintained their intellectual zest and have not lost their appetite for the excitement of teaching. Too often, however, the men on long tenure are those who never have a chance to go elsewhere. Rooted they are, in the institution to which they went for their first teaching, and their financial restrictions, ever real, prohibit them from adventuring far from home —prohibited them even in the earlier days when the spirit was willing. Every institution has a certain number of "average" teachers—it is unfair to call them incompetent, for often they teach with a dreary, lustless minimum competence. They will stay on to retirement, protected by the American Association of University Professors; and then live on to a ripe old age, for worry is not in their make-up and they avoid the strenuous effort or the excitement that kills. Every administrator facing the situation consoles himself, even as the faculty does over the administrator it dislikes: while there's death, there's hope.

The outline of the average professor as brushed in with broad strokes is an unfair picture. It leaves unmentioned the stalwart and the valiant who carry more than their share of the load and by their unspectacular labor bring prestige to the institution. It leaves unrecognized, moreover, the peculiar brand of hideous terror that lies in wait for the prospective teacher, regardless of the level of his teaching. Compensations there are for him, the joy in seeing human personality grow, the satisfaction in watching the learning process in operation, the gratitude of the mature man who returns, at least in the proportion of one out of the ten (which was the record of Jesus with his ten lepers) to speak his word of thanks. All these—and the interior assurance that the teacher is having a hand not alone in the fashioning of minds but in the making of men.

When President Harold W. Stokes bade farewell to the faculty of the University of Louisiana, he commented that "education is a tyrannical profession, making its demands upon teachers and students alike, jealous of the way in which we spend our time, insisting that each paper, each lecture, each experiment be better than its predecessors, requiring that, in Browning's phrase, we look at 'the petty done, the vast undone.' And for all of this we are rewarded for our devotion with wisdom, knowledge and understanding, inner resources of power and pleasure—accompanied by salaries much too small."[22]

The terrors lying in wait for the prospective teacher are painfully real, and the administrator must be aware of them so that he can form his counterattack. There is, for example, the contagion of immaturity, pernicious for those who teach elementary courses. There is stimulation in the fresh, eager minds that sit in the front rows; nevertheless, the contagion of immaturity is more than a phrase and it needs carefully prescribed remedies to keep the ailment from spreading. Something is likely to happen to the teacher who spends his working hours dealing with minds which, while not inferior, at least are less developed than his own. It is so simple to adopt the I'm-telling-you attitude and voice of the average teacher. Even the shaking forefinger becomes a gesture of the profession. The teacher must consciously protect a portion of his leisure for contact with colleagues who will keep him scholarly and friends who will keep him humble.

Then, too, there is the isolation of specialization. As the teacher comes to know his more and more about his less and less, there are fewer men with whom he can talk about the one subject of which he is master. This has particular application to the small college where many of the departments have but one or two members. There is a professional loneliness which comes, a sense of being cut off from those who speak the same dialect.

One should not overlook the bugaboo—and it may not always be imaginary—of the unsympathetic department chairman who cramps the young teacher's style by his sarcasm and indifference, and impedes the young teacher's professional advancement by his refusal to retire. The waves of time wear away something of the majestic cliffs of enthusiasm and the earth crumbles and the contour of the land is changed.

* * *

REPRESSION BY ANTICIPATED RESULT

I must tell you of one actual incident by way of illustration. One of my friends, a professor of Spanish at the University of Wisconsin, had a pet project about which he made an annual campaign. This is a verbatim report he made to me of his last visit to the Dean of the Arts College in whom wisdom was compounded with granite: "I am shown into the Dean's office. I look at the Dean. I see on his face the answer is 'no.' I say 'Good day, Dean' and I walk out." In this case the wisdom of the dean was clear, but every wise ad-

ministrator knows the danger of destroying creative impulses. This system of repression to the creative impulses of the people in a university can be just as deadly in its effect as active opposition. When the two are combined, the possibilities of progress virtually disappear.[23]

* * *

There is the present danger of silt-mindedness for the average faculty man and woman, by virtue of the fact that he has allowed himself to become average. The adjective is not meant unkindly; there is the well-intentioned teacher whose mind and spirit are like the shore crevices which gradually are filled with the silt which the waves carry with their eagerness and then deposit when they retreat in reluctance.

The silt-minded do their assigned duties with a faithfulness of the hopeless. They are not negligent, but they do not do the extra which would take them out of the company of the average. Jesus's X-ray insight into life was working fully the day he talked about the extra mile, the other cheek, and the coat as well as the cloak; the implications for the teaching profession are enormous.

The silt-minded refuse to change the textbook; haven't they used the old one for twenty years, and doesn't that prove . . . ? They forgot that it proves nothing except that they, the silt-minded, have used it for twenty years.

To the silt-minded teacher, students are an unavoidable bore, something to be accepted smilingly; if the adverb cannot be mastered, then something to be accepted, an exigency of life which cannot be easily changed. They spend little time in voluntary conference with students; and as for home entertainment—why should they want to? And, further, why should the students want to come?

The administrator will quickly see both the pathos and the tragedy. The words, however, ring in his ears: "the optimum situation for learning and teaching."

He maps his attack.

There is no endeavor too great to make certain that the new faculty appointments are the strongest and most promising possible. To that end he will work with his deans and his department heads. The responsibility is ultimately his. Success in all cases is not in the theory of chance. But success in the larger proportion of cases can be expected, with vigilance and persistency, patience and foresight.

There is the necessity of aiding his deans and department chairmen to see that the inexperienced instructor is given every help in his teaching. He will need orientation to the new situation, and kindly criticism as he finds his way. Plans for in-service training will be beneficial. And praise must be given when praise is deserved.

The administrator will welcome the aid of the A.A.U.P. in reasonable protection of the established teacher against the irresponsibility of trustees or the whims and vagaries of fellow administrators. This organization's achievement in securing strong standards of tenure is a contribution to the profession. But tenure protects both the strong and the weak. Under the standards of tenure the assumption is that the administrator may not ask for a resignation, except for reasons of professional incompetence or character deficiency, after the instructor has been with the institution seven years. The standards are reasonable, but in protection for the institution the administrator must make certain that contracts are renewed up to and beyond the seven-year period for only those men and women who give promise of continuing professional growth and the quality of teaching of which the institution can be proud. This calls for a ruthless weeding out of the instructor whose teaching grade is C or even C-plus, the man who has indicated no further interest in advanced study or professional advancement, the woman who is too easily satisfied with the mere fact of appointment, the teacher whose teaching is unenthusiastically satisfactory. The procedure will bring criticism. The new appointments may be no better than the men and women they succeed. But the administrator knows that he is keeping his situation fluid, and by making change when change can be made, he is holding the departmental doors open to the exceptional teacher of zest and fire when he appears.

There is, moreover, a major responsibility which the administrator holds for those who are "on tenure." He must take every opportunity to keep them strong. What were the words: "the only function . . . to provide the optimum situation of learning and teaching."

Sabbatical leaves with pay and the expectation of study or travel of the sort that refreshes the soul and rekindles the commitment to teach—perhaps those who are reluctant to take the opportunity should be required; the strong will reach for it, the weak will hesitate. Professional conventions and meetings of learned societies bring the kind of fresh stimulation and like-minded fellowship that every man needs, and especially the teacher. Surely the college budget can be stretched once again to allow for travel, and maybe extra, for the man fortunate enough to be on the program. For the exceptional man who finds time for his writing in addition to caring for his teaching assignment, there might be the encouragement of some secretarial aid; the investment will pay dividends. The administrator can provide the opportunity to represent the college at educational meetings and neighboring inaugurations, with expenses paid; the occasional visitor to the campus who comes for the enlightenment not of the students but of the faculty, chosen by a faculty committee; study groups within the faculty, interdepartmental gatherings, reading centers, faculty rooms—in some cases the administrator can help and in others they move of their own momentum. And especially commendation should be given when commendation is deserved.

Sometimes the wind on the bay may change, and in a short time the silt which has been deposited is removed, swept out to sea. It is a curious phenomenon when it occurs; it reminds one of turning back the pages of time and starting over again.

The conscientious, secular-minded administrator will give himself relentlessly to providing that optimum situation for learning and teaching and personal growth. The conscientious, Christian administrator will do exactly the same thing, perhaps in the same way, but against a differing background of thought and for somewhat differing reasons. Both are after results, results from the teaching and from the learning. Both in their hearts know that the results will be the fruits of a later harvest. But if they can be assured that the harvest will come, they will rest content.

The reports of alumni at their twenty-fifth reunions are so devastatingly discouraging! What will the graduates of today have to report at their quarter-century reunion? What does the Christian administrator want them to be able to report? How shall he measure the harvest?

Memorable is the parable-miracle of the fig tree which Jesus cursed because of its barren condition. Leslie Weatherhead suggests that the Master was condemning a fruitless religion, which was symbolized by the barren tree.[24] Perhaps there is in the story an applicableness for the administrator in the waste of fruitless, unprofitable education which has nothing to feed the hungry. Fruitlessness is an intimation of death.

It is a recurring problem of creative leadership to know the kind of fruit to be expected from the tree.

Likewise, if one fights for victory, presumably he knows the kind of victory he is fighting for. Christopher Fry in *A Sleep of Prisoners* causes David, walking in his dream, to say to Joab:

> Are you sure it is victory, Joab?
> Are we ever sure it's the victory?
> So many times you've come back, Joab,
> With something else. I want to be sure at last.
> I want to know what you mean by victory.[25]

Interchapter.* The Measure of a Christian College

Our great difficulty is to explain to undergraduates the inadequacy of good pagans. Good pagans are entirely adequate as long as life goes smoothly. It is in the contemplation of death, it is in facing the frustration of human hopes and the negation of human values, that the good pagan falls down because he has no other resort save a stiff lip, stoicism. He has no other resource because the good pagan, like all pagans, is an idolater. He has made his God in his own image. He has made human values absolute. . . .

The good pagans on our faculties are what they are for reasons often creditable to themselves and discreditable to professed Christians. If we are to tackle the problem of secularism in our higher education, we must do so with full recognition of the intricacy of the problem. In plotting our strategy we must recognize grace where we find it, even though it be uncovenanted. Above all, we must be human even in our most basic convictions, because there is always a temptation for the ardent believer, even the devout Christian, quite unconsciously to absolutize his own beliefs and make them into an idol which obscures the mystery of God.[1]

LYNN WHITE, JR.

A CHRISTIAN college, according to our earlier agreement, is a college with earnest intent to be Christian and with habits of acting constructively and creatively upon that intent. But intent cannot be measured like endowment or enumerated like buildings. How shall one judge intent? What are the earmarks of a Christian institution?

Too long the answer has been given in terms of the church membership of faculty and students, a department of religion with the possibility of a required course, chapel services, Religious Emphasis Weeks, etc. It is an easy answer to give, for noses can be counted and requirements are specific.

* This section is entitled Interchapter for the reason that the busy reader may, if he wishes, skip to the final chapter without loss of continuity. Chapters Three, Four, and Five are intended to outline the responsibilities of the Christian student, the Christian teacher, the Christian administrator. Chapter Six will be an endeavor to point out specifically the next steps that Christian education should take. In a measure, this Interchapter is a summary and an elaboration with concrete detail of what has gone before.

The measure of a Christian college will never be found, however, in any of these specific items, whatever their relative merits. That measure must deal with imponderables and the very stuff of the spirit which makes a person Christian or non-Christian.

But first a word about the conventional answer. It is assumed that a Christian administrator will seek for dedicated men and women for his faculty. Within the freedom of making appointments for a church-related institution, he will ask regarding the candidate's church membership. It is well that he should. But if he is wise, he will probe far deeper than the name on the church roll, which may mean much or little. He is looking for men and women to whom the Church is a source of Christian fellowship, not simply a dim recollection from boyhood. He wants men and women who will gladly give of themselves and their time and their income to some branch of the great ecumenical Church. A name on a church roll may or may not be evidence of this kind of devotion.

* * *

THE ANSWER IS YES

I like the words of the college president who was speaking at the New York State Baptist convention in Buffalo on the subject of Christian education. He was aware that there was an element in the audience not too friendly to the point of view he was presenting.

His address was followed by a question period, and one of the first questions asked was by an elderly man: "This is a direct question and I want a direct answer. Do you have on the faculty of the college you come from any teachers who are not members of evangelical churches? Answer me, Yes or No."

His answer had the directness the critic had requested. "The answer is Yes, sir; and I say that with pride. We have on our faculty a Jew who is thoroughly well prepared in his field; he is an excellent teacher. And in character and kindliness and in mercy for the unfortunate, he is, I believe, one of the most Christlike men I know."

* * *

Much the same argument will hold for the incomplete measure of student church membership. It may have great significance; it may have relatively little significance. In either case it is not an adequate measure of the religious vitality of a campus.

The years of college can, it is well known, be the time when the relationship with the Church can take on fresh meaning, as the young person thinks through from a secondhand to a firsthand understanding of his faith. There is a responsibility somewhere to see that the opportunity is not overlooked. The pastors of the churches which fringe the great campuses may well undertake this task for those of their own group. Student pastors and the leaders of the church foundations will do their parts.

There is, however, the group of students who for various reasons have never been brought into the life of the Church. If the Christian college carries its organized program of religion with effectiveness, that student should be confronted with the possibility of meaningful faith. But the presentation of the college, of necessity, will remain scholarly, intellectual, and to a large degree impersonal. It is not the business of the college to save souls; it is, however, the business of the college to present religion as an integral part of life and thought; and it is the business of the Christian college to show forth to the students the substance of Christian faith and action, supported by as thoroughly Christian an atmosphere as the campus will support. The Christian college has every right to work for Christian literacy; it cannot itself be evangelistic.

But what the college as an official organization cannot do, the individuals of the organization may. There is no reason why the faculty man or the administrative staff member, the YMCA secretary or the student pastor, or the student leaders themselves may not, in warm friendship and at appropriate times, bring to the student a cordial invitation to Christian commitment and to church membership. It is the student's right to make his answer as he may choose. Having voluntarily chosen a Christian college for his own, he has no reason to resent the approach if it is made without pressure or embarrassing conditions.

The college freshman is not an isolated exception who made this answer to the faculty friend inviting him to take membership with one of the local churches: "I'd like to. I was hoping someone would ask me. Do you know, sir, you're the first man who ever thought I amounted to enough to ask me to join a church."

* * *

The Open Door

The founder of the American University of Beirut, according to Dr. Gordon Poteat, proclaimed his platform as follows: "This college is for all conditions of men without regard to color, nationality, race, or religion. A man white, black, or yellow; Christian, Jew, Mohammedan, or heathen may enter here and enjoy all the advantages of this institution for three, four, or eight years, and go out believing in one God, in many Gods, or none. But it will be impossible for anyone to continue with us long without knowing what we believe to be the truth and our reasons for that belief."[2]

* * *

As for a department of religion, so frequently offered as the earmark of Christian education, a college or university ought to have such a department, but having it will not in itself determine the Christian character of the institution. A department of religion is important, but it is of no more importance than any other major department. It stands for one of the great academic disciplines, and if that discipline is taught shoddily or if the departmental courses are the softies used by athletes to keep their eligibility, then the institution may be less essentially Christian by virtue of having such a department.

A department of religion demands the highest level of scholarly competence. It must be taught by men whose preparation is the equal of the best members of the faculty. It asks no favors; it seeks no exceptions from departmental regulations. It is content to stand on its own feet.

I have never understood the argument that a department of religion was unwise for the reason that it relieved the teachers of the other disciplines of their individual responsibility for religion in the institution. There is subject-matter content to be taught which will never be offered unless it is protected by departmental organization. The same is true of any great discipline. Moreover, the work of a strong department of religion should augment and reinforce the efforts of other departments to present their materials with religious perspectives; surely there is no strength to the argument that the department of religion per se will rob teachers in other subject-matter fields of their initiative in this matter. Is it true that the presence

of an English department relieves the teachers of history and economics and the natural sciences of all responsibility for detecting
and waylaying the young criminals who are guilty of felonious assault
upon the King's language?

One of the additional measures most commonly proposed is that
of chapel, usually required, for unfortunately, with few exceptions
—praise be for them—voluntary chapel as an actuality is nothing to
be drawn into the limelight for critical inspection. Over required
chapel the battle has raged, and on many campuses the battle has
been won in the name of freedom. But while freedom won, it is
still debatable if other qualities of the spirit did not suffer loss.

There is nothing to be said on behalf of the collegiate chapel
services—voluntary or required—which are reduced to the lowest
common denominator of physical bodies present in pews and words
spoken on an empty air. There are too many such services which
specialize in boredom. There are still campuses, however, where the
chapel service—again, voluntary or required—is a throbbing heart
of the campus, and faculty and students, together with the occasional
visitor, unite in making it a service of worship and penetrating
thought and renewed devotion.

These several items are the orthodox earmarks of the Christian
college, each with a dimension of authenticity, and yet no one of them
alone nor all together are enough to constitute a reliable measuring
rod. In his characterization of the Christian college Howard Lowry
has gone behind them all to the spirit of the institution and its
faithfulness to fundamental purposes:

The Christian college will be, therefore, a community existing around
a group of learners, both teachers and students, who confess Jesus Christ
as their Saviour and Lord. They are engaged in a serious search for the
knowledge of God and His universe and His demands upon human
life. Though they control their environment for this specific purpose,
they are not exclusive or self-contained. They invite to their inquiry
those who may not hold their premises or yet share their practical commitment. They will give others time to test, accept, or reject what they
believe, and put no halter or blinder upon minds alien to their own.
They will not hurry strangers to their faith to throw about the great
words that they themselves only imperfectly comprehend—the deep-
ening convictions of their own hearts and minds. They will not try to
cheat intellectually either the stranger or themselves or set traps such
as the eighteenth-century poet James Beattie set for his little son when
he planted cress in the garden so that it would come up to spell the

child's name and thus persuade him by the argument from design. But those who do not share the community faith must not, in turn, resent it if the Christian community of the college has some decent care and friendly desire to share with them what it believes is an authentic view of human life.[3]

When one has defined the Christian college, however, one immediately faces the reasonable and practical question, How do you measure the vitality of the Christian spirit on a campus? How do you judge the strength of intention?

If I were attempting to evaluate the religious vigor and the maturity of a college campus, I should seek my measure in the following six pieces of possible evidence. Taking them together, I believe I should have a reasonably accurate score for the institution under survey.

THE MEASURE OF STUDENT CONVERSATION

In the first place, I should want to be exposed to the student conversation of the campus. I should demand more than just a single bull session or a single chicken chatter. I should want to be a quiet mouse in a succession of corners for long days while students talked to each other and to faculty friends and to campus visitors, about themselves and their school and those items of living which seem to them worthy of a place in their conversation. I should like to listen to that conversation in the fraternity and the sorority houses, in both the lounges and the bedrooms of the dormitories, in the common gathering place of students where they go for their Coke or their beer, in cars on the highway and cars parked during dance intermissions, and also in the long country strolls which wise students still take, even when there may be automobiles available to save their footwear.

When I had listened for extended hours, I should try to forget the grammatical inaccuracies I probably heard; I should not trouble myself too much by words which, because of belonging to an ancient generation, I may not have understood; I should try to put out of mind the differences of voices and accents; and then I should try hard to assay the measure of intention toward truth and integrity that I found.

I should be inhuman if I expected all the conversation to be solemn or even serious. Life has its place for banter and trivialities, for weather inanities and the oft-repeated group judgments of the day. The bulk of campus conversation, like the bulk of all conversation, will of course probe the contemporaneous rather than the eternal and deal with the personal, especially the dual-personal of campus romance. But beneath it all would be intimations, nuances, tones and tempers, and unspoken assumptions which would give background to the speakers and illumination to their words. I might even use the following questions as a kind of scoreboard to help me in my evaluation:

Does the conversation I have heard inspire or degrade the listener's ears?

Is there an attitude of respect for others as persons in spite of differences of opinion that may come up in their exchange of words?

Are there moments when the basic issues of living are confronted honestly and in the spirit of quest? Is the conversation self-centered, or are there reasonable periods when concern is felt for others?

Recognizing the need of life at all ages for the moments of lightheartedness, were those moments clean and buoyant and genuinely lighthearted, or did they bog down in filth? Were those moments in reasonable proportion to the moments of seriousness?

* * *

Campus Leaven

It was the president of a woman's college who was speaking: "We have a new leaven on the campus this year. Many of our women spent their summer vacation profitably. It's interesting the difference it has made in our campus conversation.

"Helen worked as a summer clerk in a Woolworth Store. Barbara taught swimming at a girls' camp. Phyllis prepared bottles for the blood bank in Eli Lilly & Company in Indianapolis. Lois did office work at a metal-products company; Virginia was hostess in a metropolitan restaurant; Betty was one of the drivers of the company cars at an ordnance plant; Martha clerked at Marshall Field's; Jean was nurse's aid in University Hospital; Peggy had complete charge of the nursery in a children's convalescent home. Henrietta did office work for the Jewish Federation of her city; Doris worked in an Arkansas War Relocation Center; Norma was with an American Friends Work Camp group working with the Negroes in Indianapolis; Mildred was counselor in a Girl

Scout Camp; Ann was a gas-station attendant.
"And how they love to tell about their experiences as work-ing women."

* * *

Is studying a well-respected campus activity?

Are the students expecting both themselves and others to carry their academic program with the success which their ability entitles them to expect? Is fulfillment of academic assignments accepted as a part of personal integrity?

Is the campus attitude one of respect or contempt or ridicule-which-conceals-envy toward scholastic honor societies?

Is sex spoken of as a body function solely, or are the spiritual implications of sex accepted?

When religion is discussed, is there a sincere seeking for God, or are the reaches superficial and halfhearted?

Is there a breadth of interest in the conversation which handles issues of national and international importance?

Is there a recognition of homemaking as a creative undertaking in which persons grow in comradeship until parted by death?

Is there a constructive appreciation of the essential task of the Christian church?

Is there an essential compassion among the students, a fellowship of tolerance?

THE MEASURE OF STUDENT CAMPUS LIFE

As a second measure for the judgment of Christian vitality on a campus, I should want to learn what I could from being in the midst of the students' campus life. I should want to see all there was to see. I should ask to "listen in" on their planning committees; I should hope to hear their evaluation of their efforts; I should attempt to gain some understanding of the purposes and the accomplishments of their over-all program. I should endeavor to determine whether the spirit of the student leadership was essentially democratic, willing to listen to the opposing voice and giving ear to the wishes of a minority. I should also try to learn whether there was a sharing of student leadership among a relatively large number of the campus men and women, or whether the inclination was to crowd leadership on a gifted or ambitious few.

Obviously I should never judge on the basis of the number of events or the variety of items on the college calendar: that terrifying symbol of a college's busyness. Indeed, so-called "activities" would be but one item in the review of student campus life.

Here are some of the questions I should endeavor to answer realistically and honestly:

Is the campus government vigorous? Does it have reasonable responsibilities granted to it in writing by the faculty and administration?

Is it essentially a campus community government with both faculty and students represented, or is it a faculty government in opposition to a student government?

Is there an inclination on the part of groups to work together for a common good? Is there a sense of the importance of the total institution in opposition to the importance of the smaller groups?

Are the campus politics clean? Are they cared for with reasonable publicity? Is there an effort to bring into this campus political concern an ever-increasing number of the students? Are the best students elected to office?

* * *

A Fraternity Can Be Like a Family

"Mother, what is a fraternity?" the younger son of a family had asked, and the mother had answered, "A fraternity can be like a big family. Its members are concerned for one another, they want to see each other do his best, partly because of the fraternity and partly because of their interest in each other. Most of the boys live together in a big house. Some of them may live outside and come in for their meals. They are proud of their fraternity the way we are proud of our family, and they work for each other the way we do, too."

The mother might have answered, "This, my son, is true if the fraternity is worthy of its high ideals of brotherhood."

Fraternity life at its best can be like a family, but fraternity life at its worst can be strife and conflict, undemocratic procedures and narrow class distinction, clichés which breed bitterness, ideals that tear down, and temptations which are not withstood.

"Fraternities are like people, son; some are good and some are weak. They are like people, also, in that some are sometimes good and sometimes weak, but at their best they can be like a family."

* * *

Is the social life of the campus inclusive? Is there reasonable provision for the social development of the student who may stand in sorest need? Is democracy on the campus a word or a spirit of living?

If there are fraternities, are they aware of the men or the women who stand outside their walls? Is there an outreach of genuine friendship to the group which is not included? Is there an American Commons Club or some organization where the non-Greek-letter student may find group living?

Is there an honor system, and if there is, does it work? Is it supported by the large majority of students?

If there is no college honor system, do the majority of the students maintain and live up to their own individual code of honor?

Is cheating accepted as normal or abnormal? Is the weight of the fraternities and sororities thrown behind classroom honesty or behind getting by by whatever means one can?

Is the campus recreation truly recreative and wholesome, or is it time-consuming and destructive? Are the faculty and student leaders who may be charged with the responsibility for general recreation aware of the high purpose which recreation at its best can serve? Are these leaders organization-conscious, or individual-conscious?

Are the religious activities an integral part of the program of the campus, accepted normally by a majority of the students, or are they something aside left for the queer, strange people?

In the religious program, are there adequate channels of expression for the religious conservative and also the religious liberal? Is there any effort to find a common meeting ground of faith and understanding between these two groups?

In the campus program of religious activities, is there legitimate emphasis on both the interior life and the need for community action?

In those activities which are not labeled religious—athletic, musical, dramatic, social, etc.—is there evidence of a concern for the individual's development, a reaching for high standards of taste and conduct?

Are the student leaders open to reasonable suggestions from the campus adults, or are they determined to remake all of the mistakes of the past?

Is the position of athletics major or minor in the college thinking?

Is there large and keen interest in sports apart from the inter-collegiate competitions? Is there any active and well-liked program of intramural sports?

* * *

UNDEFEATED AND UNTIED

In 1947, when the football team of Denison University took its place as the only Ohio team and one of thirteen teams in the U.S.A. which could claim the distinction of being undefeated and untied, the college celebrated the occasion with a special service, held in Swasey Chapel.

Professor Walter J. Livingston, whose influence for clean football has been felt far beyond the bounds of Ohio, had this to say to the team and its friends:

"One of the reasons for their great success has been clean living. Our boys trained week in and week out. Training and clean living made it possible for the great comeback in the second half of the Muskingum game; held off Ohio Wesleyan during the second half of play; held an inspired Wittenberg team on the seven-yard line when there were two minutes to play. These many weeks of hard training and clean living could not but enrich our men in spirit and mind and body. That is why it is truly fitting for all of us to show our appreciation of our men and the coaches here today in our college chapel."

* * *

Is there an awareness of the difference between those sports which belong to college years and those like tennis, golf, bowling, and track which have their carry-over value in the later years?

Is the habit of betting on the outcome of athletic games prevalent?

What is the common campus attitude toward the use of liquor? When drunkenness occurs, is the response of the student leaders: He (she) ought to learn his limit? So what? Too bad anyone saw him, because it might get to the dean?

Do any of the student leaders count it their responsibility to speak to a freshman or sophomore who is drinking to excess? Would they speak to him if it were known that he (she) was just beginning to drink?

What is the campus standard on premarital relations? What proportion of the students would count such relations as permissible if the couple was intending to marry? What proportion of the campus would accept the accountability of the individual to his God for the use of his body as well as the use of his time, money, energy, etc.?

In general do the juniors and seniors feel any responsibility toward the freshmen and the sophomores: in academic matters, in social needs, in moral standards, in religious searching?

Is it popular to go to church on Sunday morning? What proportion of the college men and the women go? Do they usually go to the local church of their own denomination? If not, what determines their choice?

What proportion of the student body would be critically hostile to the Church?

What proportion of the student body who are church members would feel a responsibility to invite another student, church member or not, to go with him?

THE MEASURE OF FUNDAMENTAL FACULTY ASSUMPTIONS

In personal conversation, by means of numerous classroom visitations and also by the endeavor to see the teaching faculty through the eyes of the students, I should try to ascertain the measure of Christian vitality, as far as the faculty was concerned, by the fundamental faculty assumptions of the classroom.

I should hope by my study of faculty assumptions to learn something of the instructor's respect for truth and any possible endeavor he might be making to integrate honestly and in scholarly fashion his own Christian faith with his own discipline. Here are some of the test questions that I should make use of in my study:

Does the total impact of the classroom taken over a period of months bring respect for the basic truths of Christianity?

Is there evidence on the part of the instructor of honest searching for truth?

Is there concern among the faculty and the administration that the student body shall be drawn from a cross section of American life, with representation from foreign countries?

Is the faculty, in full cooperation with the administration, determined to keep the control of athletics in the hands of the college and not some alien group outside of administrative control?

In administering scholarships are the members of athletic teams treated with equal generosity as other needy students, but without the preferential discrimination and the character-undermining pampering which have brought disrepute to college sports?

Are faculty members aware that there is cheating in their classrooms? And if they are, will they take such steps as lie in their power to decrease it? Will they work wholeheartedly with student leaders in any endeavor to make the campus honest?

Is there a basic integrity in the classroom?

Is there reasonable consistency between the aims of the institution as publicly announced and the ideals of the faculty as expressed directly and indirectly through the classroom sessions?

Does one gather the impression that the faculty as a whole counts genuine scholarship and Christian faith as compatible?

Are faculty members willing to mention God and Christian ideals when the lecture or discussion makes such mention reasonable and even necessary?

At the proper time and in appropriate fashion, is the instructor willing to state his own religious faith and conviction?

Is the instructor reasonably available for conference before and after class and by appointment? In such appointments, is the student given an assurance of the faculty member's interest in him?

In the counseling conference, is the faculty member inclined to use the techniques of religion as well as the proved techniques of psychology?

Is the faculty home opened to students on occasion? At such times is it done from sense of duty or from a genuine desire to share the family living with young friends?

Is the instructor willing to take a reasonable amount of his leisure time for students and student activities (as he may be invited) and other manifestations of student life?

What proportion of the faculty would hold to the conventional tradition of campus life that faculty is faculty and students are students, and, like the East and the West, it is not their destiny to intermingle?

What support, by attendance and leadership and contribution, does the faculty give the local churches of the community?

If the faculty criticizes the Church, is its criticism constructive?

How many make honest effort to use summer leisure and the possible sabbatical and the normal holidays for study and research and experiences of professional growth?

How many appear to be able to live above the severe and psychologically exhausting handicap of the low salary scale which is nationally common, especially in our smaller church-related colleges? How many are unintentional victims of this cankerous anxiety?

How many of the faculty appear to get the experience of zestful living from their teaching activities? How many are unashamedly bored?

What proportion of the group appears to possess "a sense of call" to the profession of teaching? What proportion by attitude and word confesses that the choice was an error of youthful misjudgment, to be regretted but noncorrectable at this late date?

THE MEASURE OF ADMINISTRATIVE POLICIES

Nor should I neglect the administration and the trustees. By conference with the president and his deans, and if possible with some of the trustee leaders, I should try to study with special care the administrative policies of the college. Then by roaming in dusty corners and by discreet questions and discreet or indiscreet listening, I should try to determine whether the statements of the administration, both public and private, can be relied upon.

On any college campus in America the administrative policies, determined by leaders and followed through by those responsible, reveal much about the Christian intent and the Christian practices of the campus community—or their absences.

Again I would prepare for myself a list of questions that might aid me in my search.

Is there fundamental harmony between administrative policies as practiced and the statements for publication which appear in the published literature of the college?

Have the trustees assigned to the faculty full or reasonably full responsibility for the educational policies of the institution?

Is discipline administered creatively? Within democratic procedures? And with the fundamental concern for the future usefulness of the person being disciplined?

In the efforts at fund raising, is the institution honestly presented as faculty and students know it to be? In more direct words, is the college president embarrassed if at one of his campaign dinners he finds himself in the presence of a group of students and faculty who know the campus life intimately?

In the total program of administration is there an essential core of religious conviction, adequate to the education situation?

If there is a department of religion, does the administration support the highest level of competence?

Does it support other departments which make thoughtful attempt to bring religious perspectives into the classroom?

In the relations between the institution and the churches of the larger community, is the administration cordial, sympathetic, understanding?

Is reasonable care taken for the security of staff members of long service?

Within the resources of the institution, are salaries adequate, that is, receiving a reasonable proportionate place in the total college budget?

In the endeavor to increase those resources, is a fair proportion of the increase allotted to faculty needs?

In the eyes of the administration and the trustees, are the human needs of staff personnel put ahead of material needs for buildings?

Is there special administrative concern for the staff members during periods of high cost of living—that is, concern that moves into action?

Are the need and the welfare of the student a major consideration in all administrative policies?

Are there occasions in the college life, voluntary or otherwise, when the leaders and the students enter together with reverence into an experience of worship?

* * *

NOTICE TO THE PUBLIC

KOTOKU-IN MONASTERY
KAMAKURA, JAPAN

Stranger, whosoever thou art and whatsoever be thy creed, when thou enterest this sanctuary remember thou treadest upon ground hallowed by the worship of ages.

This is the Temple of Buddha and the gate of the Eternal, and should therefore be entered with reverence.

BY ORDER OF THE PRIOR

* * *

Does the administration give willing and generous support to the student religious life? In addition to "willing and generous support" does it also give a reasonable freedom of action?

Is there any genuine effort made on the part of the administration to create and maintain "the belongingness of a home community"?

Is there willingness on the part of the administration and the trustees to recognize the fundamental rights of the students—and are these rights listed in writing?

Are there channels of communication to keep the faculty and the students informed on college life and policies?

Is the administration alert to make use of the proved methods for maintaining faculty growth, such as a travel fund to professional conventions, sabbatical leaves for study and travel, secretarial aid in research and writing, public recognition of academic honors?

THE MEASURE OF CAMPUS OUTREACH

A college campus can stand in high repute academically, yet be smug and complacent toward the needs of the world around it. High grades do not of themselves guarantee world understanding and sympathy.

Already I should have learned much on the question of campus outreach from the items of student conversation and student campus life. Moreover, the study of fundamental faculty assumptions and administrative policies would have doubtless thrown additional light upon the query. Nevertheless, somewhere in the survey and as a separate measure I should want to list the items of campus life which stretch beyond the college limits. These are some of the questions for which I should try to find honest answer:

What does the campus actually do to reach beyond itself?

* * *

It's Fun to Give

If you believe in something, you support it. If you support something, the time comes when good wishes and cordial words are not enough and your hand reaches for your pocketbook. Then the fun begins. For giving is fun.

If you refuse to give, your support is wavering; and if your support wavers, it can't be that you believe in that something in any strong way. Maybe our account books, after all, offer the honest list of those things in which we really believe.

* * *

Do these measures have large support from the majority of the students? Large support from the majority of the faculty? Large support from the majority of the administrative officers?

What is the campus attitude toward foreign students? Does the administration make reasonable effort to invite them to the campus? Is proportionate aid available for foreign students? Are they accepted in all phases of campus life, including fraternity and sorority life?

Are the students aware of national and international issues? Do the majority of the students follow regularly some metropolitan daily or recognized news weekly?

Does the campus participate in national and international student conferences?

Is there campus support for the World Student Service Fund? Is there a campus Community Chest drive or something comparable? When the student gives, does he do so from generous, intelligent motives, or reluctantly as a result of group pressures?

Are there even meager evidences of personal or group sacrifice for human need outside the college gates?

What is done to acquaint the students with the actual conditions of social need and economic poverty in their own community? In their own country?

What are the measures taken by campus leaders, both student and faculty, to awaken social concern?

Is there a program of community service or group-exchange or deputation teams which offer the Christian student a worth-while opportunity to express his social concern? Is such a program supported by campus leaders?

Is there awareness of the social-action programs sponsored by the various major denominations?

If there is a chapel program, are there opportunities taken for emphasis upon the deeply religious world outlook?

* * *

Chapel Walk

Some students look far as they go along Chapel Walk. Some, in moods, see only the bricks on which they walk. Some do not see.

Jim has an examination this afternoon, and after it, a basketball game; will the prof ask a question regarding Elizabethan dramatists? Pat is social service chairman for her sorority, and tomorrow the girls are to start their new project of working with a group of underprivileged children at a nearby trailer camp. It will be a new experience for many of them. Bill is wishing a certain fraternity would bid him; he is beginning to wonder if something dreadful is wrong with him that they are so slow. June may be searching for a campus spot that will cause her brushes to dance. She has finished thirty oils in recent months, and is seeking new ideas. Mary has just come from the library; there she saw the pictures of the forty men who had given their lives for their country. Jack's picture was there, and again she pondered how different her life would have been had he been spared. Instinctively her hand touches his fraternity pin which she is wearing. Ben hopes today's chapel speaker will be interesting.

The students, except for two latecomers, have entered the chapel. There are the strains of "The Lord is in His Holy Temple" and then the doors are closed. A serviceman wrote from Iwo Jima during the Second World War: "If I could have three moments back at my college, I would choose one in the fraternity living room, where the brothers were sitting around chewing the rag; one in the gym, where the varsity was tying the basketball score with a beaut of a shot; and one on Chapel Walk, just ready to enter the chapel with the other students."[4]

* * *

In vocational guidance, are the opportunities in foreign lands for teaching or diplomatic service or business reasonably stressed?

Are the representatives of other countries invited to the campus to speak? And do they linger for campus fellowship?

Through various means, are the students made aware of the great religions of the world?

In classroom or in group discussion or in voluntary gatherings, is the cause of Christian missions presented?

Are Negroes admitted to the college? And Jews? If they are, are they welcomed? If they are not, is there effort to bring about a change of policy which would admit them?

Are the church foundations on the campus and the student Christian organizations banded together in any great world enterprise?

Is the concept of religion generally held large enough to include both a thrust upward to a Father-God and a thrust outward to a brother-man?

THE MEASURE OF TOTAL CAMPUS IMPACT

There is one additional measure: a measure containing certain of the items named above, and yet going beyond them. It is an inclusive measure and by virtue of its inclusiveness less easily defined.

* * *

A STUDENT'S PRAYER OF THANKSGIVING

Margie was a college sophomore in Ohio; Dick a sophomore in New Hampshire. Dick and Margie were in love. Neither knew that that love was not to find its expression in marriage as they dreamed, for concealed from sight for Margie around the bend of the road of time was an early and a tragic death.

On the Thanksgiving day of her sophomore year, Margie wrote to Dick. It was a letter far more searching than most of her letters. One friend called it a bread-and-butter-letter-for-life-itself. "I am thankful for so many things: for you and our love; for our parents and homes; for my many wonderfully fine friends. For [our colleges] and the opportunities they offer us; for the world so full of challenge, beauty and hope. For people whose opinions differ from mine; for the bonds of warmth and understanding that grow from the exciting discovery of mutual agreement; and for the ability to grow mentally and spiritually.

"I am thankful for inward peace; for the realization of a high goal which with God's help I shall strive steadily to attain. I am thankful for all life. The times are dark, but the future is perpetually bright, for it is always what man chooses to make it. Let us hope that our lives will help to create a more ideal one.

"For these and more I am thankful. I am thankful to God, but more than that—I am thankful for God. Without Him I would never have, nor be aware of these things, and my life would lack hope.

"I am thinking of you this Thanksgiving Day as always. I know your heart carries the same thanks and hope. May God keep you safe for me, darling, and for the years ahead that need you so badly."[5]

* * *

I should want to evaluate the Christian vitality of a campus by the total campus impact or pull. There would be fewer check questions for the last of these six measures. In fact the measure could be contained in the single query:

In the total score of the college, is the balance of the campus influence which plays upon the student in favor of Christian or non-Christian living?

Phrasing it differently: Does the total campus impact make Christian living easier or harder?

Or seeking still other words: If the institution is by our definition a Christian institution, in all the groups—trustee, alumni, administration, faculty, students—does the "earnest intent" shine through enough to be recognized? Does the outside world see anything which causes it to believe in the genuineness of the "earnest intent?" Is there anything basically different in the life of this campus under examination, either in terms of faculty attitudes or student activities or general campus faith, that marks it off from the neighboring campus which at no time aspires to the label Christian and counts its professed secularness as entirely adequate?

If the campus visitor could secure thoughtful, deliberate, full answers to this welter of questions, he would be certain to have learned much about the college. And according to his own definition of Christian faith and living, he would have some concrete ideas of the institution's success or failure as a Christian college.

For many years it has been the custom of the Board of Review of the North Central Association of Secondary Schools and Colleges to make a so-called profile of a college under investigation. The "profile chart" is a pretentious document, nearly a yard long. At the top are listed all of the items of institutional life which have been examined and adjudged: items of faculty—including degrees, organization, conditions of service—instruction, library, induction of students, student personnel services, administration, finance, institutional study, athletics.

On the left end of the chart is a division from zero to one hundred. Obviously no examiner or group of examiners would be wise enough to judge an institution by any absolute standard. What can be done, however, is to rate an institution relative to other institutions of similar organization and purpose.

For example it is possible to take the library holdings of five hundred undergraduate colleges and rate them in the order of their strength. Then it is further possible to assign each college a place on a scale of zero to one hundred. When this is done for all of the major items named above, and the scattered points connected with a single line, one has in such a profile some adequate indication of the educational strength and weakness of the institution.

No one has ever attempted to make institutional profiles on the strength and weakness of the religious life of the college. Perhaps it should be tried, under the supervision of a group of wise educational leaders, committed to the theory of the necessary integration of religion and education. Perhaps in this way we might see our Alma Mater in a more honest light as she stands in comparison with the neighbor colleges. It would be a more comprehensive and intelligent method of comparison than our present judgments based upon football victories and losses.

The friendly critic may raise the objection that the examiners could scarcely be expected to agree on their evaluations of the numerous items. It might be said in reply that some of the queries listed are thoroughly objective and can be answered with exactness. And many of those which are not would yield to careful subjective judgment.

But the critic persists. "What can the examiners take for their common definition of religion?"

That some common agreement would need to be reached is evident. That such agreement would have to go beyond a definition of religion to a working understanding of Christianity is likewise clear. For the charter of religion, however, the examiners could be asked to work within the bounds of that illumined insight which Prophet Micah had when he wrote:

> He hath shewed thee, O man, what is good;
> and what doth the Lord require of thee,
> but to do justly [that would include the measure of faculty
>   competence in its search for truth, and also much of
>   administrative policies] and to love mercy [student con-
>   versation and campus life fit here]
> and to walk humbly with thy God? [and does not humility
>   of necessity include the compassion of world outreach?]

By these means some reasonably adequate measure of a Christian college might be taken.

Chapter Six. The Way Ahead

DAVID. Corporal, the crowning son of heaven
  Thinks we can make a morning.
MEADOWS. Not
  By old measures. Expedience and self-preservation
  Can rot as they will. Lord, where we fail as men
  We fail as deeds of time.
PETER (in the pulpit). The blaze of this fire
  Is wider than any man's imagination.
  It goes beyond any stretch of the heart.
MEADOWS. The human heart can go to the lengths of God.
  Dark and cold we may be, but this
  Is no winter now. The frozen misery
  Of centuries breaks, cracks, begins to move,
  The thunder is the thunder of the floes,
  The thaw, the flood, the upstart Spring.
  Thank God our time is now when wrong
  Comes up to face us everywhere,
  Never to leave us till we take
  The longest stride of soul men ever took.
  Affairs are now soul size.
  The enterprise
  Is exploration into God,
  Where no nation's foot has ever trodden yet.
  Where are you making for? What is done
  Will never lie down: lie down, lie down!
  Where are you going? It takes
  So many thousand years to wake,
  But will you wake for pity's sake
  Pete's sake, Dave or one of you,
  Wake up, will you? Go and lie down.
  Where do you think you're going?[1]

               CHRISTOPHER FRY

THERE is always a potential hypocrisy in words; words can both reveal and conceal. Words which stand as symbols of high ideas need especially to be weighed and tested lest they carry the dynamite of easy satisfaction with generalizations.

Any writer on the subject of Christian education needs constantly to warn himself against this hypocrisy: so easy to make window dressing of shining ideals, so hard to put those ideals into daily practice; so easy to list the high objectives toward which the other man should strive and so difficult to strain one's own back and to plod on with aching legs oneself toward those objectives.

There would be a measure of hypocrisy in this book if there were not an attempt in this final chapter to be as specific and concrete as one can in terms of the present contemporary educational needs and particularly that area of education which accepts the ideal of the spirit. What are those needs today? What are the next steps that we might conceivably take?

CHRISTIAN EDUCATION NEEDS CHRISTIAN TEACHERS

There is urgent need today for a larger number of men and women coming into teaching with the fullest training which the academic world offers and, in addition, a deep commitment to teaching as a Christian vocation. Praise has already been given to the National Council on Religion in Higher Education for its significant contribution to this need. Many of their Kent Fellows have in themselves been focal points of contagious interest in experimenting with ways for bringing religion and education into genuine integration. In recent years the trek of the Danforth Fellows to graduate schools has begun, with the teaching appointment as the desired goal. The leaders of the National Council and the Danforth Foundation, however, would be the first to acknowledge that their efforts have been those of trail blazing. The great need is still unmet. With the new wave of college enrollment due in the middle fifties, we seem somehow not even to have kept abreast with the need of the situation. For the years when teaching vacancies have been limited, let the reminder be given that there is never an oversupply of good teachers.

* * *

TEN AXIOMS FOR A CHRISTIAN TEACHER

1. *A personal God is the creative and ultimately controlling force in nature and human destiny. This becomes the teacher's point of reference.*
2. *Man is capable of growth and development. In each member of the student group, there is capacity for desirable change.*
3. *Truth is at least partially discoverable, and man's partial comprehension can be accepted as real, but incomplete.*

Without this axiom the efforts of the scholar are non-sense.

4. *Truth is apprehensible by other means than "the scientific method." The Christian teacher will never yield to science and science's method the exclusive right to uncover new truth.*

5. *Human life and human personality call for the attitude of reverence.*

6. *Integrity is a basic element in all human relations.*

7. *Mutual respect and friendship constitute the highest form of relationship between student and teacher. Herein lies the urgent call for more well-trained, spiritually motivated teachers to come to the classroom with the gift of respect and friendship.*

8. *The Christian teacher is tolerant, patient, and understanding. So, too, must the secular teacher be, but it is hoped that the Christian teacher will exercise these virtues more fully and more frequently.*

9. *The goal of education is the full development of the whole man, according to his potentialities in harmony with the will of God. Secular education agrees heartily with this axiom, provided you omit the last seven words.*

10. *A Christian teacher is a disciple of Jesus Christ. Disciple means learner; so that the Christian teacher never loses his position as seeker after truth, endeavoring in his seeking to embody the spirit of Christ.*[2]

* * *

Surely the time has come when definite plans must be made on a national scale to present the profession of teaching, particularly with its opportunity for commitment to the profession in terms of Christian service, to the top minds and hearts of our college juniors and seniors. Year by year industry comes to the campus and speaks persuasively to the young men and women looking for jobs. Year by year representatives of the various professions appear for their appointment with carefully chosen men in whom they see likely candidates for their work. More recently the theological seminaries, through the plan of an annual week-end conference on the ministry held at points throughout the country, have been attracting choice men and women into that field. Of all the great professions of the world, it would seem as if teaching was the one that made least effort to fill its ranks with young men and women of its own careful choosing.

If a young man or woman goes into teaching, usually it is because of the lure of books and an innate delight in exposition which have been with him since childhood, or the friendly example and perhaps a persuasive word from a teacher whom he greatly admires.

TEACHING-PRESENTATION CONFERENCES

One concrete proposal is for a series of "teaching-presentation" regional conferences on campuses carefully selected to cover the country. In these gatherings there would be offered annually to groups of students, brought together because of their academic ability and their spiritual potentiality, the claims of teaching as a major social need of our American culture and also as an opportunity for Christian service. The first of such conferences was held experimentally in the spring of 1952.

The program allows for some of our best teachers to share their delight in their profession and to answer from rich experience the questions which students ask. In these conferences there should be a study of "vocation" and the qualities of mind and heart that rightly lead a student to make a Christian commitment to teaching as his life work.

Perhaps we will need to augment these conferences with a small group of staff secretaries who will visit our campuses to speak personally to the college students who have in themselves the makings of strong teachers.

THE WORK OF THE GRADUATE SCHOOLS

In the educational counseling that may be given these students in graduate schools, there should be recognition of two types of teachers, and it is within the power of the graduate school to prepare both. One is the specialist, who masters his discipline in all its intricacies and becomes the expert in a given field; the other, equally important these days although less readily recognized by his colleagues, is the generalist, who endeavors to equip himself with a more comprehensive and, therefore, less penetrating and exhaustive mastery of larger fields and related subjects. It is folly to hold to the one and despise the other, for both the specialist and the generalist have a permanent place in the undergraduate teaching field.

The young man or woman going on to prepare himself for teaching as a Christian vocation must be encouraged by every means to achieve for himself the fullest and best academic preparation which the graduate schools of this or any country provide in his chosen field, for nothing less than that best will prepare him to accept fully the responsibilities which lie ahead. He must be assisted with the highest and most demanding scholarship to acquire the philosophical over-view within the discipline which shall give meaning to the accumula-tion of unrelated detail.

Neither must that best and fullest preparation be limited because of the economic disadvantage of the student. Considering the fact that the teacher is never likely to receive an opulent living, it would not be fair to urge him to borrow against the day of a steady salary; therefore, ways must be found, either through the scholarship funds which the universities administer or through a series of generous fellowships offered by government or private foundations. These grants are wise investments in a country's future. They are given, not primarily because a young man needs graduate study to make a liveli-hood as a teacher, but because the colleges and the country need top-notch teachers.

It is unlikely, however, that this type of graduate training will be made possible until the graduate schools have a change of heart. At present, too often the vested interests of the individual department together with the departmental-mindedness of the professors stand as barriers to the broad cultural training that welcomes some work in philosophy to augment and give meaning to the studies in sociology and English literature and the natural sciences. It is probable that an additional year of graduate work may be necessary if this be done; but even when the student is prepared to invest this extra year, arrangements for an integrated program of study will be difficult until the department chairmen see validity in the claim that great teaching is the continuing search for understanding, appreciation, and truth, conducted within human fellowship and with a philo-sophical frame of reference which is intended to aid the student in his quest for the unity of knowledge and a life overview.

For the graduate student who is eager for theological background for his teaching of the humanities or the sciences, the obstacles are twofold. The graduate-school authorities, with few exceptions, frown upon such a diversion of interest. Why should one want to go off on such a detour when the extra time might be spent on digging deeper in one's own particular well of learning? There is little or no encour-agement from the graduate schools for the seeker. And the sem-inaries, with certain exceptions, are unequipped to care for the student who has no intention of preparing for the pastoral ministry but desires a pattern of courses to give him background and understanding for his teaching. They can offer him a miscellany of courses, but a pattern of courses: the invitation finds them unprepared.

It would be unrealistic to dream of a day when graduate schools will be deeply concerned for the student seeking to prepare himself for Christian teaching. For long years to come many of the graduate-school leaders will resist any suggestion that the graduate school, whether privately endowed or tax-supported, carries any special responsibility whatever for the nurture or the encouragement of the student who comes searching for the religious significance of his subject matter.

Are not facts facts? And is not scholarship the same scholarship for all? Facts are facts and scholarship is scholarship, but in the interpretation of facts and in the implications of the findings of scholarship men differ according to their outlook on life and their judgments, philosophical and religious, on what is significance.

The day will come, nevertheless, when some of our graduate schools will be willing to make available for those who wish them courses in the Religious Perspectives in the Teaching of the Humanities—or the Social Studies or the Natural or Biological Sciences. Perhaps in a few situations there may be experimentation within the departments of the division. And if these courses can be taught by teachers of indisputable scholarship and largeness of spirit, there will be no smiles of half-concealed contempt when the student signs for them.

In that day, our seminaries will be presenting courses for the enrichment of background for the teacher whose field is not religion or philosophy. Occasionally the teacher of economics or English literature may seek profit in the course in Fundamentals of Theology or Contemporary Religious Thinking—not that the profit will come directly in new notes for his classroom teaching, but rather in the increased understanding of the person responsible for selecting those classroom notes. Occasionally the teacher of chemistry or psychology, knowing that his vocation is certain to include the discussion of student problems, will register for the course in Student Counseling on Religious Problems. Occasionally the teacher of music or language, biology or physical education, will make time in a busy schedule for some study in The Place of Religion in Higher Education, or Moral and Religious Values in Public Education. And later, perhaps that "occasionally" may be written "frequently."

BONDS OF FELLOWSHIP

These are young persons who have chosen teaching as a Christian vocation; they have come to it with ardor, believing it to be their special form of Christian service. It is no academic question to ask how that sense of commitment and the sheen of dedication can be kept through the months and the years of the drudgery which scholarship demands of those who would achieve its degrees. It probably is not entirely the fault of the churches that so often they lose their contact with the young man and woman in the early twenties who have gone off to study at one of the graduate centers of the country. There can be a sense of deep loneliness in the struggles of the graduate student. There comes frequently an awareness of isolation, as if the student were somehow cut off from the campus fellowship which he enjoyed as an undergraduate and from the community fellowship which was his in adolescent days and will be his in years to come.

In the early years of teaching the sense of isolation may increase for some teachers. The demands of the initial months of teaching are usually heavy—demands for patient understanding of immaturity, for simple articulateness, for assurance of accuracy and exactness. Colleagues are friendly, wanting to be helpful. The institution, whether small or large, has made its overtures of welcome. But at the present time the atmosphere of many of our colleges and universities, both tax-supported and church-related, is essentially secular. The young instructor wonders if he was in error when he dreamed that he might teach in the service of God.

The National Council on Religion in Higher Education has done admirable work in holding its Fellows together within the bonds of fellowship through its Week of Work. The Danforth Foundation is attempting a similar endeavor in the annual Conference on Christian Teaching. But these groups are small, and an infinitesimal fraction of college teachers is touched.

Elton Trueblood once suggested the formation of a Guild of Christian Teachers. His objective has been achieved in the newly formed Faculty Christian Fellowship, which held its first national gathering in 1953.[3] As the name announces it is essentially a fellowship—a group without formal membership. There are no doctrinal demands, no ecclesiastical allegiances, no theological conformities. As in the universal invitation, whosoever will may come.

Wide difference of opinion must always be welcomed. Within the limits of the Christian heritage, broadly interpreted—for the adjective *Christian*, like the adjective *Faculty*, is offered in the name as a possible focus of unity—there is room for all who come seeking fellowship. It is the hope of the leaders of the Faculty Christian Fellowship that in the way ahead those sharing in this larger fellowship may be influential in offering to their own campuses the experience of togetherness for all who would seek to maintain the highest scholastic ideals of the teaching profession, while insisting that those ideals are not hostile to a larger integration between religious faith and academic competence. Such a campus fellowship may save the new instructor from the spiritual hauteur of "I, only I, am left." And at the same time it may be one more center of activity to see how this working integration of faith and scholarship can be achieved.

The years ahead hold plans for additional national conferences for the Faculty Christian Fellowship, but first there is much to be done on a regional level where travel costs can be kept modest and the sheer weight of numbers does not enforce silence on the timid. It is the purpose of the Executive Committee, moreover, to undertake special studies and bibliographies "on such issues as academic freedom, the social responsibility of professors, and the nature and purpose of the university, as well as on theological questions." In all of this there is the urgent hope that the leaders of the Fellowship will seek to make relevant and explicit for the academic community "Christianity's unique understanding of the nature of knowledge and truth, its doctrines of the nature and destiny of man, its view of the significance of creation and redemption for the understanding of the world and the function of society and its affirmations regarding the goal and nature of history."[4]

There is one additional service which the Fellowship can provide the Christian teacher. It can be the liaison body, both for understanding and for exchange of fellowship, between American groups and the several movements of Christian professors throughout the world—especially in England, Europe, and Asia. At present the American teacher knows little of the stirrings within the various national professorial groups of other countries. They, in turn, are ill informed of the changes taking place in American educational thought. If the Faculty Christian Fellowship can provide channels of appreciation and exchange of ideas and personnel between the Christian teachers of America and those of other nations, it will have rendered valiant and unique service.

At present there is no place in the Faculty Christian Fellowship for the graduate student. Perhaps in time this omission can be cared for. Or, perhaps, others may seek to plan for a Graduate Student Christian Fellowship which shall hold similar objectives for those preparing themselves for teaching.

A great corps of Christian teachers is not going to come by happy accident. So far as it comes, it will come with the combined efforts of those who hold such an ideal desirable, by a continuous recruiting process, by an unrelenting drive for the best academic graduate study available, and by all the other means that can be found to keep religious faith alive and growing during a time when the concentration on a job of scholarship may be almost completely absorbing. And yet to do less than this is to encourage the divorce between scholarship and religion which has so often characterized our higher education. To do less is to agree to the common secular assumption that the relation between the academic and the religious is distant and unimportant.

THE NEED OF OUR TEACHERS IN SERVICE

The obligation, however, is twofold. There is a need to see that a larger number of our choice young people with a sense of Christian service come into teaching. There is also the need of seeing that something is done for the teachers now in service who are troubled by their own religious illiteracy. They accept with eagerness the concept of the Christian teacher, and yet their own ignorance of the basic Christian assumptions sometimes makes it impossible for them to follow through.

Early in the decade of the fifties certain of the great American academic centers began offering summer work in religious subjects exclusively for teachers of the nonreligious disciplines. They were seeking to make available to the teacher who was successfully engaged after finishing his own graduate study some understanding both of the basic tenets of the Christian faith and also the contemporary thinking on the place of religion in education. Union Theological Seminary in New York City, the University of Southern California, Southern Methodist University, and the University of North Carolina were the first to inaugurate the program. The Danforth Foundation made available at each of these institutions a series of Teacher Summer Scholarships, including tuition, fees, board, and lodging.

* * *

OVER THE PORTAL

Over the portal of the allied cemetery in North Assam, where lie the bodies of many of our American soldiers who fought in India and Burma during the Second World War, stand these words: "Tell Them That We Gave Our Todays for Their Tomorrows."

* * *

The courses which were offered were for the most part elementary in nature. These were to meet the needs of the teachers in history and chemistry and art and agriculture, whose devotion to their own discipline had kept them unaware of the new developments in the field of religion and the recent developments in contemporary religious thinking. There were courses in theology, modern approaches to the Bible, religious counseling, social ethics, and usually a seminar in "The Problems of Religion in Higher Education."

The goal of such summer courses was dual: to strengthen the individual's own Christian faith, thereby making him intellectually more aware of the best religious thought of his day; and second, to give him specific aid how he, as a teacher of sociology or physics or engineering, might bring Christian presuppositions to his classroom in ways that were entirely acceptable academically.

What has been done is only a small beginning. The response, however, has been sufficient to justify the belief that herein lies a field of adult education which is new and untouched. And if support can be found, such opportunities for summer study, geared to the special need of the teacher, should be continued and, if the demand is sufficient, increased in number.

In the field of public education, similar summer endeavors have been made. A seminar-workshop for public-school administrators was first held at Union Theological Seminary in 1952 and continued in 1953. In recent years at other academic centers, study groups in "Moral and Spiritual Values" have been organized for public-school teachers, both within the university summer sessions and as independent gatherings.

As Christian teachers, we have often failed to see the tremendous effort which the task demands. The integration of religion and education is not a matter of sprinkling holy water on the conclusions of secular scholarship. Neither is it a matter of providing a pious picture frame for the classroom.

THERE IS SCHOLARLY WORK TO BE DONE

One reason why the work of the Christian teacher has not been highly esteemed by his secular colleague is that he, the Christian, has never given it, in his own thinking, the kind of high importance which it deserved. We shall not have the Christian teacher doing his best until we have had a series of explorations made by scholars of undisputed ability in terms of each of the individual disciplines and its relation to Christian faith—"Explorations into God," to use Christopher Fry's phrase.

These studies, when they come, must be made by men who are masters of two disciplines—both the subject-matter field in which they teach and the discipline of religious thought. They will come as the second step in a program of which the Hazen Foundation's admirable series "Religious Perspectives in College Teaching" was the first.

It would be folly at the present time for the college-teacher-average-church-member, no matter how sincere, who has done no concentrated reading in the field of theology, who knows little about the movement of contemporary religious thought of our day, to attempt to bring not necessarily the last word but, shall we say, the tenth-to-the-last word on the integration of religion and the subject matter of which he may be master. There must be scholarly colonists to follow the scholarly trail blazers.

One of the present hazards in the area of religious counseling is the steady output of pamphlets and books pretending to be wise correlation of the truths of religion and psychology-psychiatry, whereas, for the most part, the religionist who writes knows little of his psychiatry except in popular distortions and the psychiatrist who writes has a most perfunctory and inadequate idea of his religion.

* * *

I Should Like

A group of alumnae gathered for their tenth reunion. The conversation quickly turned to what they wished they had done when they were college students. Here are their "I Should Likes."

1. *To have insisted on some leisure time each week for the reading I wanted to do, rather than to have read only what others prescribed.*

2. *To have made room for a variety of college activities, even at the sacrifice of great proficiency in any one.*

3. *To have spent more time with those students who because of family background or racial heritage were "different," rather than to have sought out only those who echoed my own thinking.*

4. *To have believed the faculty members when they said they were offering us friendship and to have gone halfway to meet them.*

5. *To have sought out and encouraged more hearty discussions on important issues, particularly those on which I was not informed.*

6. *To have planned my day to allow a few minutes each day which I was free to waste without a bad conscience; the sense of being driven was disheartening.*

7. *To have seen that I gathered some appreciation of art and music and the theater so that I knew a little of how to enjoy a picture, a symphony, a play, or a movie.*

8. *To have arranged my summer vacation to bring me a variety of new experiences of travel or work in a factory or one of the community-service projects sponsored by national church groups.*

9. *To have found time to care for my spiritual development at least as fully as I cared for my physical development.*

10. *To have written home letters which would have shared the years with my folks and in later years, when bound, would have revived for me many memories which are now forgotten.*

* * *

An outstanding example of a significant work in this field is that excellent volume *The Individual and His Religion* by Gordon W. Allport of Harvard. Dr. Allport is master of the two fields. Being master, he can show the interrelations and the basic agreements as well as the basic disagreements. He speaks the two vocabularies; and the vocabularies of psychology and of religion are like those of cousin languages —Spanish and Italian, for example.

One of the fundamental needs of Christian education is for the scholarly services of outstanding teachers who will take from one to three years, first to acquaint themselves fully with the presuppositions of Christian faith within the best of historic and contemporary thought, and then to strive for the largest integration of those presuppositions and their own academic discipline. There is no blueprint for such exploration. He who set forth would be the adventurer in virgin land.

If adequate funds could be uncovered through generous individuals or farsighted foundations, would it not be possible to find two or three leaders in each of the great subject-matter fields who would be willing to take time from their teaching to engage in as thorough and rigorous scholastic endeavor as they are capable of, seeking the interrelations of the best religious thought of our day and the best scholastic understanding of their special discipline?

In the field of biology, for example, what are the scientific presuppositions and also the Christian presuppositions that the Christian scientist brings to the classroom? To what degree can they be reconciled as working principles of knowledge? How does the nature of the Christian God fit into the pattern of life which the biologist has uncovered through his exacting scientific studies? What have the biological sciences to offer us in terms of a new and fuller understanding of God? And of life and being? What is the relation of nature and God? And together, what do the biological sciences and Christianity have to say about the nature of man, for both are avenues through which God discloses Himself?

In *College Teaching and Christian Values*, my friend, Arthur W. Lindsey, in an admirable essay points the way to some of these answers. He laments that more is not being done to effect a larger speaking acquaintance between the two areas. "Men of the church," he writes, "have regarded biology as of limited significance, and some biologists, since they have found no supporting evidence for religion in their researches, have been avowed atheists. The two groups show little evidence today of reaching a common understanding, and if the biologist is to extend his influence on human life beyond the boundaries of applied science, no problem can offer him greater opportunity."[5]

There is, however, one statement in the essay which gives the reader pause: "The teaching biologist is first of all a scientist." It is true, as Dr. Lindsey points out, "His primary obligation is to give his students an adequate foundation of the facts of his science, a sound appreciation of its principles and relationships, and the necessary training in the methods of procedure."[6] But are the insights and understandings of religion totally foreign to this foundation of facts, this appreciation of principle, this training in the method of procedure? Dr. Lindsey seems to suggest that any concern that the biologist might express for religion and its contribution to science would be in the nature of an afterthought—something to be added if the classroom hour were stretched for a few final moments. One gathers the picture of the Christian student expected to be appreciative for the crumbs that fall from the scientist's table.

Is there not a possible approach to this total problem of the integration of religion with the academic disciplines that can start not with the teacher being *first* the biologist or the historian or the anthropologist, nor yet with the teacher being *first* the Christian; but rather with the teacher being *first* a seeker for truth, believing truth to be God's truth, in all fields which are open to him.

Take the seeker who is the teacher of biology. The biological sciences will have much to offer him as his chosen discipline, and as a faithful scientist he will follow. Because he is a seeker after truth in the field of a major science, he will acquaint himself with other sciences, recognizing their distinctive content and yet endeavoring to find as many items in common that might be said to belong to science *per se*. His studies in psychology, chemistry, and physics will yield new understanding, and he will make every effort to achieve a synthesis of those understandings and principles which are common to all these fields. Should there be points where contradiction appears between the findings of the various sciences, he will hold them compartmentally until the time when the synthesis can be made. Only if he is a man of little mind, and thereby unworthy as a teacher, will he divide his mind into separate divisions for the completely separate content of biology, psychology, chemistry, physics, ignoring the correlative aspects of these fields. Indeed, were he to aim at such independence of the sciences, the new findings in each of these fields, with their heavy emphasis on correlation, would laugh him to scorn.

Can the scientist not come in the same spirit to the insights and understandings of religion? The synthesis between religion and his scientific discipline will not be the relatively easy one that it was for the companion sciences. Biology is based on factual data far more than religion, which must take its stand in large measure on faith, but never a faith which has the incredible for its foundation. Religion is based on faith far more than biology, but even biology has its place for faith when the scientist proceeds in the dark toward a possible but unknown segment of truth. Like Columbus, he too by faith is trusting "the soul's invincible surmise."

Inevitably there will be large areas of the irreconcilable, and the scholar, whether teacher of science or of religion, will accept this compartmentally, hoping for the day when human wisdom will extend its grasp. But one of the inviting opportunities for the Christian teacher of biology today is that of seeking for the numerous places where the two great fields of learning and endeavor overlap. There are areas where they speak to each other. Dr. Lindsey concludes his essay, "Probably few men would think of biology as a promising subject for the teaching of Christian principles; but it is the science of life and human lives are a major concern of Christianity. Can the teaching biologist give his best service without some effort to bring them closer together?" And when he makes that effort, Dr. Lindsey might have added, you have your Christian teacher.

As the teacher gives himself to such integrative studies, searching with all the faithfulness and honesty of the scholar for the largest possible and mutually contributing synthesis, how will he make available these results of such efforts? His results can be made available and useful in three different ways.

First, through the kind of scholarly study to which we are accustomed, in books written for the colleague who has mastered the vocabulary of the discipline, or in learned articles that can be prepared and presented before conferences or in learned journals.

Second, in terms of seminars or summer conferences that might be opened exclusively to the teacher in the academic discipline. If this were to be done, a considerable amount of time would have to be used in acquainting these teachers of biology or history or anthropology with the vocabulary and the concepts of contemporary religious thought before their leader could go on to the larger synthesis which would be the purpose of the gathering. But would not the attraction be great for the teacher in psychology, if it were possible for him to have a summer session with a man like Gordon W. Allport of Harvard, esteemed and respected for his scholarship? Would it not be equally helpful to the teachers of philosophy, if a man like Theodore M. Greene of Yale were available to point out, in a concentrated period of study, the interrelations of philosophy and the Christian faith? Would not the teacher of history find his horizon expanding through the study of the forces of religion in history, under a historian-scholar of repute, such as E. Harris Harbison of Princeton? One might go on through the list of the academic disciplines.

The third expression of that intensive study on the part of the scholar-leader would be, it is to be hoped, in the preparation of textbooks which might substitute Christian perspectives for the secular perspectives which are so common in our textbooks today. Sister Annette Walters of the College of St. Catherine has written of this need out of her own experimental endeavors to bridge the gulf:

The problem of integrating psychology with the rest of the liberal arts curriculum is a crucial one in the Christian college. The typical textbook writer either is not a Christian or else assumes that his religion is one thing and psychology another, and that there is no connection between the two. The teacher who uses such texts (and must, because there are no other books equally readable or sound scientifically), must somehow help his students to bridge the gap between what they are learning about man's nature in other classes, and what is assumed in the psychology book.[7]

Such texts must have the full validity of high scholarship. Anything of the shoddy or the hastily done will be more seriously out of place here than elsewhere. The secular texts make the tremendous assumption that religion is unimportant, and whether important or not can have no possible relation with academic findings. The text written with religious perspectives will likewise make a tremendous assumption, namely, that religion is of major importance to man and has direct relationships with the highest known findings of contemporary scholarship. Such texts will in candor point out those areas where the presuppositions of religion and the subject field are in agreement; with equal candor they will point out where the principles of the discipline appear to be in contradiction to the substance of religious faith.

There is scholarly work to be done. It must needs be done within the complete freedom of academic research. The best of scholarly procedures must be employed and the findings must be honestly reported. Only those well qualified by training and by eager desire are competent to undertake it. But if the right men can be found and given full support financially and scholastically, their results, as made available in scholarly papers, in teacher seminars, and in new texts, may date a new period in Christian education.

OUR TEACHERS COLLEGES

Any effort to look ahead and to suggest possible remedies for our present over-secularized education would be unrealistic and incomplete if large attention were not given to the numerous and powerful (in part because of numbers) state teachers colleges, where tens of thousands of our elementary and secondary school teachers are prepared annually. It is difficult to generalize on this group of institutions. Being subject to state law and to the control of state educational boards, they vary widely. In some states, the normal schools, so called, are still strong with a normal-school pattern of education dominant. In others—Ohio, for example—the normal schools have become undergraduate colleges, and these, in turn, are in process of becoming universities, with full-fledged divisions of graduate studies. In some situations, the teachers college is allowed large freedom to develop a program of general education, which includes philosophy and not infrequently, where legally possible, religion. In others, the hand of the professional "educationalist" is strong, and general education is kept leashed in the backyard while the front door is opened to the long procession of courses in pedagogical methods.

In the area of religious values, the scene of the state teachers colleges ranges from abundance to poverty. There are state teachers colleges where the department of religion is an integral part of the administration and the emphasis on moral values and character is as strong as in many liberal church-related institutions. On the other hand, there are institutions where all work in religion and philosophy and ethics is completely barred from the curriculum under the specious argument, "Our job is to train teachers to teach." In one such institution the president committed himself by saying, "I would discharge any teacher whom I knew to be guilty of bringing moral and spiritual values in the classroom. We're a state teacher-training institution."

It is most important that the teacher of English know his Shakespeare. It is most important that the third-grade instructor know the best ways of teaching the art of reading. It is also important that both of these teachers shall have some answer to the questions that may be asked, either in class or out, "What makes right right?" and "Why is wrong wrong?"

The laws of our states differ widely in their interpretation of the place of religion in public education. It is untrue to conclude that the present "wall of separation between the Church and the State" prevents all interchange. There is a considerable number of state institutions with departments of religion where standard courses about religion are taught as any other discipline is taught, sponsored by the institution or by cooperating denominations. New departments of religion are still being established in our state schools.

But even where state law and public opinion are opposed to teaching about religion, there is nothing to prevent and much to approve the building of sound courses in philosophy, including courses in basic moralities and ethics, which Bernard Iddings Bell calls "the science of the Good Life." With our American ethical and moral standards as variable as they are today, obviously such courses could never be taught dogmatically. The presence of such an elective in the curriculum would, however, assure the thoughtful prospective teacher of the opportunity to grapple under wise leadership with some of the fundamental moral and ethical and social problems of our day. The judgment is growing stronger that this is something essential in the preparation of our teachers for tomorrow.

There are, moreover, signs on the horizon of significant things to come.

The American Association of Colleges for Teacher Education (AACTE) was formed in 1948 as the result of the merger of three national bodies concerned with the training of teachers. The Association's membership comprises approximately three hundred institutions of various types, but all with a major concern for teacher education—state teachers colleges, colleges of education, municipal teacher-education institutions, and a smaller group of strong liberal-arts colleges with departments of education. It is claimed for the Association that its member institutions prepare approximately 65 percent of the elementary teachers and 45 percent of the secondary teachers in the nation.

In 1953 the AACTE officially took recognition of the need for attention to moral and spiritual values in the curricula of both the elementary and secondary schools, and in turn in the teachers colleges where the leaders of these schools receive their training. A Committee on Teacher Education and Religion was formed. There is significance in the name. The emphasis was to be not on moral and spiritual values—that phrase which has become pale with much use—but on religion; and the decision was made with full understanding of the obligation of the state teachers college to work harmoniously with all of the nation's religious groups, as well as with those who call themselves religionless.

The committee was charged by the AACTE "to propose a program calculated to give greater emphasis to religion as an aspect of edu-

cation in the preparation of teachers in all member institutions."
In the first report issued by this committee, there was this concrete
proposal for action:

... a factual study of religion characterized by deliberate aim and definite
plans to deal directly and objectively with religion whenever and wherever
it is intrinsic to learning experience in the various fields of study. Within
that area the principal aim and emphasis should be an intelligent
understanding of the role of religion in human affairs.

This emphasis may be considered as distinct from two other aims:
the development of religious literacy among prospective teachers . . .
the other, the development of a sense of individual commitment in
encouraging students to explore the resources of religion as a basis for
durable conviction. It is the view of the committee that the emphasis
on *teaching about religion* offers the most *immediate opportunity* for
developing programs which are both appropriate to the responsibilities
of colleges preparing teachers, and consonant with legal and practical
limitations upon the colleges.[8]

The *modus operandi* of the committee will be to select a given
number of teacher-training institutions which are willing to work
cooperatively with the coordinator of the project, both as experimental centers for the development of teaching materials, units of
work and such studies as may lead to courses, and as demonstration
centers where these materials can be tried and tested. The second
stage of such an endeavor must be the making available to all colleges and universities concerned with teacher education the results
and materials produced and found worthy by the pilot institutions.

In the Interchapter "Seeds of Hope," there was mention of the
carefully documented study made under the auspices of the American Council on Education and reported in the volume *The Function of the Public Schools in Dealing with Religion*.[9] This material,
commonly referred to as the Linton Report, had earlier set the pattern of thought, more recently repeated in the AACTE committee
findings, that "a factual study of religion [is] the best approach to
a solution of the problem confronting public education in dealing
with religion."[10]

It is the expectation and hope of the American Council that its
study will be used as a basis for experimentation and demonstration
in a selected group of public-school systems and teacher-education
institutions.[11]

Obviously there is strong similarity in the plans of the AACTE

Committee on Teacher Education and Religion and the proposals of the American Council's Committee on Religion and Education. It is important that the AACTE committee make wise and large use of the materials so carefully gathered and documented by Dr. Linton and the cooperating committee. If in the uncertain years ahead these two major programs for bringing the study about religion into public education can develop cooperatively, there is good reason for hope that something of genuine significance can be accomplished for American public education. True, these are projections for the future; nevertheless, the way ahead is brighter because of the high expectation which these two groups have encouraged.

During the time that intensive work is being done in carefully selected pilot institutions, there will be opportunity to bring before the individual college and university through conference and summer workshop, through faculty consultation and campus visitors, the national educational situation with its achievements of the past and the present and its hopes for the future, its proud strengths and its unfilled needs.

In December, 1951, a national conference was held at New Haven, Connecticut, on "Religion in the State Teachers College." No effort was made to reach final judgments by vote of the more than a hundred administrators and faculty members who were present. The purpose of the conference was frankly exploratory. It raised questions, important questions that are demanding careful answers, such as the one contained in the Introduction to the published report of the conference:

State teachers colleges are to a degree unique in facing obligations at [the levels of the college and the public schools]. As state colleges they share the broad responsibility of any college and university in providing curricular and noncurricular experiences for the religious growth of students entrusted to them. At the same time they are training prospective teachers who must come to grips with religion and values in the public schools. What should the state teachers colleges do to meet this dual responsibility?[12]

It is important that in the years ahead similar conferences shall be held, either on a regional or national basis, to explore what is being done to bring religious values into the teachers colleges and the public schools, and also what might be done, with full legal authority and with community approval. Major decisions for local situations are not made by national conferences; but national conferences have their part in creating awareness of local need, and also the presence of local opportunity.

THOSE COLLEGES ASPIRING TO BE CHRISTIAN

The continuing study project "What Is a Christian College?" conducted under the auspices of the Research Committee of the Commission on Christian Higher Education of the Association of American Colleges,[13] has already had the desired result of stirring a number of church-related institutions to study intensively their campus situation. But there is a second and equally important consequence: it has produced a strong sense of fellowship among the colleges that call themselves Christian, and among their leaders. What the Faculty Christian Fellowship can possibly mean to the individual Christian teacher this research project has been meaning to many Christian colleges.

Any effort to organize these colleges into one more strong national organization would be divisive and repetitious; already they have their connection with the commission referred to above. But there is need for the occasional gathering of these leaders on a regional or national basis to discuss leisurely and profoundly the issues which are unique to their institutions. Raymond F. McLain, the director of the study "What Is a Christian College?" has suggested that every fourth year might be a reasonable time for such a gathering. He has further made the interesting suggestion that such a quadrennial conference of Christian colleges should include not alone the conference-harassed president and dean but representatives from all the constituencies of the college: students, faculty, administration, trustees. And one might name the alumni.

Such a conference through many of these groupings would desire to investigate all possible sources of income for the Christian college. This is a major issue for any day. But there are other urgent problems which can profitably be studied, first within the limited homogeneous group and then later within the full assembly. The major assumptions of the Christian colleges are not and cannot be those of the state universities; nevertheless, when the Christian colleges come to the great task of curriculum building and to the persistent problems of academic freedom, racial segregation, faculty-student relationships, campus democracy, etc., they are prone to set their discussions not upon the assumptions of their own institutions but upon those of their tax-supported neighbors.

Locally within the institution and nationally through the means of a conference such as Dr. McLain suggests, the time is ripe for the Christian college to dig deeply into these and other problems which profoundly affect the life and integrity of the institution, and to scrutinize its findings against the background of the accepted Christian assumptions.

WANTED: PILOT EXPERIMENTS

It is strange that there have come in recent decades so few outstanding experiments on individual campuses in the ways whereby the spiritual life of the college can be more richly and intensely cultivated. Perhaps a striking exception to this statement is the pattern of Religious Emphasis Week. In itself, however, this was no new program, but an extension and an elaboration of the earlier "Week of Prayer" which was common in many of our church colleges under a variety of names.

In the past several decades this program of invitation to both faculty and students for intense concern for the things of the spirit for the period of a week or less has been exceedingly popular, both in church-related colleges and on state-university campuses as well. The meaningfulness of the program has differed according to the strength of the leadership and the careful footwork done by the planning committees. At its best, it has brought a genuine sense of vision and illumination. At its worst, there has been a repetition of clichés and pious phrases which has increased the contempt of the irreligious for the things of religion and confirmed the campus pagans in their assurance of adequacy. On too many campuses today the program of Religious Emphasis Week is settling down into a crystallized form which is being accepted as routine, having its values, to be sure, but without the attraction or the strength of novelty which it once had.

Recognizing this state of affairs, certain campuses have sought variety in the conventional pattern. Illinois Wesleyan University, for example, has made a blueprint for campus consideration which covers a college generation. A year each is being given to the four general themes: What Is Truth? What Is Beauty? What Is Right?, and What Is Goodness? Instead of concentrating the study and discussion in a single special week, it is spread throughout the year, with a monthly emphasis.

Bucknell University took *The Crisis in the University* as the study book on which it built one of its highly organized Religious Emphasis Weeks. Then, in an endeavor to continue the spirit of the Week, it arranged for three special periods in the interval between the annual Weeks, when special lecturers came to the campus for the more intensive discussion of themes suggested by Sir Walter Moberly.

If the values of the Week, under whatever name it may be called, are to be preserved, special effort must be made to maintain its freshness of approach and its democratic planning, with continuing care for the mountain of detail without which the significance is so often lost. There will be gain, however, if more of our colleges experiment with new approaches and new imaginative plans, lest in a devotion to what has been we lose sight of what might be.

In the educational world generally the recent decades have brought forth a series of significant experiments in the processes of teaching and learning and in the whole area of campus living. One thinks of the Harvard tutorial plan, the Princeton preceptorial system, the Yale housing program, and at the name of Chicago one's mind leaps to the multitude of experiments which came forth from that institution under the provocative leadership of Robert Maynard Hutchins —experiments now honored more in memory than by continuation.

Nor have smaller campuses been without their own experimental efforts: Antioch, with its experiential learning and also, although far less publicized, its experiments in community government; Berea, Blackburn, and Park Colleges, with their student work programs designed not alone for the financially needy but also for those who can learn through the daily work assignment a sense of responsibility; Hiram, with its one-study plan and the invitation to concentrate for a given period on a single subject.

But in the field of moral and religious education, there have been relatively few significant efforts at experimentation. It was not so much that our colleges loved the old, but rather that their leaders lacked the imagination—and the incentive of burning need—to conceive the new. Where shall one look for significant experimentation? One thinks of the Sunday-morning Burrall class, with its student attendance exceeding a thousand, and its many allied activities, which Stephens College has sponsored since the class's founding in 1921. One may recall numerous campuses where thoroughly commendable religious programs are maintained, but no other major endeavor of originality comes readily to mind.

Education for spiritual development will be much enhanced if there can be on a dozen major campuses—and by major one does not necessarily mean either size or prestige, but rather campuses of genuine academic integrity—well-conceived experiments in the emphasis upon the things of the spirit. The very lack of experimentation suggests a smug satisfaction totally unwarranted with conditions as they are. It may be questioned whether the progress can be made which is so devoutly desired and urgently needed until there can be that kind of cross-fertilization which comes when ideas are conceived in new wrappings and ideals are planted in newly fertilized soil.

If the answer is made that our need is for men not experiments, the reply can be offered that men will, in their enthusiasm, blaze new trails. And if the budget maker intervenes to complain about the lack of funds, the answer can be made that there is enough genuine concern on the part of individuals and groups of individuals in the country that financial undergirding can be found for ideas worthy of wise and carefully planned experimentation.

The need is there and for the present it goes unfilled.

THE INSTRUMENTS OF COMMUNICATION

There is still one additional effort that deserves brief mention in any listing of "next steps" if we are to meet the needs of our moral and religious scene, nationally viewed. It is the suggestion of the fullest and strongest means of communication.

The Christian Scholar, from its first issue of March, 1953, has given promise that it will serve the faculty member as a periodical both scholarly and Christian. The necessity of keeping its discussions fresh and pertinent, of holding its reports of current experimentation to the significant and the timely, will never be editorially easy. But the task of Christian journalism is not easy. The hazards which confront it, hazards of fatiguing repetition and safe conventionality of idea and phrase, are greater than those of secular journalism.

For the college student there have been two praiseworthy journals, each of which has commanded a respectable reading. *The Intercollegian* is the publication of the National Student YMCA and YWCA and the Student Volunteer Movement; *motive* has been sponsored since its first appearance in 1940 by the Board of Education of the Methodist Church. *The Intercollegian* by its purpose has been in part an organizational periodical. *motive* has been allowed unusual freedom to cover the total field of student interest, and within a small budget has done so with remarkable success, first under the editorship of Harold A. Ehrensperger, whose hand molded the initial policies of the paper, and, since 1950, under Roger Ortmayer. To the critical reader, the denominational control has at no time been evident or objectionable.

Both *The Intercollegian* and *motive* have suffered from financial limitations; with larger budgets, both periodicals might have taken on new strength, which in turn might have brought larger circulation. Is there reason to believe that there is a potential circulation for a strong student journal of religious thought larger than that held by either *The Intercollegian* or *motive*? If such a periodical were to emerge beyond the talk stage, it would have to meet and face the strenuous competition of the popular pictorial magazines. Its Christian appeal would have to be—as indeed the appeal of both *The Intercollegian* and *motive* now are—strictly and strongly ecumenical. Such a journal is manifestly impossible at the present time without a substantial subsidy for an initial period of years. But such a journal might conceivably be the instrument of Christian leadership in the student world.

The suggestion has been made that either *motive* or *The Intercollegian* or both periodicals in merger might become the nucleus for such a journalistic venture, if the controlling boards were willing. Or there is the alternative that the new magazine should be a fresh undertaking.

THE FACULTY MAN IS THE KEY

If the faculty member in large numbers is the competent teacher plus the enthusiastic Christian, making that miracle fusion that produces the Christian teacher, he will see his post in the under-graduate college as an opportunity for something more than impart-ing historical dates or chemical formulae; then the students will inevitably catch something of the contagion of both learning and faith which the classroom can offer. And as a consequence, we may have trained not minds alone but men equal to the opportunity of an American democracy.

One of the most interesting manifestations of this concern for an enlarged spiritual outlook of education is the series of week-end faculty conferences which has come about in recent days under the variety of leaderships suggested in the first Interchapter. The common theme for these gatherings is: How can the spiritual values so necessary for good living be brought into the patterns of our American education?

Another plan is for the extension of the program of campus visitors. For a period of years it has been common for colleges to welcome outstanding resident guests in the area of music and art and literature. More recently there has been an effort to extend this principle of visitation to distinguished religious leaders. During successive years Gerald Heard spent an academic quarter on the campus of Washington University, where his lectures and fellowship contacts were of large value to students but, perhaps, especially to faculty. Many faculties appear to desire this kind of visitation, assuming always that they will have a hand in the choice of visitor.

Moreover, on the individual campuses themselves, where there is a nucleus of faculty men and women reaching for this larger concept of their profession, there have been groups meeting regularly for study and discussion of the problems as they affect their own campus situation. In some cases this has been a group of both faculty and students, so that the over-all picture of campus life could be considered with concern for both of the two generations who have engaged to occupy the same house.

All of this experimentation is testimony to the importance of the faculty man seeing his job in the light of the eternal—or, if those words be offensive to some readers, seeing his work in its moral and ethical and spiritual implications which make of teaching not a trade but a glorious profession.

There is acknowledged danger in searching for new patterns when the need of the hour is less for new patterns than for stronger leadership. It is always tempting to put the blame of failure on organization rather than on the human personnel which conceives and controls organization.

The area of religious and spiritual values in education is cultivated first by those teachers who are concerned for the moral and spiritual responsibilities of their appointments and who see the hour in the classroom and the conversation in the counseling chamber as the occasion wherein man's mind touches man's mind for the enrichment of both lives.

This area, moreover, is cared for by the chaplain or religious coordinator—the person responsible to the administration for the over-all spiritual life of the campus. His teaching assignment may be great or small, his title may vary, but his responsibility is clear. There is also the third group without direct responsibility to the administration, representatives of the churches or of the great Christian organizations, such as Young Men's Christian Association and its companion organization for women, which work exclusively with students. These three groups of leaders control, for success or mediocrity and sometimes for sheer moral failure, the so-called religious life and activities of the campus.

One of the next steps suggested for the decade ahead is the recruiting of a larger number of well-qualified college students who see teaching, for them, as a Christian vocation, and undergirding them with the best graduate training and in addition a continuing attention to their spiritual needs. But the college chaplains and the student religious workers likewise need careful recruiting and also attention to the problem of training.

Too often it has been assumed that the pattern of ministerial training was right and best for the man committed to the work of the college chaplain; then, if he saw fit to prepare himself for college teaching, in addition he could complete his doctorate. Perhaps the assumption was correct, but there are many doubting Thomases. And the doubt can best be resolved if representative men now in the chaplaincy, together with administrative educational and religious leaders who are in a position to judge the chaplains' work, can meet together for an uninhibited session on the preparation and training of today's college chaplain. The conclusions ought not to be limited by the training now available in our seminaries and graduate schools. It must be assumed that when the profession knows its own clear mind, it will be possible to find academic centers which will make this training available.

In large measure the same situation holds for the student worker, whether student pastor, director of a church foundation, or the leader of the campus student Christian movement. The easy answer that these men, too, need the rigorous discipline in Christian thought and pattern of homiletical training that the theological seminaries offer the men entering the ministry may or may not be the wisest solution. But until studies can be made of the in-service experiences of these workers and critical judgments gathered from those in position to evaluate their work, we shall not have either confirmation of the "easy answer" or reasonable refutation.

The success of the college chaplain and the director of the denominational foundations will in considerable measure rest on the support or lack of support given to religious living by the leaders of the college faculty. Plans have been suggested for the recruiting and training of the teacher; suggestions have been offered for summer seminars and workshops whereby the teacher in service may acquaint himself with the best of contemporary religious thought.

One additional proposal deserves to be considered: a program of postdoctoral study in theology and allied subjects for the teacher of the humanities, the social studies, the natural and biological sciences, who is willing to take a full year off from his professional commitments for the intensive study which will bring him a fuller religious background for his living and teaching. There may not be many seeking such opportunity; and of those who come, it is unlikely that any neatly packaged group of courses will be the answer to their need. Rather there must be individualized answers to individual needs. In addition to courses of study now available, there should be invitations for these scholars to pursue their own research, especially in fields which combine religion with their own discipline.

At present, of those who seek such opportunity, many may be deterred for financial reasons; families demand support and expenses continue even in postdoctoral years. For the man whose teaching experience has revealed the promise of large competency and success both in the area of scholarship and human relations, it would be a tragedy if he were kept by financial inadequacy from such further enrichment of his teaching.

It has been the not uncommon experience in American education that when the institutions offered their best, and students—in this case student-scholars—recognized their need of that best, ways were found to make the intellectual adventure possible. Even so may it be with a program of postdoctoral research for those properly qualified.

THE WAY AHEAD

The way ahead is a long way and a hard way. For the traveler it is important that he know where he is going and the direction he will need to follow if he is to arrive at his destination. It would be folly to grow rhapsodic over the scenery that may lie ahead when there are hazards besetting the present stage of the journey.

In the very act of promoting Christian education and in genuine concern for the fulfillment of the ethical and spiritual needs of our campuses, we dare not overlook the dangers which beset the effort.

They are the dangers of furthering the divisiveness which stains the pages of historical Christianity, of narrow-mindedness which sees not beyond our own back yard, of callous superiority and hideous smugness, the dangers of organizing new groups in an already overgrouped profession just for the claim of personal or organizational glory, and ever with us the danger of rousing that dread apparition of intolerance. Beset with dangers such as these, we shall walk warily, in compassion and the spirit of the great Teacher. From these temptations and, as the old Scottish prayer read, "all other beasties," good Lord deliver us.

* * *

COMMENCEMENT PASSES BY

Gene, with a quiet smile, who plans to be a surgeon; he will make a good one, for he combines conscientious scholarship with a warm faith in people, and his hands are capable. Marilyn, whose four years have brought, among other things, a new understanding of the sincerity and the power of words. Her verses are already beginning to claim recognition. John, whose ambitions are unified by a desire to come close to the life of a small rural community; he may farm, he may go into social work, he may preach, but at least he knows he wants to work with country folk. Ruth, whose first two years won her the title of playgirl; she still deceives the unknowing, but we of the campus are aware that beneath that glamorous loveliness there is the stuff of great womanhood. Her ambition to go into scientific research is no idle choice. Earnest and Fred and Warren, who are headed for business and will bring to it trained minds, habits of perservance, and a sense of world responsibility. Mary, who plans matrimony for her career; like an earlier Mary, she will make a good mother, pondering many things in her heart. Fred and Jim, who dream of graduate school and new worlds of ideas to conquer. Bill, who knows the inner compulsion to be a Christian minister, and a faithful servant of his God. Fanny, who came from an under-privileged family and, having learned much, goes back with gratitude. Sam and Gretchen, who have carried, without parental aid or encouragement, the load of four years; they plan to go on together, united first by their need for companionship and then by their love. Ronnie, who has learned democracy, and Jane who taught herself to live above her family's wealth.

Together "with all the rights and privileges and responsibilities appertaining" to the magic diploma go congratulations and good wishes.

* * *

Periodically through the centuries men have tried to make of education this essential combination of mind and heart. But the passion for factual information was great, and the standards of the profession became increasingly secular. The task was hard and the methods to be followed in giving pre-eminence to the spiritual not clearly seen; it was easy to let self-contentment reign when once it could be proved that Operation Learning had fully been launched. And, too, in our own country the representatives of the churches were not agreed on the nature of the religion which was to be embodied in the lessons of the public school. The school leaders, therefore, discouraged and uncertain, slackened their efforts and concentrated on the half of their job which had full community approval.

The time is upon us to make another determined effort to find ways whereby education can be academically strong and spiritually enlightened. Some may choose to call it Education for the Good, not with any elation of superiority but in recognition that education to be complete must aid in the search for the Good. Many of us will prefer to call it simply Christian education, although by the very title we must know that we cannot ask for acceptance or agreement on the great doctrines of the Christian Church among the American public where only half make nominal claim to church affiliation. By Christian education we shall mean the full restoration in our teaching of the place which religion has in the molding of history, and especially the part which the Christian religion has played in the making of our American life and culture. We shall mean also the search for the values and the ideals of life which Jesus Christ set forth to the world two thousand years ago.

The way ahead can start from our church-related colleges and those independent colleges which are free to experiment. There is room for a larger measure of Christian education in most of these institutions than one commonly finds. If the members of the administrative staff will carry the burden of creative leadership, if the faculty men and women will accept the terrible responsibility of the teacher, if the students by at least a slight majority are those who would gladly learn, then some exciting and most significant ventures may be made in an education that is truly God-centered.

The way ahead, moreover, can start from the campuses of our state-controlled institutions. We know that we can teach courses *about* religion in the tax-supported schools of practically all of the states. The law and public opinion have accepted, with few exceptions, the campus activities of the great church foundations and the student Christian movements. These can be greatly strengthened. And with complete fairness to the educational constituency which may be offended by the label Christian, there can be endeavors in new and better ways—as we are able to find them—to care for the unfilled moral and spiritual needs of young America.

On that way ahead let our Christian administrators and our Christian teachers, in company with our Christian students, set forth with gladness and humility—gladness at the importance of the task before them, humility that they have been chosen in our day for a part in the effort. To that gladness and humility let there be added faith —faith that, with intelligence and patient vigilance and spiritual sensitivity, education can be brought to care more wisely and more fully not alone for minds but for men.

Æ, in "On Behalf of Some Irishmen Not Followers of Tradition," has written lines that may be construed as a parable of these frontiers to Christian education:

> We hold the Ireland in the heart
> More than the land our eyes have seen,
> And love the goal for which we start
> More than the tale of what has been.[14]

Acknowledgements

The author acknowledges with thanks his debt to the individuals, periodicals and publishing houses, listed below for permission to use copyrighted material.

Edith Lovejoy Pierce for use of "Main Street, U.S.A." from *Wind Has No Home*.

The Macmillan Company for use of material from Moberly, *The Crisis in the University*, McGrath et al, *Toward General Education*, Coatsworth, *Country Poems*.

The Westminster Press for use of material from Lowry, *The Mind's Adventure*.

Oxford University Press, Inc. for use of selections from Fry's *A Sleep of Prisoners*.

Harcourt Brace and Company, Inc., for use of selections from T. S. Eliot, *The Cocktail Party*.

The Eucalyptus Press, for use of the selection from Thurman, *The Greatest of These*.

William Sloane Associates, Inc. for use of the selection from Anderson, *Winterset*.

The University of Illinois Press for use of material by Robert M. Hutchins and Archibald MacLeish from *Ferment in Education*.

The Beacon Press for use of material from Liebman, *Psychitary and Religion*.

"Time" for use of material from their columns.

The Church Society for College Work for use of materials from *Church Review*.

"Intercollegian" for use of materials from their columns.

Footnotes to Chapters

Preface

1. Nels F. S. Ferré, *Faith and Reason*, p. 46, New York, Harper & Brothers, 1946.
2. Reprinted from *Time*, with permission. Copyright Time, Inc., 1951.

Chapter One

1. Elizabeth Coatsworth, "Lullabye," from *Country Poems*, New York, The Macmillan Company, 1942, p. 64.
2. Taken from Nansen-Haus Essay #1, January, 1951, p. 3, Olaf Brennhovd, Director.
3. From a personal letter written by Dr. Bjerne R. Ullsvik to Dr. Wm. J. Hutchins, President Emeritus, Berea College.
4. Gordon Keith Chalmers, *The Republic and the Person*, Chicago, Henry Regnery Company, 1952, pp. 164-165.
5. Harold Cooke Phillips, *In the Light of the Cross*, New York, Abingdon-Cokesbury Press, 1947, pp. 120-121.
6. Robert Maynard Hutchins, *Freedom for Education*, Baton Rouge, Louisiana State University Press, 1943, p. 104.
7. Sequel to the story of the German applicant: When the registrar received the transcript of courses and grades, it was apparent that the young man already had the equivalent of the American A.B. He was, therefore, advised to apply to a university able to offer him graduate study.

Interchapter

1. *Time*, November 5, 1951.
2. Patrick Murphy Malin, *The Contribution and Task of the National Council on Religion in Higher Education* Bulletin XII, Nov. 1949, New Haven, National Council on Religion in Higher Education, p. 5.
3. Seymour A. Smith, *The 1950 Directory of the Fellows of the National Council* (pamphlet), Introduction.
4. *The Vitality of the Christian Tradition*, George F. Thomas, editor, New York, Harper & Brothers, 1944.

5. *Liberal Learning and Religion*, Amos N. Wilder, editor, New York, Harper & Brothers, 1951.

6. *The Edward W. Hazen Foundation 1925-50*, New Haven, Hazen Foundation, 1950.

7. Hoxie N. Fairchild, *et al*, *Religious Perspectives in College Teaching*, New York, The Ronald Press Company, 1952, p. iv.

8. *Ibid.*, p. iv.

9. *The Consolidated Report of the Six Faculty Workshops of 1952 in the Research Study Project What Is a Christian College?* Prepared by Raymond F. McLain, 297 Fourth Avenue, New York 10, New York.

10. *The Christian Scholar*, March, 1953, p. 55.

11. "Religion in Higher Education, The Program of Faculty Consultations," *Educational Record*, October 1946, p. 422; later reprinted as a pamphlet by the Hazen Foundation.

12. "Colleges, Faculties, and Religion," *Educational Record*, January 1949, p. 52; later reprinted as a pamphlet by the Hazen Foundation.

13. *Ibid.*, pp. 57-58.

14. The University Christian Mission of the National Council of Churches, although intended primarily as work among students, has been most helpful in extending the services of its missions to faculty. For a fuller account of its efforts see *A Six Year Review of the University Christian Mission 1947-53*, James L. Stoner, Director, University Christian Mission, 297 Fourth Avenue, New York, New York.

15. The booklet is available as a Bulletin of the Bureau of School Service, College of Education, University of Kentucky, Volume XXV, No. 1, September, 1952.

16. Educational Policies Commission, *Moral and Spiritual Values in the Public Schools*, National Education Association, 1201 Sixteenth Street NW, Washington, D.C., 1951, p. vi.

17. *Ibid.*, pp. 77-78.

18. *Ibid.*, p. 6.

19. *The Relation of Religion to Public Education: The Basic Principles* (A Report on the exploratory study made by the Committee on Religion and Education), Washington, American Council on Education, 1947.

20. *The Function of the Public Schools in Dealing with Religion*, Washington, American Council on Education, 1953.

21. *Ibid.*, p. 83.

22. See p. 176.

23. *Religion in State Teachers Colleges, A Report of a National Study Conference on Religion in State Teachers Colleges*, New Haven, Yale University Divinity School, 1952.

24. *The Crisis in the University*, Sir Walter Moberly, London, SCM Press Ltd., 1949.

25. From Howard Lowry's *The Mind's Adventure*, published 1950, Westminster Press, copyright 1950, W. L. Jenkins. Used by permission.

26. *The University and the Modern World*, Arnold S. Nash, New York, The Macmillan Company, 1943.

27. *The Task of the Christian in the University*, A Grey Book of the World's Student Christian Association, A. J. Coleman, New York, Association Press, 1947.

Chapter Two

1. Sir Walter Moberly, *The Crisis in the University*, London, SCM, Press, 1949, pp. 51-52.

2. *Ibid.*, p. 105.

3. *Ibid.*, p. 103.

4. Moberly, *op. cit.*, p. 101, quoting *General Education in a Free Society*, p. 39.

5. Moberly, *op. cit.*, p. 104. For the full presentation of Sir Walter's argument, see pp. 99-105.

6. Homer Rainey, quotation taken from a mimeographed copy of the address, pp. 10-11.

7. Howard Lowry, *The Mind's Adventure*, Philadelphia, Westminster Press, 1950, p. 83.

8. With the auspicious beginnings of the National Council of the Churches of Christ in the USA, it is the increasing hope of many Protestants that there will be forthcoming from the officers of the Council candid and carefully considered statements of policy which will provide courageous leadership for the forces of Christian education.

9. Emlyn Williams, *The Corn Is Green*, Act 3, New York, Random House, 1938, pp. 152-153.

10. Moberly, *op. cit.*, p. 56.

11. From *A Sleep of Prisoners*, by Christopher Fry. Copyright 1951 by Christopher Fry. Reprinted by permission of Oxford University Press, Inc.

Chapter Three

1. Joshua Loth Liebman, ed., *Psychiatry and Religion*, Boston, Beacon Press, 1948, p. xii.

2. This is a paraphrase rather than an exact quotation from Sherwood Eddy, *A Pilgrimage of Ideas*, New York, Farrar & Rinehart, 1934, p. 58.

3. "The Younger Generation," *Time*, November 5, 1951, p. 46.

4. Frederick Prokosch, "Elegy," from *New Poems: 1940*, Oscar Williams, ed., New York, Yardstick Press, 1941, p. 145.

5. Catherine Drinker Bowen, *Yankee from Olympus*, Boston, Little, Brown & Company, 1944, p. xii.

6. Edith Lovejoy Pierce, "Main Street, U.S.A.," from *Wind Has No Home*, privately printed, 1950.

7. Edward A. Fitzpatrick, *How to Educate Human Beings*, Milwaukee, Bruce Publishing Company, pp. 129-131.

8. Rainey, *op. cit.*

9. Quoted in Moberly, *op. cit.*, p. 269.

10. Lowry, *op. cit.*, pp. 137-138.

11. Moberly, *op. cit.*, pp. 290-291.

12. Fred B. Millett, *The Rebirth of Liberal Education*, New York, Harcourt, Brace & Company, 1945, p. 73.

13. Educational Policies Commission, *The Education of Free Men in American Democracy*, Washington, National Education Association, 1941, p. 63.

14. Mark Van Doren, *Liberal Education*, New York, Henry Holt & Company, 1943, p. 60.

15. Howard Thurman, *The Greatest of These*, Mills College, Eucalyptus Press, 1944, p. 3.

16. *Report of the Trustees of the Ford Foundation*, Detroit, September 27, 1950, p. 14.

17. Albert C. Outler, from an unpublished lecture.

18. Sir Richard Livingstone, *On Education*, New York, The Macmillan Company, 1945, p. 86.

19. T. S. Eliot, *The Cocktail Party*, Act. II, New York, Harcourt Brace & Company, 1950, p. 134.

20. Theodore O. Wedel, "The Church and the University," *The Church Review*, January, 1950.

21. Nels F. S. Ferré, *Strengthening the Spiritual Life*, New York, Harper & Brothers, 1951, p. 59.

Chapter Four

1. Archibald MacLeish, "The Terrible Responsibility of the Teacher," from *Ferment in Education*, Urbana, University of Illinois Press, 1948, pp. 48-49.

2. Eliot, *op. cit.*, Act I, p. 96.

3. Julius Seelye Bixler, "Reflections on the Art of Teaching," *The Independent School Bulletin*, November 1951 (taken from the original manuscript).

4. Moberly, *op. cit.*, pp. 68-69.

5. *A College Program in Action, A Review of Working Principles at Columbia College*, by the Committee on Plans, New York, Columbia University Press, 1946, p. 63.

6. Lowry, *op. cit.*, p. 107.

7. Albert C. Outler, from a stenographic report of an unpublished lecture given at the Christianity on the Campus Conference, Camp Miniwanca, August 31, 1951.

8. Earl J. McGrath, et al., *Toward General Education*, New York, The Macmillan Company, 1948, pp. 133-134 (italics not in original).

9. John Baillie, *Invitation to Pilgrimage*, New York, Charles Scribner's Sons, 1942, p. 20.

10. Jacques Barzun, *Teacher in America*, Boston, Little, Brown & Company, 1945, p. 222.

11. Dexter Merriam Keezer, *The Light That Flickers*, New York, Harper & Brothers, 1947, p. 6.

12. Oliver Wendell Holmes' "Deathless Line to a Katydid" must serve as warning to the sensitive teacher: "Thou sayest an undisputed thing in such a solemn way."

13. McGrath, et al., *op. cit.*, p. 135.

14. Erwin Schrödinger, Preface to *What Is Life? The Physical Aspect of the Living Cell*. New York, The Macmillan Company, 1946, p. vii.

15. Frederick W. Stewart, "The Well of Troubled Water," *Christian Education*, March, 1942.

16. Keezer, *op. cit.*, p. 108.

17. Barzun, *op. cit.*, p. 108.

18. Maxwell Anderson, *Winterset*, Act III, contained in *Eleven Verse Plays*, New York, Harcourt, Brace & Company, p. 125.

19. *The Intercollegian*, February, 1950 (taken from original manuscript).

20. Lowry, *op. cit.*, p. 82.

Chapter Five

1. Howard Thurman, *The Greatest of These*, Mills College, Eucalyptus Press, 1944, pp. 15-16.

2. Moberly, *op. cit.*, p. 26.

3. *Ibid.*, pp. 26-27.

4. Edgar J. Goodspeed, *A Life of Jesus*, New York, Harper & Brothers, 1950, p. 190.

5. Eleanor Roosevelt, *This I Remember*, New York, Harper & Brothers, 1949, p. 193.

6. John Steinbeck, *A Russian Journal*, New York, Viking Press, 1948, p. 11.

7. Rainey, *op. cit.*

8. Sholem Asch, *One Destiny*, New York, G. P. Putnam's Sons, 1945, p. 30.

9. The author is indebted to Albert C. Outler for the substance of this paragraph.

10. Henry P. Van Dusen, *God in Education*, New York, Charles Scribner's Sons, 1951, pp. 80-81.

11. Moberly, *op. cit.*, p. 265, quoting Pusey, *Collegiate and Professional Teaching and Discipline*, p. 25.

12.   Robert M. Hutchins, "The Education We Need," *Ferment in Education*, Urbana, University of Illinois Press, p. 31.

13.   Paul Hoffman, *Peace Can Be Won*, New York, Doubleday & Company, 1951, p. 130.

14.   Melvin E. Haggerty, *The Evaluation of Higher Institutions: The Faculty*, Chicago, University of Chicago Press, 1937, p. 118.

15.   James Gray, *The University of Minnesota, 1851-1951*, Minneapolis, The University of Minnesota Press, 1951, p. 389. Dr. Beard's article in the *New Republic*, January 19, 1938, was in part responsible for the action.

16.   Hutchins, *op. cit.*, p. 44.

17.   James Bryant Conant, *Education in a Divided World*, Cambridge, Mass., Harvard University Press, 1948, p. 174.

18.   Leslie D. Weatherhead, *When the Lamp Flickers*, New York, Abingdon-Cokesbury Press, 1948, p. 99.

19.   Kalman Seigel, *The New York Times*, series beginning May 10, 1951.

20.   Albert C. Outler, from a stenographic report of an unpublished lecture given at the Christianity on the Campus Conference, Camp Miniwanca, September 1, 1951.

21.   Sir Richard Livingstone, *The Future in Education*, New York, The Macmillan Company, 1945, p. 2.

22.   Dr. Harold W. Stokes, from a mimeographed statement made to the faculty of Louisiana State University upon the occasion of his resignation, 1951.

23.   *Ibid.*

24.   Leslie Weatherhead, *op. cit.*, p. 77.

25.   Christopher Fry, *op. cit.*, p. 27.

Interchapter

1.   Lynn White, Jr., "Why Are Our Faculties Secular-Minded?" *The Church Review*, October, 1949.

2.   Gordon Poteat, "Can a University Be Christian?" from a mimeographed press release of an address (unpublished) given at Denison University, 1949.

3.   Lowry, *op. cit.*, pp. 102-103.

4.   K. I. Brown, "Chapel Walk," *Missions*, May, 1946.

5.   K. I. Brown, ed., *Margie*, New York, Association Press, 1947, p. 153.

Chapter Six

1.   Christopher Fry, *op. cit.*, pp. 47-48.

2.   These axioms are the work of faculty committees studying in seminars at the Christianity on the Campus Conference, Camp Miniwanca, 1949.

3. See first Interchapter, p. 28.

4. Taken from *A Proposed Draft of Recommendations* (mimeographed), prepared for the Park College Conference, June, 1953.

5. Arthur W. Lindsey, "Biology," in *College Teaching and Christian Values*, Paul M. Limbert, ed., New York, Association Press, 1951, p. 36.

6. *Ibid.*, p. 37.

7. Sister Annette Walters, "The First Course in Psychology: The Psychology of Persons," *Journal of General Education*, April, 1947, p. 189.

8. Taken from *A Report of the Sub-Committee on Teacher Education and Religion* of the AACTE, May, 1953, pp. 2-3, unpublished.

9. See first Interchapter, p. 20.

10. *The Function of the Public Schools in Dealing with Religion, A Report on the Exploratory Study made by the Committee on Religion and Education*, Washington, American Council on Education, 1953, p. 85.

11. *Ibid.*, p. 87.

12. *Religion in State Teachers Colleges, A Report of a National Study Conference on Religion in State Teachers Colleges*, New Haven, Yale Divinity School, 1952. Introduction, p. 3.

13. See first Interchapter, p. 27.

14. Quoted in Amos N. Wilder, *The Spiritual Aspects of the New Poetry*, New York, Harper & Brothers, 1940, p. 23.

Index

A.A.U.P., 137
Adams, Henry, 87
Æ, 191
Allen, Henry E., 37
Allport, Gordon W., 172, 175
American Association of Colleges for Teacher Education, 178-180
American Baptist Assembly, Green Lake, Wisconsin, 35
American Council on Education, 29, 32, 33, 179
American Education and Religion: The Problem of Religion in the Schools, 37
American Tradition in Religion and Education, The, 36
Anderson, Maxwell, 12, 104
Antioch College, 183
Asch, Sholem, 122
at Denison, xiv
Axioms for a Christian Teacher, 163

Bach, 12
Baillie, John, 96
Barr, Stringfellow, 81
Barrymore, Ethel, 51
Barzun, Jacques, 97, 102, 125
Beattie, James, 144
Bell, Bernard Iddings, 178
Berea College, 28, 183
Bixler, J. Seelye, 87, 96
Blackburn College, 183
Board of Education of the Methodist Church, 184
Bower, William Clayton, 31, 35, 36
Brand, 105
Brubacher, John S., 36
Bucknell University, 183
Burrall Class, 183
Butts, R. Freeman, 36

Calhoun, Robert L., 24
Chalmers, Gordon K., 9, 36

Character Building and Higher Education, 37
Chicago, University of, 21, 31, 183
Christian Education, 29
Christian Scholar, xiv, 29, 184
Church and State in Education, 36
Church, College and Nation, 36
Church Society for College Work of the Protestant Episcopal Church, 30
Coatsworth, Elizabeth, 1
Cocktail Party, The, 80, 85
Colby College, 87
Coleman, A. J., 35
College Program in Action, A, 90
College Reading and Religion, 37
College Seeks Religion, The, 37
College Teaching and Christian Values, 37
Colleges, Faculties and Religion, 29
Columbia University, 33, 90
Commission on Christian Higher Education of the Association of American Colleges, 27, 29, 30, 180
Commission on Christian Higher Education of the National Council of Churches, 28
Committee on Religion and Education of the American Council on Education, 32, 35, 37
Committee on Religion in Higher Education of the National Student Council of the YMCA and YWCA, 29
Community Campus Chest, 156
Conant, James B., 132
Consolidated Report of the Six Faculty Workshop of 1952, The, 27
Contribution and Task of the National Council on Religion in Higher Education, The, 23
Contribution of Religion to Cultural Unity, The, 25
Corn Is Green, The, 51

Counseling, A Christian Context for, 25
Crisis and Hope in American Education, 36
Crisis in the University, The, xiv, 35, 39, 123, 183
Cuninggim, Merrimon, 37

Danforth Associate, 26
Danforth Foundation, The, 26, 92, 162, 167, 169
Danforth Graduate Fellowships, 27, 162
Danforth, William H., 26
Danny Grads, 26
Dante, 105
Darwin, 42
Denison University, 39, 150
Department of Elementary School Principals of the NEA, 35
Dewey, John, 11

Eddy, Sherwood, 62
Education and Crisis, 36
Education—Christian or Pagan, 36
Education in a Divided World, 132
Education of Free Men in American Democracy, The, 76
Educational Policies Commission of the National Education Association, 31, 35
Ehrensperger, Harold A., 185
Eliot, Charles W., 124
Eliot, T. S., 80, 85
Elliott G. Roy, 7, 36
Emphasizing Moral and Spiritual Values in A Kentucky High School, 31
Espy, R. H. Edwin, 37
Evaluation of Higher Institutions, The, 125

Faculty Christian Fellowship, The, 28, 110, 167-169, 181
Fairchild, Hoxie N., 25
Faith and Reason, x
Ferment in Education, 85, 124
Ferre, Nels, X, 84
Fitzpatrick, Edward A., 72
Fletcher, Basil A., 36
Ford Foundation, 79
Freedom for Education, 14
Friutjof Nansen International Student Haus, 4
Fry, Christopher, 60, 139, 161, 168, 171
Function of the Public Schools in Dealing with Religion, The, 33, 37, 179
Future in Education, The, 133

Galileo, 42
Gauss, Christian, 37
General Education in a Free Society, The Harvard Report, 8-9, 40
Ghirlandaio, 106
Glaucon, An Inquiry into the Aims of Education, 36
God in Education (Jacks), 36
God in Education (Van Dusen), 36, 123
Goodspeed, Edgar, 117
Gorky, 106
Gray, James, 128-129
Greatest of These, The, 79
Greene, Theodore M., 175

Haggerty, Melvin E., 125
Harbison, E. Harris, 175
Hartford, Ellis F., 31
Harvard Report, The: *General Education in a Free Society*, 8-9, 40
Harvard Tutorial Plan, 183
Hazen Associates, 24, 26
Hazen Conferences, 24
Hazen Foundation, The Edward W., 22, 24, 26, 29, 35, 37, 92, 171
Heard, Gerald, 5, 65, 98, 186
Henry, Virgil, 37
Hiram College, 183
Hoffman, Paul, 125
Holmes, Oliver Wendell, 64
Horton, Mildred McAfee, 71
How to Educate Human Beings, 72
Hutchins, Robert M., 14, 124, 131, 183

Ibsen, Henrik, 12
Illinois Wesleyan University, 182
In the Light of the Cross, 9
Independent School Bulletin, 87
Individual and His Religion, The, 172
Intercollegian, The, xiv, 107, 184-185
Invitation to Pilgrimage, 96

Jack Horner, 6-7
Jacks, M. L., 36
Jackson, Robert H., 48
Japan, 154
Jeffreys, M.V.C., 36
Johnson, F. Earnest, 32-34, 37
Journal of General Education, 176
Journal of Higher Education, xiv

Keezer, Dexter, 98, 102
Kent, Charles Foster, 23
Kent Fellows, 162
Kent State University, 34

Leavis, F. R., 74
Liberal Education, 77
Liberal Learning and Religion, 24, 37
Liebman, Joshua Loth, 61
Life of Jesus, A, 117
Light that Flickers, The, 98
Limbert, Paul M., 37
Lindsey, Arthur W., 173-175
Linton, Clarence, 33, 180
Livingstone, Sir Richard, 36, 80, 133
Livingstone, Walter J., 150
Lowell, A. Lawrence, 119
Lowry, Howard, xiv, 35, 45, 74, 91, 144

Macalester College, 81-82
MacLeish, Archibald, 85
Madden, Ward, 37
Malik, Charles, xiii
Malin, Patrick M., 25
Margie, 158
Maritain, Jacques, 44
Mason, Robert E., 36
McGrath, Earl J., 92-93, 99
McLain, Raymond F., 27-28, 181-182
Michelangelo, 105
Mind's Adventure, The, xiv, 35, 45, 74
Missouri State Teachers Association, 34
Moberly, Sir Walter, xiv, 35, 38, 39,
    40-41, 60, 76, 88, 113, 116, 123,
    183
*Moral and Spiritual Values in Educa-
    tion*, 35
*Moral and Spiritual Values in the Pub-
    lic Schools*, 31-32, 35
Moral Values and Secular Education, 36
motive, xiv, 184
Mount Mary College, 72
Mozart, 12
Muskingum College, 150

Nash, Arnold, 35
Nason, John W., 29
National Council on Religion in Higher
    Education, 21, 23, 26, 29, 162, 167
National Education Association, 32, 76
*Nature and Role of the Christian Col-
    lege, The*, 28
New Education and Religion, The, 36
New Haven State Teachers College, 34
New York Times, The, 132
Niebuhr, Reinhold, 25
Niles, John Jacob, 113
North Carolina, University of, 169

Objectivity, 10, 107-109
Ohio Wesleyan University, 150

On Education, 36, 80
One Destiny, 122
O'Neill, J. M., 36
Ortmayer, Roger, 185
Outler, Albert C., 25, 29, 92-93, 127,
    133

Park College, 28, 183
Peace Can Be Won, 125
Peer Gynt, 105
Phi Beta Kappa, 69
Phillips, Harold C., 9
Pierce, Edith Lovejoy, 67
Pilgrim's Progress, 117
*Place of Religion in Higher Education,
    The*, 25
Place of Religion in Public Schools, The,
    37
Poteat, Gordon, 143
Princeton University, 183
Prokosch, Frederic, 64
Psychiatry and Religion, 61
Public Schools and Spiritual Values, The,
    36
Pusey, Edward, 123

Rainey, Homer, 43, 120
Ramachandran, G., 95
Rebirth of Liberal Education, The, 76
*Relation of Religion to Public Educa-
    tion: The Basic Principles*, 33, 35
*Religion and Education under the Con-
    stitution*, 36
*Religion in Higher Education, The Pro-
    gram of Faculty Consultations*, 29
Religion in Public Education, 36
Religion in the State Teachers Colleges,
    180
Religion in the State University, 35
Religion of College Teachers, The, 37
Religious Emphasis Weeks, 183
*Religious Perspectives in College Teach-
    ing*, 25, 35
Religious Values in Education, 37
Republic and the Person, The, 9, 36
Rockefeller Foundation, 33
Roosevelt, Eleanor, 117
Russian Journal, A, 118

Schaper, William A., 128
School and Society, xiv
Schrodinger, Erwin, 99
Schweitzer, Albert, 96
Secularism, xi, 30, 82, 140
Seigel, Kalman, 132
Shaw, George Bernard, 12

Sistine Chapel, 105
Snavely, Guy E., 112
Southern California, University of, 169
Southern Methodist University, 169
Spiritual Problems of the Teacher, 25
Spiritual Values in the Elementary Schools, 35
Steinbeck, John, 118
Stephens College, 43, 183
Stewart, Frederick W., 101
Stokes, Harold W., 134
Strengthening the Spiritual Life, 84
Strozier, Robert, 21
Student Volunteer Movement, 184

Task of the Christian in the University, The, 35
Teacher in America, 97
Teacher Summer Scholarships, 26
Teachers College—Columbia University, 33
Teachers Colleges, 30, 176, 180
Teaching Economics With A Sense of the Infinite and the Urgent, 25
Teaching of Religion in American Higher Education, The, 37
Teaching-Presentation Conferences, 164
Tead, Ordway, 25, 37
Thayer, V. T., 36
This I Remember, 117-118
Thomas, George F., 23, 25
Thurman, Howard, 79, 111
Time, xiv, 21
Toward General Education, 92-93, 99
Trueblood, Elton, 167
Tydings, J. Mansir, 31

Ulich, Robert, 25, 36
Union Theological Seminary, 33, 169-170
United Student Christian Council, 28
University and the Modern World, The, 35
University Christian Missions, 30
University of Minnesota, The, 1851-1951, 35, 125, 128-129

Van Doren, Mark, 77
Van Dusen, Henry P., 36, 123
Vitality of the Christian Tradition, The, 23

Walters, Sister Annette, 176
Wardha, 95
Washington University, 5, 65, 186
Weatherhead, Leslie, 132, 138
Wedel, Theodore O., 82
What Is a Christian College, 181
When the Lamp Flickers, 132
White, Lynn Jr., 140
Whitehead, Alfred North, 80
Wilder, Amos N., 24, 37
Williams, J. Paul, 36
Williams, John Fred, 31
Winterset, 104-105
Wittenberg College, 150
World Student Service Fund, 156

Yale University, 183
Yale University Divinity School, 34
Young Men's Christian Association, 184, 187
Young Women's Christian Association, 184, 187